Transoceanic Studies
Ileana Rodriguez, Series Editor

Oriental Shadows

THE PRESENCE OF
THE EAST
IN EARLY AMERICAN
LITERATURE

Jim Egan

The Ohio State University Press · Columbus

TO KIERAN AND LIAM

Copyright © 2011 by The Ohio State University.
All rights reserved.

Library of Congress Cataloging-in-Publication Data
Egan, Jim, 1961–
 Oriental shadows : the presence of the East in early American literature / Jim Egan.
     p. cm.—(Transoceanic studies)
 Includes bibliographical references and index.
 ISBN 978-0-8142-1161-8 (cloth : alk. paper)—ISBN 978-0-8142-9262-4 (cd)
 1. American literature—Colonial period, ca. 1600–1775—Asian influences. 2. American literature—19th century—Asian influences. 3. United States—Civilization—Asian influences. I. Title. II. Series: Transoceanic studies.
 PS159.A85E35 2011
 810.9'3585—dc22
                          2011013985

Paper (ISBN: 978-0-8142-5627-5)
Cover design by DesignSmith
Type set in Adobe Caslon

COnTEnTS

Acknowledgments		ix
Introduction	From Bradstreet to Poe	1
Chapter 1	The Colonial Body Travels East in Anne Bradstreet's Poetry	19
Chapter 2	How West Becomes East in Colonial Georgia Poetry	40
Chapter 3	Humanity's Eastern Home in Benjamin Franklin's Oriental Tales	75
Chapter 4	Edgar Allan Poe's Oriental America	95
Epilogue		121
Notes		125
Works Cited		147
Index		163

aCknOwlEdgmEnTS

Brown University provided support of various kinds for this project, including several Humanities Research Fund grants. I also received an Undergraduate Teaching and Research Award from Brown University toward research for the third chapter. Anne Jonas served as my research assistant for this UTRA, and I offer her my deepest thanks. Not only did she assist me in the mundane tasks that had to be done, but she also shared her extraordinary insights, contributions that made the chapter clearer, richer, and more revealing. Even though the UTRA I did with Joseph Shapiro and Theodore Schell-Lambert was not directly related to this book, the conversations we had regarding the research they performed helped shape my thinking on issues at the heart of *Oriental Shadows*. I offer them my thanks as well. The Department of English staff, including Marianne Costa, Jane Donnelly, Lorraine Mazza, Suzanne Nacar, and Marilyn Netter, offered invaluable support, as did the staff at the John Carter Brown Library, including Susan Danforth, Kimberly Nusco, and Ken Ward.

I owe a debt of gratitude to those colleagues and friends who read parts of the manuscript at various stages, shared their own work, or discussed issues relevant to the manuscript: Robert Battistini, Ralph Bauer, Michelle Burnham, Thomas Hallock, Mark Kamrath, Edward Larkin, Suchetta Muzumdar, David Shields, Timothy Sweet, Leonard Tennenhouse, Edward Watts, and Roxann Wheeler. I'd also like to thank those who participated in the Harvard Early American Workshop at which I presented my work, especially Joanne van der Woude, whose comments and collegiality are much appreciated. I'd also like to thank those who attended my talk at the Warburg Institute. I owe a very special thanks to Garrett Sullivan for suggesting me to the Warburg Institute, and I want to express my appreciation as well for the innumerable other ways in which he has offered his support over the years. Malini Johar Schueller and William Scheick provided especially helpful comments as readers for The Ohio State University Press. Their reports helped me understand the strengths and weaknesses of the manuscript, and the book profited from their insights. I am deeply grateful for Sandy Crooms's enthusiasm, interest, and support. I feel extraordinarily lucky to have stumbled upon such a remarkable acquisitions editor.

At Brown, I am very fortunate to work in a department with thoughtful, engaging, and insightful graduate students. My conversations with them over the years influenced the book in ways both obvious and subtle. At the risk of leaving out some former and current students whose words have helped make the book better, I would single out Keri Holt, John Melson, Sian Silyn Roberts, and Stephanie Tilden. I am equally fortunate to have supportive and insightful colleagues both inside and outside the department. This book has benefited especially from conversations with Stuart Burrows, Jean Feerick, Philip Gould, William Keach, and Kevin McLaughlin. Tamar Katz's incisive remarks taught me a great deal about vital literary issues, and the importance of her consistent, unwavering friendship defies adequate description. Outside of my department, Caroline Frank deserves special thanks for sharing her work with me. Her research has had a profound effect on my own work on figures of the East in early American writing. Susan Smulyan offered support and guidance as well as much laughter, not to mention a perspective that often helped me see things in a more reasonable light.

The members of my writing group, Dian Kriz, Robert Lee, and Joanne Melish, offered incisive, trenchant comments on early versions of several chapters. They also asked the kind of remarkably insightful questions about this project as I was just getting started. On top of all this, our engaging, supportive, and just plain fun lunches lifted my spirits when it seemed easier simply to let myself fall into the chaotic abyss of archival research rather than complete the manuscript.

When he served as a librarian at the John Carter Brown Library, Richard Ring helped me see both the material book and literature in radically new ways that have reshaped my interpretive practices. The value of our friendship, though, far exceeds the great professional profits I have accrued from his help as a librarian, and the importance of his good humor, support, and wisdom are beyond measure.

I owe my greatest debt to my family. Their inquisitiveness, joy, wisdom, and love can be found on every page of this book. Kieran and Liam have taught me more about literature than the most sophisticated and insightful scholarly writings, and they have taught me even more about the world outside literature. I have never met such remarkable people, and I feel blessed to have them in my life. I feel at a loss to express adequately my love for Lisa and my gratitude for the support and love she has given me. Her laughter, intelligence, and touch remain with me wherever I go. Her patience, courage, and clear vision have helped me see the world anew. Always have. Always will.

INTRODUCTION

From Bradstreet to Poe

The specter of the East haunts the literature of colonial British America and the new United States from the earliest promotional pamphlets to the most aesthetically sophisticated works of art of the American Renaissance. Take, for instance, the writings of John Smith, hailed as the author of "the first American book."[1] Having traveled through virtually all parts of the known world in his quest, first, to do battle with Muslims, and, then, to help subdue New World Natives, Smith singles out "Cathay and Chyna" as "the most famous Kingdomes in the world."[2] Or let us choose another beginning point, the poetry of the devout New England Puritan Anne Bradstreet, labeled the "first authentic poetic artist in America's history" by one critic and identified by another as the poet who brought "forth a newborn, New World poetry."[3] To whom does she compare the most revered monarch of her age? She finds the fittest comparison to Queen Elizabeth in "*Zenobia*, potent Empress of the East."[4] Edward Taylor casts the human soul's most "Elemental Frame" as a "China Dish" in one poem, then in another uses the very same figure of a "China Dish" to represent the beauty of God's creation.[5] In the most popular book other than the Bible in seventeenth-century New England, a book whose 1,800-line poem "The Day of Doom" was memorized by schoolchildren in New England for over a century, Michael Wigglesworth tells his readers how "The *Eastern Conquerour* was said to weep, / When he the *Indian* Ocean did view."[6]

Lest we think those closer to the founding of the United States lost their appetite for the East, we find, quite the contrary, that the men and women who put their very lives on the line to help bring the United States into being turned Eastward just as much as, if not more than, America's first British colonists. In the same month the Declaration of Independence was signed, no less a figure than Benjamin Franklin compared the British Empire itself to "a fine and noble China Vase." Apparently, Franklin quite liked the phrase; he repeated it seven years later in a letter to an English correspondent who was worried that the new "confederation [of states] may be annihilated" by dissension from within. Franklin sought to assuage his correspondent's fears by assuring him that "there is sense enough in America to take care of their own china vase." Figures of the Orient leave their mark long after the Revolution, too, even—and perhaps especially—among those writers who have traditionally been cast as the founders of a distinctively American literary tradition. Take, for instance, Washington Irving. While we know Irving as the author of the *Sketchbook,* we tend to forget those works devoted exclusively to the East that were enormously popular among nineteenth-century readers, including *A Conquest of Granada* and *Tales of the Alhambra.* We need look no further than Nathaniel Hawthorne's hypercanonical *Scarlet Letter* to find another instance among many other possible examples of the presence of the East in the very period during which the nation's literature came of age. For Hawthorne characterizes Hester Prynne, that most American of creations in his most penetrating examination of American history and culture, as having "in her nature a rich, voluptuous, Oriental characteristic."[7]

Figures of the East served important rhetorical functions for American writers not only in radically different historical periods but also from remarkably different—indeed, sometimes even combative or contradictory—ideological, regional, religious, political, and personal perspectives. Those who advocated colonization for the sake of empire, those who saw it as part of the Lord's work, and those who envisioned it as a way to wealth all turn Eastward to make their case. British American writers in Massachusetts call on these figures, as do writers in Pennsylvania and the staple colonies such as Virginia and Georgia in the South. Male writers use these figures, but then so, too, do female writers. Figures of the East appear in the most celebrated of works from the period by the most widely praised of authors, and they appear just as often in works known only to the most well-read specialists in the field. These figures can be found in those works popular in the period, and they can be found in those works passed over by contemporary audiences.

The extraordinary interest in the people, places, and things of the East shown by British American readers and writers from the sixteenth well into the nineteenth centuries should hardly surprise us. After all, Europeans recognized the landmass that would come to be called "America" only after countless ships sailed west in Christopher Columbus's wake in hopes they might locate a quicker route to the riches of the East. Even after Europeans and people of European descent living in America realized the glaring flaws in their geographical knowledge by acknowledging the existence of a considerable body of land separating them from the East Indies, these very same people continued to invest enormous amounts of money, time, and labor, not to mention the lives of many a sailor, searching for a Northwest Passage that would accomplish what had eluded those earlier voyages, but this time with an ironic twist. Those who sought a Northwest Passage after the European recognition of America sought not just a quicker route to the East, but also, it is important to point out, a quicker route to the East that specifically avoided the New World as much as possible.[8]

For many in Europe and America, then, the New World was as much an obstacle as an opportunity. Scholars long ago established that many Europeans and Anglo-Americans before 1800 viewed North America as the home of unparalleled possibilities for the less fortunate and potential profit for all. We have focused significantly less attention on the implications of the determined effort on both sides of the Atlantic, on the one hand, to find a Northwest Passage but also, at the same time, to produce Eastern goods in America. This effort cast America's chief value in terms of the place that Europeans had wanted America to be but was not. In this way, at least, America's value derived from its relation to the East. British American colonists as well as those who helped forge a new nation thus lived in the shadow of a land they neither occupied nor equaled. The discursive systems of the British American colonies and new nation, systems that helped give meaning to the lives of the first Anglo-Americans, came into being by establishing their value in terms of what they were not; they established their value, that is, by serving as pathways to the true object of European desire, not as communities whose value derived from what they and they alone had to offer.

If America could never be the East, British American writers and those of the new nation could, at least, use the infinitely greater cultural power granted Eastern people, places, and things in their own quest for acknowledgment as a truly civilized community by European and Creole intellectuals. Writers in the British American colonies and the early United States used these figures to ward off accusations that the people who lived in the many communities springing to life across the Eastern Seaboard of North America lacked the necessary refinement and gentility to be classified as truly "civilized" peoples.⁹ As I hope to demonstrate in the chapters that follow, some of the most important British American writers, in a variety of forms and for a variety of reasons, show remarkable consistency in their contention that the way early American culture could equal—and perhaps even surpass—its supposed social superiors in Europe was for American literature and culture to become more Oriental. That is, writers of what we have come to call early American literature offered the East as a solution to America's inferior civilized status by suggesting that America become more civilized, not by becoming more European—or perhaps not only by becoming more European—but by adopting aesthetic styles and standards long associated with an East cast as superior aesthetically to both America and Europe.¹⁰

Before I lay out this argument in greater detail, though, I must first address a fundamental question of terminology on which the argument depends. It is all well and good to argue that early American writers turned to figures of the East to argue for the civilized nature of colonial culture, but such an argument depends entirely on what counts as "East." In the chapters that follow, the case for the importance of figures of the East in early American literature has been made using definitions of the "East" contemporaneous with the writings on which each chapter focuses. Doing so leads us not only to different definitions of what counts as East and West on the globe but also to sets of assumptions about the relation between the various parts of the globe, and sets of associations attached to various parts of the globe, that differ from modern ones. It is not, in other words, simply that the writers in question divide the world differently than we do. For the most part, the writers examined in this study attached different concepts, values, and ideas to particular places and peoples on the globe than we do. Since these concepts, values, and ideas were integral to producing a text's various meanings and implications, we must pay them special attention here. These unstated assumptions, rules, and associations constitute what I call a "symbolic spatial economy."

I use the term "symbolic spatial economy" to indicate the unstated set of assumptions that form the complex, sometimes contradictory, system of symbols that allow the ideas, images, and concepts associated with any particular geographic space on the globe to seem only natural. Words relating to physical geography are, after all, no less figurative than words that do not refer to physical spaces on the globe where people live, work, and die. "India," for instance, refers to the spot on the globe we have come to call "India" but not because of some inherent relationship between "India," the signifier, and "India," the actual place being signified.¹¹ Just like any other word in a language, those words referring to particular spaces on the globe carry with them not only a literal meaning—the literal space on the globe to which the word refers—but also a range of connotations. Words relating to spaces on the globe, that is, carry symbolic resonance just as any other words in the language do. These symbolic associations are not random, but they do not necessarily correspond to what can be considered objectively true of the people and places of that region of the earth. They make sense only in the context of some larger signifying systems, what Foucault has famously called "discursive systems." Words relating to physical geography, I would suggest, are the products of the subset of those signifying systems relating to geography, a subset that structures and organizes the symbolic meanings attached to physical space, a structuring system that can be likened to an economy. This system teaches us not only to associate certain parts of the globe with certain ideas, images, and concepts, but also and in the same moment teaches us so well that the very productive capacity of the system becomes invisible to us. We come to think of the associations that grow out of this economy as preexisting our way of understanding the world rather than being borne directly out of that understanding.

Of course, as integral parts of larger systems of meanings, the associations attached to any distinct space on the globe are not isolated from or unrelated to the associations linked to any other part of the globe. Indeed, they are, ultimately, dependent on one another for their meaning. In this way, if the images associated with one spot on the map are altered, other spots that are unrelated geographically might, through this change in associated imagery, also undergo a change. The symbolic spatial economy, then, represents a fluid and flexible way of organizing the world rather than a static monolith of meanings.

In order to see the symbolic spatial economy at work in the texts under investigation in this book, I have used the definition of "East" operative at the time of the work about which I am writing. This is not to say that a single, uniform definition of the "East" existed across even a single language community during the period. Not only did the "East" include different parts of the globe at different moments in British American writing over the period, but disagreements over just which parts of the globe should be classified as "East" and which as "West" occurred during the period as well. The proper category for the land and people of Greece, for instance, was a source of considerable dispute. Was it in the East or the West?[12] No matter what precise region one's definition of the East included in this period, though, the "East" for all British American and early national writers included a much larger section of the map than we currently assign it, and the discriminations we make between and among, for instance, the Far East, Southeast Asia, the Middle East, and so forth, simply did not exist. The East for Anglophone writers well into the nineteenth century included both China and Persia; it included North Africa and Russia; it included Turkey and India; and sometimes it included Egypt. During the period this study covers, Jerusalem and other Christian holy lands were considered part of the Orient.[13] As Martin W. Lewis and Kären E. Wigen point out in *The Myth of Continents,* classifying such a vast geographic territory with an enormously diverse collection of cultures "into a single regional category was seldom questioned" until late in the 1800s.[14] This does not mean that writers in the period saw no difference between the people and/or products of these various locales. The "hither" East was sometimes differentiated from the "farther" East. Hegel was the first to draw "sharp and essential distinctions between different parts of Asia" when he cast "hither" and "farther" Asia as "essentially different from each other."[15] Hegel, though, was the exception rather than the rule. The vast majority of European and Anglophone writers before and immediately after Hegel understood the East as a single region whose communities, however different, constituted a distinct part of the globe whose peoples shared certain fundamental characteristics and features.

At least until the middle of the nineteenth century, then, the "East" not only covered an enormous portion of the globe but also cast as a single unit groups of people with very different institutions, beliefs, body types, and customs. While the people who inhabited this region were not cast as identical to one another, the logic that allows for these different peoples and places to be categorized together, as a single though diverse unit, gives some sense of how, at times and in important ways, these differences could be overlooked in favor of what were understood to be fundamental similarities. That the figure of the "East" could be understood to include all these different peoples tells us something about the way British American and early national writers organized the world in which they lived. At least at the level of the figure, the similarities between what we consider disparate places on the map exerted more power than those differences that, at least from the perspective of the discursive system in operation at the time, were of secondary significance.[16]

The geographic "East" signified in the figures this study investigates was hardly an empty space, though; nor were its inhabitants utterly powerless in the process of social construction. Quite the contrary. As I note above, a diverse and rich group of peoples and cultures lived in the enormous geographic area classified as "East" by Americans before 1860, and many of these communities played crucial roles, in some cases, even the dominant roles, in the world's economy in this period.[17] Given this study's specific focus on figures of the East in the discursive system of British America and the early United States, though, I have largely avoided discussion of the role played in the production of those meanings attached to figures of the East during this historical period by those who lived in the East at the time or, for that matter, by individuals from Asia who travelled to or lived in Europe or British America in the seventeenth through nineteenth centuries. The absence of such people and/or groups of people from this study should not be taken as an implicit argument that they had absolutely no impact on the implications of the figures under investigation. Compared with the impact of more local practices of book production, distribution, and readership, though, the influence of Oriental peoples on the meanings of the figures I consider was small enough that it need not be treated in detail here.

The binary division of the globe by peoples of European descent into the different regions of "East" and "West," with their attendant symbolic associations, is, itself, a social production rather than an unmediated representation of a preexistent physical geography, a production whose emergence can be witnessed at the very beginning of the period this book covers. The dominant modern meanings of "East" and "West" were forged during the early modern period.[18] As Jerry Brotton demonstrates, "Geographical antecedents of the geographers of the early modern world lacked any perception of a directional 'east,' or even of the very distinction between the geographical and symbolic concepts of 'west' and 'east.'"[19] Brotton goes on to argue that while "no . . . geographical or imaginative line of demarcation firmly existed between a political East and West in the early modern world," such a conception developed only gradually from the 1500s through the 1700s when "Europe as a geographical and political entity" began to emerge.[20] Instead, up through the late seventeenth century—the very period when Bradstreet produced her poetry and when it was published in Boston—"the east was not a separate, mysterious space antithetical to the developing ideals of European civilization," Brotton shows, but, on the contrary, a space "filled with myriad territories from which early modern scholars imbibed spiritual, intellectual, and material sustenance."[21]

In examining works of American literature in relation to geographic space, I am not treading new ground but following in footsteps that begin at the field's very roots. Scholars in the 1920s who succeeded in legitimating American literature as a worthwhile field of academic study used Frederick Jackson Turner's "frontier thesis" as the basic structuring element in the development of a distinctly American literature.[22] A cursory glance at the titles of some of the most important works of scholarship on American literature before 1860—from *Virgin Land* to *The Fatal Environment* to *The Lay of the Land* to *American Incarnation: The Individual, the Nation, and the Continent*—shows how geographic figures have helped shape the way we understand writing classified as American.[23] More recently, the field has witnessed a resurgence of interest in the problem of space, especially in relation to writing before 1900. Ralph Bauer's *The Cultural Geography of Colonial American Literature* insists, "We must place literary history in the context not only of the historical but also of the spatial dialectics that were foundational in the making of modernity," while Martin Brückner's *The Geographic Revolution in Early America* investigates the importance of geographic space by examining the way in which "the construction of the American subject was grounded in the textual experience of geography."[24] Such works have enabled my very ability to reconstruct the symbolic spatial economy of the period so that I can see the many figures of the East appearing right before my eyes as I read through the archive of British American and early national writings.[25]

Just as I am hardly the first scholar to investigate American literature in relation to matters relating to space, so, too, have previous analyses directed our attention toward various aspects of the Orient in early America. Before Edward Said's *Orientalism*, scholars generally took references to the Orient in early America as evidence of the diversity and open-mindedness of the canonical figures of America's literary tradition. As examples of this trend, I would point to Frederic Ives Carpenter's *Emerson and Asia* in 1930 and Arthur E. Christy's *The Orient in American Transcendentalism* two years later, as well as Dorothee Metlitsky Finkelstein's *Melville's Orienda* in 1961 and David Reynolds's discussion in *Faith in Fiction* (1981) of the Oriental tale in America before 1830. More recent works such as A. Owen Aldridge's 1993 *The Dragon and the Eagle: The Presence of China in the American Enlightenment* follows in this tradition, as does Arthur Versluis's *American Transcendentalism and Asian Religion*, also from 1993, which offers without question the most detailed study of Orientalism in nineteenth-century American literature. While conceding Said's point that Transcendentalist writers practice some intellectual colonialism in their adaptation of Oriental materials for their purposes, Versluis adheres more closely to the perspective established by Christy. Versluis reads American Transcendentalists' use of Asian religions not primarily as an instance of the kind of Orientalism Said identified but, instead, as evidence of the willingness of these writers to embrace even the most "esoteric" ideas. While I argue that figures of the East played a key role in the way early American authors sought to present themselves as part of a civilized culture, Versluis argues that engagement with Oriental religious materials was "at the center of the entire American Transcendentalist movement."[26]

Scholars writing in the wake of Said and in the fields of postcolonial and colonial discourse studies that grew exponentially after *Orientalism* have, first of all, pushed their inquiries even further back into America's colonial history, directing attention to pre-Revolutionary writings as well as those of the nineteenth century. These scholars' reexamination of the influence of the Orient in pre-Revolutionary British America has led them to point out the sometimes explicit, sometimes implicit links between various forms of power inherent in representations of the Orient as well as the relation these representations—and the various powers they invoke and produce—have with questions of imperialism and empire in particular. So Hilton Obenzinger argues in *American Palestine* (1999) that representations of the Holy Land by nineteenth-century American writers can best be understood through the lens of theorists of settler colonialism, while Malini Schueller's *U.S. Orientalisms* (1998) adapts Said's Orientalist model to show what she identifies as various kinds of Orientalism in American literature from the Revolutionary period to approximately 1890. While these Orientalisms, Schueller shows, do not cohere into a single narrative, collectively they illustrate how images of the Orient were crucial to the formation of notions of U.S. nationhood. Timothy S. Marr and Fuad Sha'ban take us further back into the American past than Schueller does in examining seventeenth-century materials in their demonstrations, in *The Cultural Roots of American Islamicism* (2006) and *Islam and Arabs in Early American Thought* (1991), of the connection of Islam to American identity.[27]

In some ways the most relevant predecessor to *Oriental Shadows* can be found in an essay not specifically devoted to an examination of the East at all, Michael Warner's provocative "What's Colonial about Colonial America?" Toward the end of his piece, Warner argues that the "spatial imagination of colonial culture has tended to be ignored" by scholars. In order to make his case, he points out that "England's movement into America was in most ways parallel with its movement into India," a fact of which Warner reminds us with examples from contemporary writings well known to British Americans of the seventeenth and eighteenth centuries.[28] This observation leads Warner to remark that "it is surprising how invisible India has been in the history of Anglo-American colonialism."[29] Warner contends that our focus on the incipient nationalism of explicitly nonnational colonial writing blinds us to the spatial imagination that would understand India and America as fundamentally connected. I think he is absolutely correct in this. American nationalism provides its own symbolic spatial economy that serves its own interests. In paying close attention to figures of the East in early American writing, I hope to expose the workings of a prenationalist spatial imagination—what I am calling a symbolic spatial economy—that, partly through the very writings investigated in the rest of this book, helps produce the distinctively modern way we in the United States tend to understand the people and places on the globe and their relation to one another.

Scholarship has played its role, too, as Warner notes, in teaching us how to imagine the relation between different spaces on the map. We can see such instruction in the work of those very scholars who were crucial in establishing the unstated assumptions that would help provide the intellectual foundations for the study of early American literary studies. Perhaps the most distinguished and certainly one of the most influential of those scholars, Perry Miller, acknowledges the fascination for all things Oriental expressed by American writers of the 1830s, 40s, and 50s, but in order to establish what he considers the native Americanness of American literature, Miller acknowledges the Oriental influence only to suggest its lack of true importance.[30] In what would become one of his most influential pieces, Miller asks in "From Edwards to Emerson" whether "New England's transcendentalism [was] wholly Germanic or Hindu in origin."[31] Miller concedes the point that the literary theories espoused by nineteenth-century American writers "were importations, not native American growths, . . . extracted from imperfect translations of the Hindu scriptures."[32] He concedes, in other words, that a superficial reading of nineteenth-century American literature shows that these writings owe a substantial debt to ideas imported—however imperfectly—from the Orient. Miller wants us to see that what he calls "a deeper reading" will reveal what seems counterintuitive: that the Pantheistic writings of nineteenth-century American writers who were openly hostile to traditional Christianity owe their greatest intellectual debt to the staunchly, unflinchingly Calvinist writings of the American Puritans who brooked no dissent when it came to matters of God.

We have yet to find a fully satisfactory answer—and we never will—to the problem of continuity at the core of "From Edwards to Emerson."[33] What relationship does the writing produced by those colonists living in North America—who were, after all, a group of people who generally reacted with alarm at the slightest suggestion they had relinquished their claims to being British by living so far removed from their homeland—what relationship does writing produced by such people bear to the literature produced by the citizens of nation who fought a protracted and bloody eight-year war designed specifically to free themselves from the very state to whom they had pledged their allegiance? By what logic, scholars have asked from the birth of scholarly interest in American literature, do we justify the yoking together of pre- and post-Revolutionary writings from the communities that would become the United States into a single, unbroken narrative? The issue of whether a continuity exists between the writings of the British American colonies and those in the United States relies itself, of course, on the questionable assumption that the writings of those colonies can be made to form a unified, coherent collective entity themselves. We might view the writing produced in Britain's American colonies instead, for instance, as constituting a series of related but distinct discursive systems. But let us say we accept the premise that an object called "colonial American literature" exists and can be studied. If, as Benedict Anderson has noted, all nationalist movements necessarily rob the graves of their ancestors in order to provide the nation with a history of its own, how, as scholars, do we understand the relationship between those whose graves are robbed and those who resurrect the corpses for their own purposes?[34]

Of course, such attempts to demonstrate a continuous literary tradition that extends from colonial to postcolonial times necessarily rely on a sometimes implicit, sometimes explicit theory of Americanness. The coherence of these narratives depends, in other words, on identifying some distinctively American characteristic or characteristics of American literature so that even those works that expressly announce themselves as something other than American can be included in our national narratives. Some scholars have shown how American works seem to bear distinctive stylistic features that differentiate them from, for instance, the literature of other nations written in English. Scholars often point to the shaping power of experience to produce a distinctly American brand of writing. We have learned a great deal over the years about what appear to be thematic concerns that seem to be peculiarly if not exclusively American. Much work has been done to identify those genres and/or formal structures whose origins can be traced to the colonies or the new nation. Others have taken a different tack by trying to tie together the various strands of America's literary history by using the place of a work's publication, where the author was born or where he or she lived during a crucial period of his or her life, or some complex combination of these criteria, as the basis for a unified story of America's literary heritages. Still others have pointed out ideological commonalities among those works that have achieved canonical status that serve, along with the critical presuppositions that are used to interpret those works, to maintain the very notion of a unified American literary tradition in spite of much evidence to the contrary.

I do not propose in the space of this introduction, or, for that matter, even in the rest of the book, to solve the problem of continuity that has haunted the field of early American studies since its inception and that will, we can be confident, continue to bedevil scholars for as long as such a field exists within the discipline. The use of figures of the East by those writers we have labeled as "American" represents simply another important and, heretofore, overlooked way of understanding the relationship between pre- and post-Revolutionary American writing. Figures of the East in early American literature provide no more of a master narrative that defines all of early American literature than did figures of the wilderness or the frontier. These figures of the East in colonial British American and early national writing do reveal a distinctive tradition of figurative language that begins in the formative years of colonization and continues unabated through what has been called the "flowering of narrative" in the middle of the nineteenth century. Put differently, one of the many ways the works I examine in what follows and, I would also suggest, any work produced during the period of this study mark themselves as American can be seen in the work done by the figures of the East used in the text. In the complex set of characteristics that distinguish the literary tradition of what we have come to call American literature, they share a bond in the way they represent the relationship between what they cast as the "East" and "West."

We can see one way in which American writers' relation to figures of the East would have been different when we look at some of the work done on figures of the East by scholars of British literature of the same period. So, for instance, Ros Ballaster convincingly demonstrates in *Fabulous Orients* that we should read fictions of the Orient published in England from the late seventeenth through the eighteenth centuries in relation to the burgeoning expansion of Britain's empire in India and the East more broadly. Our interpretation of these tales, Ballaster insists, must take into account England's status in the world community as a tiny island nation bent on extending its power across the globe to ever-more-distant communities. If Oriental tales published in Great Britain helped British readers imagine their own relation to empire differently, then those readers whose relation to empire was different before they even picked up the magazine and began to read would have necessarily taken different meanings from those very same words. For representations of the "East" must have born at least some subtle trace, for British American and early national readers, of the commercial, political, military, and economic interests those in Great Britain, British America, and the United States harbored in this region of the globe. But the expansion of the empire looked very different, and indeed, meant something very different, to readers in London than to readers in Boston, New York, Philadelphia, Charleston, and, to be sure, the even more remote outposts of Great Britain's empire in North America. The relation of these British American readers to the most basic laws and liberties associated with Great Britain differed from those of readers in London, Oxford, or Exeter simply because of where they lived. If where you were on the globe helped define your status within Great Britain, then where you were on the globe necessarily defined your relation to even those imaginary representations of every other place on the globe.[35]

British American and even early national readers thus occupied a triangulated relationship to figures of the East. Figures of the Orient would have been read in British America and the early United States in relation to Europe's position to the Orient. A wide range of recent scholarship demonstrates British American writers' "cultural dependence," to use Lawrence Buell's term, on standards of taste drawn from Britain in particular and Europe in general.[36] British America's cultural dependence on Great Britain has been cited by Leonard Tennenhouse as one piece of evidence illustrating American literature's fundamentally diasporic nature; it has been used to demonstrate the distortion of a related literary tradition by Paul Giles; and Buell takes this dependence as evidence that America produces the world's very first postcolonial literature.[37] However one explains this dependence, though, scholars from a wide variety of methodological approaches agree that British American writers kept their glance firmly fixed on the mother country across the Atlantic for guidance on cultural and aesthetic matters, even if they often claimed to reject what the Old World had to offer. Their relation to the figure of the Orient, then, was necessarily triangulated by Europe's relation with the Orient, a triangulation that marked British Americans as necessarily different from those in Europe whom they sought to emulate. The works examined in the chapters that follow, then, are American—at least in part—because of the way they ask their readers to imagine themselves in relation to the figurative category of the geographical "East," and, in this way, these figures of the East provide one significant foundation among many for a distinctly American literary tradition. The "Eastern imaginary," the sometimes contradictory but nevertheless systematic ways in which the East was imagined, was different, in other words, in British America during the years of this study than in Great Britain.

This triangulated relation to an East invested with great cultural power did more than simply help British American writers address their fear of provinciality, their fear that those in Europe were absolutely right that America had no legitimate claims to civilized status. Their use of these figures in the hopes of establishing their own cultural bona fides offered readers in the colonies and early United States—and even, in some cases, England and the rest of Europe—new ways of imagining the relation between East and West. This new way of organizing the world, this new way of organizing the set of figures that constituted the symbolic spatial economy of the period, offered a new shape to economy that cast Europe as the cultural, economic, and political center of the globe. For America to gain in status, the East must be downgraded in stature. In becoming more like the East to please its so-called betters in Europe, America drains power from the East as Europe becomes even more firmly situated in the center of global power and prestige. For Europe and America to become more important in the symbolic spatial economy, the East must be displaced. All things, in this new symbolic universe, emanated from a European center. Europe occupied the center of a globe rather than its former position at the very edge of relevance and power.

Given the extraordinary number of such figures contained in the archive of British American and early national writing, I make no claims that this study represents a comprehensive description of the varied uses of figures related to the East in the period. Nor do I aim to map out a linear narrative of historical development in the use of what is an extraordinary variety of figures carrying a wide range of associations that extends approximately one hundred and fifty years. Instead, I offer case studies of four especially provocative uses of figures of the East that, upon close, textual analysis, harbor important implications for our understanding of the formation of a distinctly American literature within what we commonly recognize as American culture. I will discuss the implications in more detail in the epilogue, but, for now, suffice it to say that close attention to figures of the East in these instances forces us to rethink just how seventeenth-, eighteenth-, and even nineteenth-century American writers sought to demonstrate the significance of American social environments. From the start, they looked to the East, rather than simply either to the land before them or to hallmarks of European refinement, for the terms through which they should be judged. American writers' sense of themselves as members of a distinct community grows as much, in other words, out of the use of figures of the East as it does out of any encounters with the environment, real or imagined, or any effort to adapt European models of cultural refinement. The East, in other words, plays a key role in the story of the emergence of a distinctively American set of literary traditions.

I have chosen to offer case studies of four provocative instances rather than offer a catalog that neatly divides the use of such figures into discrete categories for several reasons. First of all, such a comprehensive approach would be virtually impossible for one scholar to accomplish given the extraordinary number of figures in the archive. Part of the goal of my book is to demonstrate to scholars that such figures exist in the first place and are important. Second, I believe the best way to interest literary scholars—as opposed to, say, historians—in this archive is to demonstrate the figurative richness of the material and its relevance to important issues in the study of American literature. This simply cannot be done in an "inventory."

Each chapter thus makes its case by marshalling evidence drawn primarily from a close reading of the language of the text under analysis. These close readings of literary texts, though, occur only after first situating the specific work in the context of its production, distribution, imagined audience, and/or genre, historical factors that scholars working on the history of the book in the early modern Atlantic world have taught us are particularly important in understanding texts of the period. My decision to employ a methodology that relies primarily if not exclusively on figurative rather than more traditional "historical" evidence grows out of my conviction that, in the words of Henri Lefebvre, "[r]epresentations of space . . . have a substantial role and a specific influence in the production of space."[38] Far from ignoring or dismissing the historical, though, such an approach takes literature—and all practices of representation—as a crucial component in the production of history rather than as merely reflective of the political, social, economic, and other so-called historical events and phenomena. For such an emphasis on figurative analysis allows us to see the birth of the very categories historical actors developed to understand the world around them. "If," to return to Lefebvre, "space is produced, if there is a productive process, then we are dealing with *history*."[39] Historical events such as the Navigation Acts passed by Britain's Parliament in the eighteenth century, for instance, or the dramatic political and social events that occurred in India in the centuries covered by this study play an important role as well in the production of those categories colonial British Americans used to experience their world. When the evidence has indicated that historical events played a role in the way the writers discussed in this book figured what they considered the "East," such events have been included in the analysis.

Each of my four chapters focuses on a single author's use of figures relating to places, peoples, and things understood as Eastern at the time of the literary work's production and/or circulation. The four authors whose work I have chosen to analyze—Anne Bradstreet, James Kirkpatrick, Benjamin Franklin, and Edgar Allan Poe—offer glimpses into important historical periods, geographic regions, cultural formations, and aesthetic developments that are encompassed by an object of study, American literature before 1850, that not only includes many disparate regions but also spans the very historical period that gave birth to distinctly modern ways of organizing the world. These authors include a female member of the highest ranks of seventeenth-century New England society, a devout Christian, whom critics have labeled the first American author; a writer of relatively modest social background living in the staple colonies who wrote poems celebrating Britain's use of the colonies for commercial gain before returning to England to gain fame as a physician; a businessman from the mid-Atlantic whose work as a printer served as a prelude to his crucial role in British America's Revolution for independence; and an author born in Boston, and raised in Virginia, who would challenge efforts to evaluate literature using nationalist standards during the period of America's first great literary productions. While these authors are drawn from a range of geographic regions and historical periods, and while their works cover a variety of topics and genres, the work of three of these four has come to play a prominent role in the way we tell the story of America's literary history. I have chosen to focus so much attention on such canonical authors from some of the most important periods in early American literary history in order to demonstrate how figures of the East—so long neglected in our study of this literature—in fact serve vital literary functions in writings by authors who have come to be understood as crucial to the emergence of a distinctly American literature.

Chapter 1 focuses on the New England poet Anne Bradstreet (c. 1612–72). Bradstreet's writings demonstrate more clearly than those of any other colonial British American writer how references to the East in early American writing have been hiding in plain sight. Bradstreet wrote far more about the East than she did about any other topic, yet figures of the East in her poetry have received virtually no scholarly attention. Careful attention to two of her poems, "The Four Monarchies" and "An Elegie Upon that Honourable and Renowned Knight Sir Philip Sidney," shows how Bradstreet ties colonial British Americans to the East and, in so doing, brings colonial British America into the realm of civilized nations. Bradstreet rests the colonists' claims to civilized status on the bodily ties her poems establish between Alexander the Great and colonial British Americans. As part of the same imagined body as the great conqueror, Britain's American colonists share in the exalted social status Alexander gains from his Eastern conquests.

In order to demonstrate that figures of the East played a role in writing from the colonies to New England's south, we turn our attention to commercial images associated with the East that can be found in materials relating to the promotion of Georgia in the 1730s and early 1740s. Chapter 2 focuses primarily on "An Address to James Oglethorpe, Esq" (first published in 1732–33), written by James Kirkpatrick (c. 1700–1770) in support of the new colony's efforts to paint itself as a rich source of commercial goods that were associated with China and India. In its vision of a Georgia overflowing with Eastern goods, Kirkpatrick's poem collapses the very distinction between the geographic East and West. The collapse elevates, the chapter argues, what British America has to offer the world, for it suggests that America gains its value by helping Britain look more civilized by allowing it to look more "Eastern. The East occupies the position in this poem of the place to be emulated, of the transcendent signified that seems to provide the ultimate source of value, and the poem quite pointedly and explicitly asks us to imagine America's value in relation to what it classifies as "Chinese" and/or "Eastern" standards and objects rather than in terms, either, of the distinctive products to be found in the American environment or of some resemblance to the mother country of Great Britain.

While the first two chapters investigate writings from colonial British America, the third chapter focuses on late-eighteenth-century literature in circulation at the moment of the United States' birth as a political entity by examining the Oriental tales written by Benjamin Franklin. Franklin's "Eastern tales" use the ideas, images, and conceptions linked to the category of the "East" to define the "human" itself, a "human" that is understood in opposition to one of the key terms of the Enlightenment with which Franklin is so often associated: reason. Franklin suggests that the notion of "reason" on which Americans operate has the curious effect of leading to uncivilized behavior, and he offers a model of civilized behavior for Americans to emulate drawn from a specifically Orientalized East. Thus the truly civilized human in Franklin's Oriental tales is an Eastern man.

The final chapter suggests one way in which figures of the East provide the glue that binds America's colonial and national periods of literary production together. Focusing on Edgar Allan Poe's spoof of *The Arabian Nights*, "The Thousand-and-Second Tale of Scheherazade," the chapter argues that Poe casts what he considers an Eastern aesthetic as superior to aesthetic theories trumpeted by American literary nationalists. Scheherazade's aesthetic theory becomes the model for American literature to emulate, a model that, if followed, would allow American aesthetic products to be considered in the same breath as those of more civilized communities. In suggesting that this superior, Orientalized vision of literature could serve as a model for the United States, Poe's story offers a way for American culture to be included in the category of civilized nations by having American aesthetic theory become more Oriental.[40]

BY WAY OF concluding these introductory remarks, let me briefly return to Perry Miller's attempts to cleanse America's seemingly most American nineteenth-century writers of their Oriental influences. Miller's generation of scholars sought to create a space for American literature in the university, a place that would be valuable in its own right, as derivative of traditions to be found nowhere else in the world. Miller asks us to ignore the Oriental influence on American Transcendentalism as a way of establishing a continuity between pre- and post-Revolutionary literature that allows for American literature to stand, as it were, on its own. A careful examination of the archives of British American writing tells us that Miller—and those who wrote in support of his project—had it backwards. A close examination of the writings of this field demonstrates the need to highlight rather than ignore references to what the colonists and citizens of the new nation would have called the "East." In place of Miller's trajectory of Edwards to Emerson, then, I offer an alternate line of descent in American literary history. At least for the pages of this book, I would like us to imagine American literature flowing from Bradstreet to Poe—from, that is, the poetry produced by one of seventeenth-century New England's most orthodox Puritan thinkers, for whom poetry served as a means of glorifying God, to the nineteenth-century writings of a man who championed the production of art for art's sake amidst accusations of insanity, ill-mannered behavior, drug abuse, and atheism. These two writers share a common figurative bond that stretches across the centuries and ideologies, and they stand as representatives of a bond that can be found in the literature of the period in general.

CHAPTER 1

The Colonial Body Travels East in Anne Bradstreet's Poetry

Anne Bradstreet wrote far more poetry concerning Alexander the Great, well over 1,000 lines, than on any other topic or person. Let me put this another way. Bradstreet devoted more poetry to Alexander than to her husband, her children, her grandchildren, her father, or her mother, either individually or combined. She devoted more lines of poetry to Alexander than to one of the most important icons of her age, Queen Elizabeth, or to one of the most important political events of her time, the English Civil War. She wrote more poetry about Alexander than she did about the New England Way or her life in the New World. She wrote more about Alexander than she wrote about her experiences as a woman. She wrote more poetry about Alexander than she wrote about Native Americans, the people who were the Puritans' sometimes combatants, sometimes allies, but who were always involved in some way in seventeenth-century Puritan New England and English thinking. In fact, we might never have had a published work from her in the first place had Bradstreet not been quite so fascinated with Alexander. After all, virtually all of the material on Alexander appears in "The Four Monarchies," and this poem alone, as Jane Eberwein points out, "takes up more than half of *The Tenth Muse.*" "Without its sheer mass," Eberwein continues, "it is improbable there ever would have been such a book." As Eberwein goes on to note, "[I]t is Alexander that dominates the poem."[1] One might even say that *The Tenth Muse* is as much about Alexander as it is about any other topic.

Given the interest Bradstreet demonstrated in all things relating to Alexander, how could it be that scholars have paid so little attention to "The Four Monarchies" in general and to Alexander in particular? Why have we chosen to focus our interpretive attention on Bradstreet's other poetry, even though we know Bradstreet devoted an extraordinary amount of her time and energy over many years to "The Four Monarchies," more time and energy, it seems clear, than she spent on any other piece of writing? Even more importantly, what can be learned about Bradstreet's writing and, more broadly, colonial British American writing and culture from a more careful analysis of the figure of Alexander as he appears in "The Four Monarchies" and Bradstreet's other poetry?

I suspect that we have ignored this poem and, more specifically, the figure of Alexander who dominates it, because the poem and person seem to have little to tell us about what is specifically colonial and/or American about colonial British American poetry, culture, and life.[2] The first book of poetry published in England by an American poet provides us with no scenes of encounters with Indians, adjustments to the wilds of America, descriptions of America's distinctive landscape, meditations on colonial political squabbles, or colorful portraits of colonial life in general.[3] Instead, Bradstreet fills her poetry with references to "antique Greeks" such as Alexander, and she provides us with detailed scenes of England regaining its strength after the Civil War so that it can "lay waste" to "Turkey."[4] Bradstreet recounts stories of "barbarous" people, "sottish kings," and incestuous relations in the East.[5] She writes of Egyptian revolutions. She devotes hundreds of lines to scenes set in Asia and "less Asia" in which she speaks of "Asiatic coast[s]" alongside "Asiatic cowardice."[6] She writes of the "manners, habit, gestures" of the "luxurious nation" of Persia.[7] Bradstreet does write about "Indian Kings," but she uses the phrase without exception to refer to Southeast Asian royalty rather than Native Americans leaders.[8] She compares Queen Elizabeth to the "potent empress of the East" and follows Alexander's attempts to conquer what she refers to as the "East" as he relentlessly battles to "his empire extend / Unto the utmost bounds o' th' orient."[9] While a colonial British American poet wrote these words, the images in the lines seem to ignore rather than engage with what William Spengemann has labeled "American Things."[10] Yet, depending on how one counts what should be classified as "Eastern Things," at least a third of Bradstreet's poetry is devoted to references just like those above.

In an effort to begin filling this void in scholarship concerning the significance of "Eastern things" in Bradstreet's poetry, this chapter will analyze her representation of Alexander the Great.[11] Such a focus on Bradstreet's portrayal of Alexander will require investigation into the figure of the East in the Puritan New England poet's verse. This is true first because, as I noted above, the poem in which Alexander appears most often, "The Four Monarchies," contains many references to the East, and these references are most prominent in the section of the poem in which Alexander takes center stage, Bradstreet's versification of the third monarchy. Even if, though, Bradstreet had written of Alexander in "The Four Monarchies" without once mentioning any people, places, or things associated with the East, we still would have had to consider the region in some fashion in our analysis of Bradstreet's representation of Alexander given the frequency with which writers in the early modern period connected him to the region. Alexander's connection with the East—both his confrontation with it and the allure that it held for him—were such integral parts of his seventeenth-century image that it was virtually impossible to speak of him without invoking the specter of the region he ultimately failed to bring under Western control. In the early modern world in which Bradstreet lived, Alexander's very identity—the qualities, characteristics, and features with which he was associated and which served to define him as a distinct character—was inextricably bound with the East.

Before we consider the significance of the East in Bradstreet's representations of Alexander, we must first understand the paradoxical qualities associated with the region when Bradstreet wrote. As the dominant political, economic, and military power throughout most of recorded history—at least as Bradstreet and her contemporaries tell the story of human history—the East stands in the way of the desire expressed by many in England and her colonies to extend the range of Protestantism's hegemony across the globe. Indeed, given the Ottoman Empire's attempts throughout the sixteenth and seventeenth centuries to bring more of Europe under its political control through military conquest, Bradstreet's brand of Christianity seemed, at least to many of its supporters in Europe, to be in a fight for its very life with its foes to the East.[12] Our historical vantage point looks at the late seventeenth century as precisely the period when the Ottoman Empire began its slow decline. This perspective was not available to Bradstreet or her readers. When English Puritans and their allies in the American colonies viewed their plight in light of what was happening around the globe as a whole, they tended to see a world dominated by countries and worldviews they cast as fundamentally "Eastern," countries and worldviews that had, in their opinion, turned hostile toward the "true" religion of Christianity to which the East had given birth. They still viewed the Ottoman Empire, in other words, as a real, ongoing threat to Christendom's way of life.

But this view of the East as purely or even primarily a threat to the West fails to account for other, more positive ways in which the East was understood by people writing in English around the time Bradstreet composed her poetry. Indeed, we should be careful to avoid reading back onto seventeenth-century New England writing a strict East–West binary that would come into life in the nineteenth century. Bradstreet wrote and revised her poetry before Orientalism came to dominate what in the introduction I called the symbolic spatial economy.[13] As Daniel Vitkus points out, "'the East' was not yet the clearly defined geographic or cultural category that it would become"; an "imaginary construct" that cast East as diametrically opposed to West "was yet to be built."[14] In this moment of history before Orientalism took hold, Bradstreet and her contemporaries found much to emulate in Eastern people, places, and practices.

For one thing, the East was the birthplace of Christ and the geographic location of the events in the Bible. New England Puritans associated the East, in other words, with God's representative on Earth, the being with whom all Puritans longed to be one in the afterlife, and they considered the East the holiest of lands by virtue of its being the birthplace of the being they considered humanity's savior. In addition, for those communities who longed for a seat at the table with the truly civilized nations, the East's status as the center for centuries of the civilized world provided an image of what it meant for a nation to be truly civilized, an image that had received the sanction of historians and educators for centuries. If, as scholars have long noted, the people in Britain's American colonies learned what it meant to be refined by aping the ways of their supposed betters in London, early modern Europeans and British Americans looked, in a similar way, still further East for behaviors and practices to emulate that would allow them to claim that they, too, should be counted as civilized people.

In order to explore the ways in which the sometimes paradoxical qualities these issues, ideas, and images attached to the East come to life in Bradstreet's poetry, this chapter will focus on the two poems in which Bradstreet mentions Alexander the Great: "The Four Monarchies" and "An Elegie upon that Honourable and renowned Knight, Sir Philip Sidney." Each of these poems appears in the two seventeenth-century editions of Bradstreet's poetry over which we believe she had some control, *The Tenth Muse*, issued in London in 1650, and *Several Poems*, printed in Boston in 1678.[15] "The Four Monarchies" of *The Tenth Muse* is unfinished.[16] It abruptly ends during the early years of the last monarchy. She was unable to finish the poem before she died, so the version to appear in *Several Poems* is also unfinished.

This second version of Bradstreet's longest poem contains relatively minor revisions. The most significant revision can be found at the end of the section on the fourth and final monarchy when Bradstreet attempts to explain, in a 27-line "Apology," her inability to complete the poem. The London elegy to Sidney, on the other hand, underwent significant revision before it made its second appearance in Boston in 1678. At some point after the poem's initial publication, Bradstreet substantially revised her memorial to Sidney, trimming it from approximately 150 to just under 100 lines. We will, in the pages that follow, need to consider the nature of some of these revisions as they pertain to Alexander.

The chapter is divided into two sections. First, we need to examine the connection Bradstreet makes in her poetry between Alexander and the East. Therefore, the first section focuses on Bradstreet's representation of the East in general in "The Four Monarchies." This discussion is followed by a careful consideration of the way she portrays Alexander in relation to the East in the poem. Our examination of the Great Conqueror reveals that the figure of the East in Bradstreet's poetry served as both a threat and a model, an object of debilitating fear and intense, unsatisfied, and unquenchable desire. Once we have considered Alexander's connection to the East in "The Four Monarchies," we then turn our attention to the implications Bradstreet's vision of Alexander has for our understanding of the two versions of her Sidney elegy. Bradstreet uses Alexander in both versions of this poem as a way of sneaking the colonists into identity categories from which they were usually excluded. Through the magic of figurative language, Bradstreet engages in what I think can accurately be described as a kind of imaginary grave robbery in which colonial corpses rob classical ones of their very identities. She does this when she represents Britain's American colonists as being part of the very same body politic as Alexander. Through this rhetorical sleight of hand, she ties to the East all those living on the very far reaches of England's burgeoning empire and, in so doing, brings colonial British Americans into the realm of civilized nations. In this poem, Bradstreet grounds colonial British American claims to be civilized on classical figures associated with the East rather than, for instance, by turning our attention to the new world that lay before her or the peoples and places she and the colonists had left behind in Europe. In order to see how she accomplishes these rhetorical feats, we need to turn now to the poem, "The Four Monarchies," in which Bradstreet focuses our attention most often on Alexander and the East.

WHILE FIGURES of the East play a key role throughout Bradstreet's poetry, the Eastern focus of *The Tenth Muse* and *Several Poems* grows primarily if not exclusively out of what is by far the longest poem in either collection and the longest poem Bradstreet ever wrote, "The Four Monarchies."[17] The poem is divided into four sections corresponding to each of the monarchies that—according, at least, to seventeenth-century historians—had governed the world from just after the Great Flood until the fall of the Roman Empire. At approximately 3,500 lines, the poem is more than five times longer than Bradstreet's next longest poem, the approximately 600-line "Of the Four Humours in Man's Constitution." We should hardly be surprised that even 3,500 lines of poetry would be insufficient to cover so vast a topic as the history of the world and, in fact, Bradstreet never finished the poem.

Bradstreet explains in what, at first glance, appear to be the final 13 lines of the third monarchy that she is "done" with a poem whose "errors" make her "blush."[18] Any careful reader of Bradstreet knows better than to take the explanation she offers here—that the "task befits not women like to men"—at face value, and we are even less inclined to do so in this case given that these 13 lines announcing her decision to abandon the poem are followed by another 10 lines in which she proclaims that, after "some days of rest," she has decided "To finish what's begun" (1. 3412; 3422–23). Even her newfound energy proves insufficient to the task at hand, though, and the final lines of the version of "The Four Monarchies" in *Several Poems* announce one last time that Bradstreet will be unable to complete the task. But not for lack of effort. She speaks of the "hours" she spent and the "weary lines" she "penned" in an effort to fulfill her "desire" to "prosecute the story to the last" (1. 3560–65). Try as she might, though, a "raging fire" destroyed her most recent additions to the poem, and, in the end, she decided she could not see the history of the world through to its completion (1. 3566). If nothing else, Bradstreet's repeated efforts to finish so gargantuan a project after so many years and in the face of so many daunting personal obstacles suggests the great importance she attached to this poem.

If it is to be expected that a poem aiming to versify world history would end up being the longest poem Bradstreet ever wrote, so, too, should we hardly be surprised, given the history of the world up to that point, that "The Four Monarchies" focuses attention on the East. Bradstreet and the histories she adapted and/or used as background for her poem had little choice but to concentrate on matters associated with the Eastern part of the globe, for Europe and the West had played relatively insignificant roles in the shaping of world history up to that point. The Eastern orientation of the historical record in "The Four Monarchies" reminds us of what any seventeenth-century reader would have known but we might have forgotten: far from being the dominant imperial and/or economic power it would later become, England and its European enemies and allies had long been second-tier communities whose clout on the world stage paled in comparison to the political and economic entities to their East. The very development by Western writers in the middle ages of the concepts of translatio studi and translatio imperii—the march of learning and rule from East to West—indicates that Europeans were well away of the East's historical supremacy over the West, and the continuing invocation of these concepts by Britain's American colonists in the seventeenth and eighteenth centuries shows that people of English descent living in the colonies were equally aware of their culture's own inferiority in comparison to those to be found in the East.[19] The theory might even be understood as motivated by a deep anxiety about the West's place in the hierarchy of civilized nations. If those in the West found themselves less advanced when they looked back over the historical record, why not lay claim to greater learning and eventual rule in a yet unrealized but no doubt inevitable future?

The greater learning and the vast body of sophisticated cultural products to be found throughout history—learning and products that account in part for the sense of inferiority out of which theories such as translatio studi and imperii grow—confer on the East a cultural sophistication to which those of English ancestry can only aspire. We catch a glimpse of the great cultural power attached to the East in the way Bradstreet's poem suggests that one can never be East enough. All of the rulers to be found in the first poem's first book want to control territory to their East, including rulers who lord over what would seem to be the very center of Eastern power. So even though the poem begins in what it calls the East, Assyria, it nonetheless demonstrates the grandeur of one of the very first rulers mentioned, Ninus, by showing how he extended his reign even further east throughout "all the greater Asia" (1. 64). The focus on the East as the object of insatiable desire becomes clear when control of virtually the whole of Asia fails to satisfy Ninus's successor, his widow Semiramus. She dies leading her armies on "[a]n expedition" even further "to the East" (1. 130).

The poem does not bother to tell us where in the East she led her armies. Instead, the East remains an undefined region here and elsewhere in "The Four Monarchies," a region whose precise boundaries matter less than its function as a signifier of desire for accumulation, wealth, and status. One cannot be entirely successful, the poem suggests, nor can one ever be entirely satisfied with one's position in the world, unless and until one conquers the East as a whole, a region that lacks a whole from the Western point of view because those who seek to master it continually and obsessively fail to offer their own definition of its boundaries. As a demonstration of this, the poem puts on display ruler after ruler from greater and lesser Asia, each of whom embarks on quest after quest in the hopes of conquering some region even further to the East, only to end up defeated because, without fail, some part of the East remains just beyond his grasp.

We might expect the poem to be less fixated on the East once the center of world power moves westward to Greece and Rome. Instead, precisely the opposite turns out to be the case. The poem fixes our gaze even more frequently on the Eastern parts of the world as civilization advances, at least according to translatio studii and imperii, toward its inevitable European home. For the third book in "The Four Monarchies" concentrates almost exclusively on Alexander's quest to bring the East under his control.

As if this were not enough to show the outsize focus Bradstreet here gives the desire to conquer the East, we must remember that the obsession with the East during the Grecian monarchy does not end with Alexander.[20] In Bradstreet's retelling of the history of the world during the third monarchy, the desire for the East becomes the defining goal not simply of the period's main character but of all those who follow in his wake. From the moment we are introduced to Alexander until Rome succeeds Greece more than 3,000 lines later, the poem allows us no diversion from its myopic fixation on the East. We are first treated to Alexander's plans for conquering Persia and Asia, then to the details of his military successes and failures as he aims to bring his vision to reality. When Bradstreet tells us of the various places and peoples he subdues while he leads his army in battle, of the treachery Alexander encounters and the cruelty he inflicts, she never fails to specify where on the globe these deeds occur. We hear of his crossing the "River Granic" and the "Black Sea," and, when Alexander draws near Persia, she tells us how his order that his ships sail by the mouth of the Indus flood has the unfortunate result of having those boats get stuck upon the flats and mud (1. 1675; 1691; 2360–75). Alexander's death brings no end to the obsession with all things Eastern. Bradstreet's treatment of how his descendents, disciples, and enemies seek to realize his vision lasts another 800 lines. Whether or not Bradstreet consciously chose to spend so much more time on a section devoted exclusively to the East, the effect is the same as if it were conscious. When we get to the Grecian monarchy, the focus on the East explodes into a downright obsession from which the reader cannot escape.

Bradstreet's engagement with her material grows as the story becomes more focused on the East. Of all the monarchies, the Grecian clearly holds the most interest for Bradstreet.[21] Suddenly, in the section on Alexander and the attempt to conquer the East, Bradstreet finds her muse. She devotes over 1,700 lines to the Grecian monarchy but only 1,600 lines combined for the Assyrian and Persian. She wrote twice as many lines about the Grecian monarchy, in other words, than she did about any other monarchial period in spite of the fact that the Persian monarchy lasted far longer than the Grecian. Bradstreet thus devotes more verse—1,000—to things of the East in this single section of this monarchy than she does to the various rulers and their travels and concerns in either of the first two monarchies. Indeed, the first two monarchies combined amount to only 1,600 lines. She writes over 1,000 lines about Alexander and the East alone.

Bradstreet's greater focus on the East in the Grecian monarchy derives, at least in part, from the fact that this is the section of the poem in which a figure claimed by the West as its own—Alexander—comes remarkably close to bringing the East under his dominion. Bradstreet focuses so much attention on the East in this part of the poem, that is, because this is the moment when the West seems capable of defusing the threat posed by the East and absorbing its antagonist's cultural legacies into its own traditions. To incorporate the East into the West, though, poses a threat as grave as the one Alexander's political domination of the East wards off: turning Turk. How does one incorporate the cultural legacies of the East into the West without corrupting Western cultural products and practices themselves with Eastern influences? The way to satisfy the desire to incorporate the East into the West, Bradstreet suggests, is to obliterate the distinction between East and West in the first place, and Alexander, according to Bradstreet, does exactly this.

Alexander's very body, the poem suggests, defies geographic boundaries and cannot be contained by geographic space. It is not just, Bradstreet insists, that Alexander wants to extend his dominion beyond his home country. Alexander does more than simply "scorn" being "confin'd" to "Grecia" alone (1. 1621–23). Bradstreet extends Alexander's reach beyond the mere globe by insisting that all of geographic space itself would barely contain Alexander's body parts. The very "universe" itself, Bradstreet informs us, would "scarce bound [Alexander's] vast minde" (1. 1621–22). Bradstreet associates not only his body but also his very identity with geographic space. His "fame," she tells us, will "last whilest there is land" (1. 2577–78). At the very height of his power, when he has brought "All countries, kingdoms, provinces . . . From Hellespont to th' farthest ocean" under his control, Alexander is made to "oft lament" the fact that "no more worlds" remained "to be conquered" (1. 2508–9, 2601–2).

We see this aspect of Alexander's character as well in the way Bradstreet highlights the Great Conqueror's constant motion over geographic space as once-powerful monarchs fall one by one in the face of his seemingly invincible armies. He moves over so much space so quickly that geographic borders themselves—and distinctions such as East versus West—are called into question. Scanning the lines of poetry on any page from "The Third Monarchy" takes us in a matter of seconds across hundreds of miles of often rugged, mountainous territory. So it is that in fewer than 100 lines Alexander moves from Gaza to Jerusalem to Egypt to Syria then back to Egypt until, finally, he ends up in Phoenicia. Even death fails to halt his body's movements, for Alexander continues his journey even after he dies (1. 2775). His dead body travels for two years before being laid to rest in Macedonia. After so much motion, so much movement over so much space, we are led to ask, how can such a figure be contained within a single geographic region?

Alexander's ability to obliterate geographic boundaries—boundaries that, we must remember, signify at the same time a cultural divide that prioritizes Eastern cultural history over Western cultural history—provides the very means by which the West can triumph over an East of the West's imagination. Let me explain how this paradox works in "The Four Monarchies." We must remember, first, that at the time the poem was written and as the poem itself demonstrates in the people, places, and incidents it describes, only the East could lay claim to a long, uninterrupted history of social, political, and economic dominance. Second, we need to keep in mind that Alexander serves in this poem and elsewhere as a representative of the West. Third, we should recall the paradoxical nature of the Eastern imaginary. It is not that Bradstreet or other early modern writers want simply to adopt the ways of the East so that they can be seen to be just as civilized and refined as those who lived in the communities authorized as truly civilized in world history. After all, the East is both a model for those in the Western world to emulate and a threat to the religious, political, and economic aims of those in the West. Bradstreet wants to use the refinement of the East as a model that can be adapted by those in the colonies so that they can take on the refinement attached to the people and places of the East, but she wants them to take on this refinement while simultaneously retaining their own identities as people of the West. She wants her fellow colonists to use the East so that they can claim to be civilized and English at the same time, all without becoming, through the incorporation of Eastern things, an Easterner herself.

Succumbing to the charms of the East is precisely what trips up Alexander in the end. While he absorbs one group of people after another into his and the West's political and cultural orbit as he relentlessly defeats one army after another in the space of only a few lines of verse, he ultimately fails to lead the West to what Bradstreet would have considered its rightful place at the head of the civilized world because he succumbs to the lure of the East. Armies pose no obstacle to him. He defeats each one that crosses his path. Instead, Alexander fails to conquer the East, according to Bradstreet and her sources, because he goes native. We see this in his rejection of what Bradstreet casts as distinctively Protestant moral codes. He behaves more like one of the monarchs of the East from the earlier books than like someone who lives by the Christian God's laws. Once he has extended "his empire" not only to "th' farthest ocean" but even more crucially "to the utmost bounds o' the' orient," once the extension of his empire has created an army defined by its "monstrous bulk," not only does his wealth grow "boundless" by the extraordinary breadth of his rule but also, and more importantly, "Him boundless made in vice and cruelty" (1. 1945–46). Freed from abiding by Protestant moral codes once he has obliterated the distinction between East and West by bringing the people and places of the East under his command, Alexander sets fire to whole towns, puts to death former allies for no discernable reason, and pursues power for power's sake alone.

It is one thing for Alexander himself to adopt Eastern ways, but it is even more threatening to the purity of the Western tradition to insist, as Alexander does, that his subordinates follow his lead. This, Bradstreet suggests, is the final straw. This is what ultimately brings about the Great Conqueror's death. Alexander suddenly and without warning, at least according to Bradstreet, adopts the "manners, habit, gestures . . . [and] fashion" of the "conquered and luxurious nation" of Persia (1. 2166–70). Not satisfied with keeping his fashion tastes to himself, Alexander goes so far as to insist that "his nobility" do the same. Lest we miss the implication of his turning Turk, Bradstreet informs us that his "captains" were "grieved" at the transformation these seemingly stylistic changes produce. For Bradstreet claims that his Captains lament the change they see in his very "mind" that these new "manners" bring about (1. 2171–72).[22] It should not surprise us, then, that after an evening of drinking, Alexander's subordinates are able to overtake him. If even so great a leader as Alexander, even so ruthless and successful a military tactician as the Great Conqueror, cannot wrest control of the East without succumbing to the threats posed by its so-called corrupt ways, what hope does the West as a whole have of succeeding where so exemplary a figure has already failed?

In order to answer this question, we must return to an earlier point: that while Bradstreet associates the figure of Alexander with the East, she shows that his quest for ever more territory to his East ultimately stems from the inability of space to contain Alexander. He conquers because the world cannot contain him, and so he holds open the possibility of space lacking geographic distinction at all. He cannot be contained within the boundaries of the West but seeks to obliterate those boundaries through conquest. Once the world is his, the boundaries that had defined the world—East and West—will be obliterated. In using Alexander as the figure for a space in which geographic divisions no longer apply, though, Bradstreet necessarily claims this philosophical position for the West. The destruction of these boundaries would usher in the continual, never-ending, nevermore threatened triumph of the West over an East that threatens precisely because it has dominated the world for all of human history. We in the West can learn from Alexander's example, Bradstreet's representation of Alexander here seems to suggest, to avoid going native by obliterating such geographic distinctions in the first place. Since it is a figure from the West who embodies this position and potentially brings it to life, though, the West gets to define the world after it has lost its divisions. It is in this way that Bradstreet can suggest that the West can eat its geographic cake and have it too. For once geographic distinctions are obliterated, the world becomes one because it is one as the West imagined it. No one need fear becoming Easternized in such a world, for this world owes its nativity to the West.

This is not, of course, the way history went. Alexander failed to conquer the East, and European Christians continued to perceive the East as a threat to their religious and political systems. The European monarchy had yet to occur when Bradstreet wrote, and the Ottoman Empire continued to pose a potent threat to any hopes the West might have. But in spite of Alexander's failures, the dream lives on in the poem in his descendents. His failure signals not the impossibility of the West's success but its potential to match the East.

"THE FOUR MONARCHIES" makes no explicit connection between the British American colonists and Alexander. None of the few scholars over the years who have analyzed the poem have detected any attempt to use the people, places, and events in Bradstreet's verse history of the world as allegories for any aspect of New England life.[23] To see the connection in Bradstreet's poetry between the colonists, Alexander, and the East we must turn to a much shorter of Bradstreet's writings, "An Elegy Upon that Honourable and Renowned Knight Sir Philip Sidney." As I noted earlier, Bradstreet wrote two very different versions of this elegy, one published in 1650 in *The Tenth Muse* and the other in 1678 in *Several Poems*. She dramatically shortened the Boston version of the poem, transforming a 150-line poem into one of barely 95. To achieve this newfound brevity about Sidney, Bradstreet not only removed entire sections of the work but also reworked and reordered other parts. Commentators have generally found both versions unsatisfying—hardly surprising given that this appears to be Bradstreet's first attempt to write an elegy—but they have been especially critical of the second version. Rosamond Rosenmeier, for instance, finds the "religious and erotic enthusiasm" at the heart of the first version to be absent entirely from the second.[24]

The changes in the Boston version make Alexander even more central than he was in the London elegy, in spite of the fact that his name appears less often in the revised version of the poem. We see this in the way Bradstreet reduces the number of people to whom she compares Sidney. Since comparisons are one way a poet defines his or her subject, one way, that is, the poet helps us understand the ideals and ideas with which the subject is to be associated, then fewer comparisons means fewer ideals with which to be associated. The narrower range of comparisons thus allows us to see the subject with a sharper focus, and in the process of doing so strengthens the connection between the subject and the person to whom he or she is being compared. We see precisely this sharpening of focus in Bradstreet's Boston elegy. In London, Sidney merges his identity with two figures, Apollo and Alexander. Sidney, the poem contends, has such a "deep share" of Apollo's "Deity" that the two become indistinguishable.[25] On numbers alone, though, Alexander rates above Apollo in *The Tenth Muse* version of the poem, for Sidney not once but twice becomes Alexander. Bradstreet speaks at one point of "Princely *Philip*" and later tells us that "Philip *and* Alexander" lie "*both in one*" in Sidney's grave.[26] In addition to these two instances in which Sidney becomes someone else, Bradstreet analogizes Sidney with several figures in *The Tenth Muse*. He is directly compared to both Mars and Vulcan in *The Tenth Muse*. For the 1678 version of "An Elegie," though, Bradstreet removes all but one of these comparisons. She retains only the image of Alexander and Sidney merging in Philip's grave. He becomes, that is, more like Alexander in Boston if for no other reason than that he is less like anyone else.

Bradstreet's comparison of Sidney with Alexander alone would not warrant our interest. It is the way she uses the occasion of an elegy to Sidney to show how the colonists are part of the same community that includes Alexander that is unique. Before we examine the way she connects Alexander to the colonists in both versions of the poem, before we can appreciate, that is, the remarkable rhetorical feat she accomplishes in using this trope to bring the colonists into the civilized world, we need to understand the level of conventionality that the comparison of Sidney with Alexander had achieved when Bradstreet first began "An Elegie." By the time Bradstreet started her memorial to Sidney, Alexander had been used so often by other Renaissance writers as to have been rendered cliché. "Sidney's earlier elegists," as Raphael Falco points out, "again and again compare the dead hero to Alexander."[27] Bradstreet even co-opts one of the most common themes among those elegists when she claims that both combined qualities of the poet with those of a warrior, or both were, in her words, "*Heire to the* Muses, *the* son of Mars *in truth.*"[28] Of course, in elegizing Sidney at all, Bradstreet was choosing a topic that itself had long ago become a cliché. Sidney died in Holland in October of 1586, and the elegies began flooding what would pass for a print market in 1587 only to peter out a few years later. Bradstreet finished the first version of her Sidney poem in 1638.[29] This would mean that Sidney had been dead almost fifty years, and the elegiac tradition that memorialized him almost as long. In short, Bradstreet chooses a defunct subgenre to honor a long-dead poet in terms that only replicate the praise the subject had already received.[30]

But if her comparison was conventional, the relationships she posits between colonial, English, and Greek bodies offers a radically different spatial economy that aims at nothing less than the transformation of conventional notions of identity. In other words, she puts a rather tired comparison in a stale genre to work by using it to sneak a new theory of identity into English discursive systems. To see how she accomplishes this remarkable rhetorical feat, we need first to see how Bradstreet obliterates the bodily distinction between Sidney and Alexander. In the "Epitaph," in the very section of the poem meant to give us the essence of the elegy's subject, when she conjures up for her readers the figure of Sidney's "bones . . . interred in stately Paul's," we read "Philip and Alexander both in one" (1. 92–95). Through Bradstreet's figurative sleight of hand, one dead body becomes indistinguishable from another. English bones become Greek bones.

And not just any bones. Bradstreet frames her elegy on Sidney as a meditation on an ideal English identity set during "her halsion dayes" (1. 1). She casts Sidney not simply as exemplary of this period but as a "patterne" that all who reside on "British land" should follow (1. 6). In calling him a "patterne" she draws on the meaning of the term at the time as, in the words of the OED, "[a]nything fashioned, shaped, or designed to serve as a model from which something is to be made." In this way Bradstreet makes Sidney a potentially productive figure who serves not only as a representative of an ideal Englishness but also as a force whose very image will re-produce itself and, in the process, continually re-produce the halcyon days in which he lived. The very bones of the pattern of ideal Englishness thus merge their identity with the figure of classical leadership.

Bradstreet does not rest at transforming English identities into Greek ones. If she had, as I noted above, we would simply have another one of the many elegies that compared Sidney to Alexander. Bradstreet, instead, uses the figure of blood to link her own body with the great Alexander and, by extension, the colonists with classical culture. Sidney serves as the pivot point in this link. In order to see how she uses the figure of her own blood to level a figurative attack on the spatial economy that would relegate the colonial English poet to a mere sideshow freak, we must now return to her revision of the "Elegie." The alteration of one phrase in the poem has generated the most critical interest and is the revision most relevant to the issues of this chapter. In the 1650 version, the speaker of the poem asks potential critics not to dismiss her praise of Sidney simply because she shared with the famous poet "the 'self-same blood.'" The 1678 Boston edition of this very same poem substitutes "English" for "self-same." Here are the lines in question:

> In all records, thy Name I ever see,
> Put with an Epithet of dignity;
> Which shewes, thy worth was great, then honour such,
> The love thy Country ought thee, was as much.
> Let then, none dis-allow of these my strains,
> Which have the self-same blood yet in my veines;
> Who honours thee for what was honourable,
> But leaves the rest, as most unprofitable:
> Thy wiser dayes, condemn'd thy witty works,
> Who knows the Spels that in thy Rethorick lurks?
> (*The Tenth Muse*, 1. 23–32)

> In all Records his name I ever see
> Put with an Epithite of dignity,
> Which shews his worth was great, his honour such,
> The love his Country ought him, was as much.
> Then let none disallow of these my straines
> Whilst English blood yet runs within my veins.
> (*Several Poems*, 1. 38–43)

Critics have generally understood Bradstreet's use of the term "self-same" in *The Tenth Muse* as a signal of her relation to Sidney and, therefore, an indication that she was born of noble blood. Some members of the Bradstreet family, in fact, at times claimed to be members of the Dudley line.[31] Critics have further wondered whether these lines were revised in a "bow to decorum" that was also a concession to the "outright criticism" she received after making such a boastful claim. Worried that she might be viewed as arrogant or as trying to trumpet her own status in a community with few if any members of noble rank, Bradstreet, critics speculate, shifted the terms of the link the poem makes between herself and Sidney from blood to nation.[32]

Before we examine whether "self-same" was a subtle way of indicating Bradstreet's membership in the Sidney clan, we should first remember that "self-same" and "English" serve the same purpose in each poem. Whether or not Bradstreet intended her line to be a subtle reminder of the noble blood coursing through her own veins, whether she altered those lines in response to criticism or simply because she felt she had overstepped the bounds of good taste, both "self-same" and "English" obliterate the geographic space that separates the colonists from those they left behind in England in order to include those living in the provinces with people living in England in the same identity category. In obliterating the geographic divide that separates English people living on different parts of the globe, these lines directly address the worry that life in the colonies necessarily and inevitably robbed the colonists of their very Englishness. "Self-same" and "English" do this because each provides a way of connecting the poem's speaker with the "Country" that owes Sidney its love given all the service he has performed on that country's behalf. "Self-same" and "English" each refer to "Country." We know this because each term is part of a clause born out of the very sentence that includes "Country." "Then" in line 27 of *The Tense Muse* and in line 42 of *Several Poems* turns the phrase to follow into a consequence of the previous sentence. Do not, Bradstreet asks all her readers ("let none"), dismiss my praise, because I am born of English blood and, therefore ("then"), like all English people, ought to praise Sidney. What she has to say in honor of Sidney, Bradstreet insists, is true regardless of her national duty.

The fact that both terms refer to "Country" suggests that "self-same" is not intended to function as a subtle nod to Bradstreet's family tree. After all, since "Country" serves as the antecedent of "self-same," it would violate seventeenth-century English notions of national and familial identities. It would, in other words, make no sense to a seventeenth-century reader. To say Bradstreet shares the same "blood" as Sidney because she belongs to the same family line relies on a biological model of community. Families are made through the literal merging of one body with another, a bodily interaction that produces yet another body out of its very own. Members of a country are not made in the same way. The members of the "English" nation cannot all trace their heritage to the same collection of bodies. They do not share the same family line. Indeed, the purity of the monarch's body depended on families procreating only with those of their own social rank. Members of the nobility, to be sure, had relations with commoners that produced offspring. These offspring were, at least in principle, excluded from the family so as to preserve the pure blood of the nobility as a whole. Bradstreet's use of the phrase "self-same blood" in 1650 to refer to all who are subject to the English monarch makes sense only if blood is understood in a figurative rather than a literal sense. It makes sense, in other words, only if she is referring to a diverse community of peoples whose connection to one another as part of a single political and cultural entity comes to life only through acts of imagination.

Before we see how "self-same" and "English" forge a link between the colonists and Alexander the Great, we must first consider one more puzzling aspect of Bradstreet's revision. Whether we think "self-same" and "English" refer to her family or to her nation, we must ask why she would claim that anyone in her audience in old or New England might "disallow" her praise of Sidney in the first place. When had either of these audiences demonstrated the slightest inclination to dismiss praise by anyone, for any reason, of its national heroes? The impulse to defend her praise of Sidney when no such defense is necessary, and to do so for two completely different audiences, suggests the lines serve a purpose other than to deflect a critical response that is virtually impossible to imagine. Both poems defend themselves against criticisms that will never be made in order to help bring the colonists into the imagined body politic of Britain. *The Tenth Muse* and *Several Poems* have very different reasons, though, for staging such rhetorical confirmations of national identity. In the case of *The Tenth Muse*, it's not so much that Bradstreet is worried that her criticism of Sidney will be dismissed because she is English. No. What worries Bradstreet is that her praise of Sidney might be dismissed because she is not truly English. The reference to the poem's speaker as a member of the "self-same" "Country" as readers in 1650 England requires those readers, after all, to confirm Bradstreet's identity in spite of then dominant theories of identity. Those theories held that Bradstreet and her fellow colonists had forfeited their claims to true Englishness by living so long in America's degenerate climate. She uses literary form to counter such claims. Who would claim that a poem in English memorializing Sidney in a way that closely mirrored earlier elegies by authors whose national identity was beyond reproach was not English simply because it was written by a woman of English descent living in America? The very imitative quality of the poem that has drawn so much fire from Bradstreet's critics over the years serves, in fact, as a testament to her nationality and helps convince her English readers to accept rather than dismiss her praise of Sidney in spite of an Englishness they might not have acknowledged prior to reading the poem.

If "self-same" encouraged readers in 1650 England to reconsider the basis for inclusion in the imagined English body politic, "English" in 1678 called on readers in New England to proclaim their right to be included in the community of English peoples in spite of their living in a foreign environment. Readers in New England who do not cite her national identity as the reason her praise should be dismissed implicitly grant her the very national status that living in America calls into question. Of course, no colonial reader in New England in the 1670s would have challenged Bradstreet's Englishness. To do so would have meant calling into question the Englishness of a recently deceased member of one of the most distinguished families in the Massachusetts Bay Colony. Bradstreet's father, Thomas Dudley, served four terms as governor and several more as deputy governor. Elizabeth White describes him as "second only to Winthrop among the leaders of the colony."[33] Bradstreet's husband, Simon, occupied a position of equal esteem, including service as an envoy to the court of Charles II in 1661, where he and others persuaded the king to restore the colony's charter. Colonists might have disagreed with the Bradstreet family on policy matters. They might have scoffed at the Bradstreet clan's claim to noble lineage. But cast aspersions on so vaunted and powerful a family's claims to Englishness? This is simply unimaginable. In using her family's distinction as a shield to defend her own claims to being as much a part of the English community as anyone living in England, Bradstreet helps defend all colonial readers against similar challenges to their own Englishness. In confirming Bradstreet's Englishness, colonial readers simultaneously attest to their own national status. After all, if Bradstreet is English even though she lives thousands of miles away on the other side of the ocean, so, too, are those colonists who are capable of reading these lines praising Sidney. When these readers refuse to dismiss Bradstreet's praise of Sidney because she owes it to him as an English person, they put to rest any doubts they might have had about their own connection to their imagined home across the ocean.

This was a fear that appears to have been more prominent in the colonists' minds in the latter half of the century when *Several Poems* first saw print than when Bradstreet first arrived in New England in the 1630s. The minister whom Perry Miller identifies as "the intellectual leader of the second generation" of New England Puritans, Jonathan Mitchell, for instance, preached in 1668, just ten years prior to the publication of *Several Poems*, that "wee in this Country being farre removed from the more keep up Learning & all Helps of Education among us, lest degeneracy, Barbarism, Ignorance, and irreligion do by degrees breake in upon us."[34] In a sermon delivered just over twenty years after Mitchell's, Cotton Mather, whose father, Increase, was Mitchell's most distinguished student, used his pulpit to warn his parishioners of the threat they faced in "that sort of Criolian degeneracy observed to deprave the children of our most noble and worthy of Europeans when transplanted into America."[35] The specter of Indianization, too, haunts New England readers of 1678 in a way that it certainly did not haunt 1650 London readers. Just one year before the 1678 publication of *Several Poems*, the very same publisher printed Increase Mather's *A relation of the troubles which have hapned in New England; by reason of the Indians there*, and William Hubbard's *A Narrative of the troubles with the Indians in New England*. Only four years later Samuel Green in Cambridge would print Mary Rowlandson's *The Sovereignty & Goodness of God*. The almost total annihilation at the hands of the Indians in the recent wars described by Mather and Hubbard would have brought the question of one's relation to one's colleagues across the Atlantic into violent relief. In prompting Bradstreet's audience to call themselves "English," Bradstreet's poem directly addresses their burgeoning fears of degeneration by providing a way for readers to establish their membership in a transatlantic English community through simple affirmation of Sidney's greatness.

As was the case in *The Tenth Muse*, the poem asks its readers to confirm the national identify of its narrator. But who among her colonial readers would think of casting doubt on Bradstreet's English bona fides? In agreeing that Sidney's merits should be praised, the Boston reader confirms his or her own status as a member of the civilized, English community in the very act of affirming the merits of a member of English nobility who died outside Europe a century before fighting a religious war for England's survival as a Protestant nation.

Now we can, at long last, see how Bradstreet stitches colonial bodies together with English ones that are, in turn, fused with classical ones. Both "self-same" and "English" ask readers to imagine the English community as a single body in which a colonial poet, and the colonists she represents, shares the same blood as a national hero such as Sir Philip Sidney. If the colonists are a part of the same imaginary English body as Sidney, whose body, in turn, becomes indistinguishable from Alexander's when buried at St. Paul's cathedral, then the colonists' bodies are just as much "one" with Alexander's as they are with Sidney's. They, too, can claim figurative kinship with the body buried in that grave. Since Alexander's very identity in both the 1650s and the 1670s was inextricable with the East, through this simple figurative magic Bradstreet connects not only Sidney's heroism with the West's complicated, indeed contradictory, feelings toward the East but also, and more strikingly for our purposes, colonial New England as well. Readers are thus invited to imagine the colonists—and, in 1678, this means that readers are invited to imagine themselves—as fundamentally linked to the West's obsessive struggle to best the East militarily and culturally.

While the differences in the ways Bradstreet's 1650 Sidney elegy and her revision of 1678 ask their very two very different audiences to affirm the national status of English colonists living in America are very important, we should not let those differences blind us to the fact that the link between the colonists and the East through Alexander remains precisely the same in each poem. Much had happened on both sides of the Atlantic in the temporal space that separates *The Tenth Muse* from *Several Poems*. One English king had been beheaded only to have his line restored some nine years later after a period of Puritan rule. London had been essentially destroyed by fire only a few years after yet another plague has devastated the population. The newly restored monarchy had passed a licensing act in 1662 that fundamentally altered the nature of English print culture as it had developed during the Civil War. New England had undergone an only slightly less tumultuous twenty-eight years. The nature of church membership had seen a drastic alteration when the Half-Way Covenant took effect in 1662, John Eliot published the first Indian bible, and thousands of colonists were killed in a war with their greatest local antagonist, the Native Americans, who suffered even greater losses. It is no exaggeration to say that New England was a different place when "An Elegie" was published in 1678 than it had been in 1650, much less 1639, when Bradstreet completed the first draft of the poem.

Yet in spite of so many momentous changes, the link Bradstreet forges between the colonists, England, and the East through Alexander remains unchanged. In each instance, in spite of so much that has transpired in the world around her, Bradstreet turns our attention to the confrontation between East and West as a way of linking the colonists with their supposedly social betters across the Atlantic. This is a confrontation that signals an attempt to better the West by showing how it can conquer the very model of civilized behavior that is, at the same time, a threat to all things a Christian held dear. It is, in other words, a connection that holds out as much danger as it does promise: danger in what might become of the colonists and England in general if they become too much like the East, promise in what hope it offers British American colonists in their quest to be accepted into the community of civilized peoples. To protect the colonial body threatened by exposure to the corrupting environment of America, Bradstreet reaches backward on the temporal axis while simultaneously stretching our imagination eastward across the globe for a figure who can protect her and her fellow colonists from whatever threat awaits them in the wilderness of America. We in the colonies are English, Bradstreet seems to say in these poems, not because we are not Indian. We are English, the elegies of both 1650 and 1678 insist, because we, like Sidney, are blood relatives of Alexander the Great. The figuration of a civilized, English identity by a colonial writer threatened by the specter of degeneration looks as much to the corrupted yet powerful conqueror of the East, then, for its sense of itself as it does to the supposedly savage lands and peoples immediately imagined to be—perhaps hoped to be—somewhere to its west.

CHAPTER 2

How West Becomes East in Colonial Georgia Poetry

The July 1732 *Gentleman's Magazine* focuses its brief summary of the inaugural meeting of the "Trustees for establishing the Colony of Georgia" on a single aspect of the occasion: the design of a common seal for the corporation.[1] The summary appears as one of a number of items in the magazine's monthly section devoted to what it calls "*Domestick Occurrences.*" There we learn that Georgia's Trustees "order'd a common seal to be made with the following Levice: One Side two Figures of Rivers resting upon Urns, representing the *Alamatha* and *Savanah*, the Boundaries of Georgia; and between them the Genius of the Colony, seated with the Cap of Liberty upon her Head, a Spear in one Hand, and a Cornucopia in the other, with this Motto, *Colonia Georgia Aug.* The Reverse is to be Silk Worms at Work, with this Motto, *Non sibi sed Allis.*"[2]

Most twenty-first-century readers are likely to find the images on this seal representing liberty, military might, and natural abundance quite in keeping with their assumptions about the United States' colonial origins, but the image of silkworms would probably surprise most Americans today. To be sure, the stories we have told ourselves about the development of the colonies that eventually formed the United States focus our attention on a variety of topics: tobacco, religious faith, clashing political ideologies, slavery, taming or despoiling the natural environment, building an entirely new nation on a new land or perpetrating an act of genocide in order to clear the space necessary for that nation, or some combination of these and other now-familiar motifs. When we note silk in our stories of America's development, though, if we mention it at all, we tend to do so in passing as a mere fantasy of America's promoters unworthy of our analysis given its subsequent unimportance.

The decision by the Trustees to single out silk as *the* representative product from what they cast on the other side of the seal as a cornucopia of goods should lead us to wonder what conceptual—as opposed to, say, strictly economic or purely historical—implications such a choice of figures might have for those of us who study British American colonial literature. Just what ideas, issues, problems, and/or images did, after all, eighteenth-century British and British American readers associate with the figure of silk that might be relevant to the study of early American literature and culture? To be sure, they would have connected silk with specifically economic concerns and possibilities, but it seems almost too obvious to say that the associations attached to a commodity of such extraordinary value would be limited to the domain of finance. If we accept the premise that eighteenth-century British and British American people connected the image of silk with a variety of ideas and issues beyond the purely economic, what might these figurative associations—related to one another in eighteenth-century British and British American symbolic systems even if they are not related in what we tend to call "fact"—tell us about the underlying assumptions that allowed at least some British American colonists to make sense of their world which we have thus far overlooked?

If we were to begin our investigation of these issues by examining what the Trustees themselves said about their choice of silk for the seal, though, we would be sorely disappointed. For no records remain of the Trustees' deliberations—if any even took place—over the decision to feature silk on the colony's seal.[3] If we have no explicit statements explaining the Trustees' logic in choosing silk, we can reasonably infer from what documents we do have that the Trustees had a choice to make. For the records of the Trustees' meetings and the promotional material they authorized show that silk was only one among many products they expected Georgia to supply, including *"raw Silk, Wine, Oil, Dies, Drugs,* and many other Materials for Manufactures."[4] So while the Trustees themselves never spell out their reasons for choosing silk as the image with which they wanted Georgia to be associated, we know that it was a choice. The choice of silk, in turn, necessarily associated Georgia with all those concepts, ideas, and values to which silk had become attached for eighteenth-century British and British American consumers, associations of which the Trustees must surely have been aware.

I think the available evidence allows us to conclude that most eighteenth-century British and British American readers of the *Gentleman's Magazine* would have expected references to silk in British American promotional material; very likely they would have grown accustomed to such allusions given that America's promoters had long been trumpeting America as a place where Great Britain could obtain a good that had become such a huge commercial success throughout Europe. In the discursive systems of 1730s Anglo-America, though, silk's symbolic associations extended well beyond its connection to the colonization of North America. For well more than one hundred years before the birth of any of Georgia's board members, silk had been linked in European culture with East Indies trade goods in general and with China in particular.[5] Indeed, the desire to obtain silk products—among *many* other goods—from the East fueled the very discovery of the New World and subsequent European efforts to produce silk on its continents in the first place.[6]

To say that British consumers had long associated silk with the "East" in general and "China" in particular begs a crucial question: just what did these consumers understand these terms to mean in the first place? I noted in my discussion of Bradstreet's *Several Poems* that not only did readers of English in the late seventeenth century understand the term "East" differently than we do today, but also that the word itself lacked stability and precision in its geographic denotation. By the time Georgia's Trustees began their promotional blitz on behalf of the colony in the 1730s, the "East" had achieved slightly more stability than it had had fifty years earlier. Georgia's promoters wrote, like Bradstreet, during the very period when the modern meanings of East and West came into being.[7] Georgia's promotional documents reflect the broader usage of the time when they include what appears to a modern reader to be an extraordinarily diverse body of regions and countries within the single category of the "East": "*Barbary, AEgypt,* and *Arabia*," "Asia" and "*Asia Minor,*" "the Kingdome of Kaschmere," "India," "Persia," and "China" are all part of the "East," as is the "East Indies" from which Great Britain gained so much of its trade in the period.

It is ironic that, by the 1730s, very little of the silk hanging in British or colonial homes, adorning the nation's bodies either on Britain's home isle or in its colonies, or being put to any of the many other uses to which British people put the fabric were actually imported from countries in what was considered by early-eighteenth-century readers to be the "East." In spite of their place of production, silk, porcelain, and other Eastern products retained their symbolic associations with Eastern cultures, styles, and aesthetics.⁸ It was its symbolic ties to China and the East rather than any material connection that allowed silk to play such a key role in the "Chinese rage" known as chinoiserie that swept all of Europe in the middle of the eighteenth century.⁹ That contemporaneous audiences connected Georgia's promotion to the East geographically and symbolically can be seen by the way in which one set of the colony's critics, who would come to be known as the Clamorous Malcontents, characterized the man who ran Georgia in its early years, James Oglethorpe. In their pamphlet criticizing the management of Georgia, the Malcontents cast Oglethorpe's own characterization of the colony as "like the Illusion of some *Eastern Magician*."¹⁰ To an eighteenth-century British and British American audience, then, the decision to affix an image of silk to all official documents from the Georgia Trustees would have seemed, perhaps, only the most bold and aggressive attempt not simply to obtain so-called East Indian goods from America but also to associate a colonization effort understood by all—even in a period in which Europe's conception of the globe was rapidly changing—to be in the West with a product conceptually linked to the worlds and cultures of the East.¹¹

In asking their readers to imagine British people living in Georgia while producing materials associated symbolically if not materially with the East Indies, Georgia's promoters faced a number of daunting practical objections. For starters, Georgia was designed to be different from previous colonies.¹² Unlike previous British colonies—those that succeeded as well as those that failed—Georgia was set up as a charitable organization. The Trustees of Georgia received permission to colonize the land between the Savannah and Alatamaha rivers for the purpose of putting to work those idle British subjects now languishing in prison for their unpaid debts.

This was by no means an easy sell. In the first place, what came to be known as the "Georgia plan" would have to fight a general skepticism toward all colonial ventures among 1730s British readers. This skepticism was born, in part, of the deep scars that appeared in the wake of the South Sea Bubble of the 1710s and 1720s, which had left many individual investors in dire straits and threatened the financial health of England itself. In addition to these concerns about American colonization, the Georgia plan in particular offered much upon which skeptics might seize. Such skeptics might well ask, for instance, what mechanism the backers planned to use to induce people thought to be congenitally lazy to transform themselves into productive laborers once they were separated from England by an ocean. Even if such undesirable elements of society could be prodded into working the land, how could the profits from their labor generate the kind of cash necessary to cover the enormous expense of transporting them to and housing them in such a forbidding territory?

Assuming the backers could credibly demonstrate that potential profits would more than offset such costs, one had to concede that Georgia's location placed it in an especially vulnerable spot. The colony's promoters unabashedly acknowledged that the colony would sit precisely between Britain's most southern colony, South Carolina, and Spain's most northern colony, Florida. Not only did they acknowledge this fact; they went so far as to use it in promoting the colony to South Carolina residents and the British government. Georgia, they claimed, would serve as a buffer, safeguarding Britons' profitable holdings in South Carolina from further incursions of Spanish troops. Were debtors struggling to work an untamed land for profit supposed to simultaneously defend it from Spanish forces who might attack at any time, transforming all the money investors had sunk into Georgia into mere American ashes? If all these challenges did not deflate the hopes of a potential contributor, perhaps the threat the local native populations would surely pose to another British settlement and, of perhaps more concern to potential contributors, by extension to any charitable contributions would be enough to dissuade even the most generous of potential patrons from giving to a project whose success faced seemingly insurmountable obstacles.

The conceptual hurdles posed by the plan were perhaps still more daunting even though they were not expressed as explicitly as the practical concerns. Whether one focused on its symbolic associations or the place of its material production, all of silk's promoters in England had, by the 1730s, conceded that it couldn't be produced in Great Britain. Silk was, all agreed, an entirely "foreign" product. By insisting on the way in which clearly "alien" goods could be produced by British subjects in the decidedly un-British environment of America, Georgia's promoters seemed to put the very Britishness of those subjects at risk. If, after all, Georgia was so much like these "foreign" regions that one could literally substitute products from this part of America for ones that had to be imported from outside Great Britain, were the English people living in Georgia to lose their very status as British while living in such distinctly "foreign" locales? If climate had anything to do with the distinctive characteristics of a nation, as many eighteenth-century theories of identity formation held, what was to become of the British men and women consigned to live in such an environment?[13] Were the economic, social, and cultural advantages to be gained by this charitable proposition so great that they outweighed the risks involved?

And what of these so-called advantages? A number of commentators in early-eighteenth-century Great Britain were already worried about the corruption of British society by an overreliance on luxury items. To them, the colonization of a region that would make silk, porcelain, and other Eastern items even easier for English consumers to obtain loomed as more of a threat than an opportunity. The production of such items in Great Britain's own colonies would only cater, these commentators argued, to desires better thwarted than encouraged. Silk gowns, porcelain vases, chinaware, and other items for the so-called refined taste threatened the very moral foundation of British culture. Was Britain's status as a "civilized" nation—for Georgia's promoters suggested that nothing less was at stake in bringing the colony's products to Great Britain—to be bought by sacrificing some of her subjects' very claims to that civilized identity by living abroad while corrupting those who remained at home by encouraging them to indulge their basest desires for material objects associated with the East?

Perhaps some in Great Britain were willing to accept such a bargain, but Georgia's promoters in both the colonies and Great Britain insisted that what they consistently cast as "Eastern" products obtained from the soil of British Georgia need not come at so high a price. In order to investigate the way in which Georgia's promoters initially cast the cultural advantages to Great Britain of the production of silk and other products in the region between South Carolina and Florida, I have examined the many writings relating to the colony of Georgia that appeared in print from the beginning of the promotional campaign that launched the colony in 1732 up through the publication of critical material by—and official responses to—the Malcontents in 1742. These writings suggest that Britain needs its own source of distinctly "Eastern" goods in America in order to maintain the nation's economic and social health, protect its strategic military interests, and elevate itself to the most elite status of civilized communities. In order to interrogate in the greatest detail the various complications and problems that such a position raises, I focus my attention in this chapter on a single poem from the promotional campaign: "An Address to James Oglethorpe, Esq," first published in *The South Carolina Gazette* in the 10 February 1732 issue and attributed by David Shields to James Kirkpatrick.[14]

I have chosen to focus the bulk of my attention in the following pages on this poem in particular in part because of its American origins. "An Address . . ." was first published in British America by a writer living in the colonies when he penned his verse.[15] Its colonial origins allow us to use it as evidence of the way at least one British American writer figured the East in relation to what he considered a New World discovered in the West in the 1730s. Like the promotional material that came out of London or that was written with a specifically British audience in mind, Kirkpatrick's, too, focuses our attention on the value of Georgia's silk in particular as a way of satisfying consumer demand while simultaneously working to enhance the civilized status of Great Britain in general. In collapsing the distinction between the geographic East and West, "An Address . . ." not only explicitly calls our attention to the metonymic qualities of the American environment but, in the process of doing so, also elevates what British America has to offer the world when its author makes the system of values that are never stated directly but which nonetheless provide the philosophical foundation for such metonymies equivalent to the values that underlie Britain's social system at large. To put this perhaps more provocatively, this writing from the British American colonies suggests that America helps Britain look more civilized by allowing it to look more "Eastern." Given this, we might be tempted to ask how such a work fits into the story of the development of British American literature—to say nothing of the broader British American cultural history—as we have traditionally told it. How, in other words, does a focus on the symbolic associations connected to a single product, silk, to which a single poem grants considerable political and aesthetic power lead us to rethink, if it does, the literary history of America? Our investigation of how the poem prompts such questions, though, must begin not with the poem itself, but with the role of silk in New World colonization before Georgia. In order, that is, to understand the implications of Kirkpatrick's use of the figure of silk in the 1730s, we must first understand how it came to be associated with the New World in the first place and the implications of those associations as they came down to Kirkpatrick's readers.

GEORGIA'S PROMOTERS were by no means the first to suggest that England cultivate silk in her New World possessions.[16] Quite the contrary.[17] They were the very last to argue that America could satisfy Great Britain's seemingly boundless desire for silk.[18] References to silk occur so frequently in the histories, sermons, poems, pamphlets, and other printed material promoting English activity in North America that it seems almost as if these writers were not allowed to talk about the colonies without talking about silk. So while some of the promotional tracts from this period provide elaborate descriptions of the possibilities for silk production in the New World, others mention it only in passing. The long lists of commodities that could be had in the wilds of America prominently featured in works promoting

America mentioned silk almost without exception. If such lists divide the New World into its various parts, in the process presenting the natural world as no more than a set of discrete objects whose value depends on their ability to be transformed into money, then silk, as a part of this list, becomes part of the very stuff that makes up and defines New World value.

To give some idea of the ubiquity of references to silk, let me provide a few snapshots from relevant works. Visions of New World silk as a source of vast riches for Old World investors appear, in fact, in the very first wave of English promotional tracts for American settlement in the late sixteenth century. Thomas Hariot lists "*Silke of grasse or grasse Silke*" at the very beginning of the list of "MARCHANTABLE COMMODITIES" the New World offers that opens *A Briefe and True Report of the New Found Land of Virginia* (1590), and, in case his reader fails to grasp the importance of silk from its pride of place, he removes any doubt by putting "Worme Silke" second on the very same list.[19] The New World promoter long credited with being the most realistic and/or pragmatic about what the genuine opportunities for the production of New World commodities were, John Smith, never fails to mention silk in his catalogs of possible New World products.[20] He mentions silk in his works almost as many times as he does Pocahontas, a figure with whom he has become forever associated in the U.S. myths of origin even as his links to silk production have been entirely forgotten. The dream of American silk producing English wealth continued up through the early eighteenth century, focusing especially on the colony to Virginia's immediate south, Carolina. The failure of some "French Protestants" at producing silk in what would become South Carolina, Thomas Ashe contends, should not be seen as an indication of the difficulties involved in such a project but, on the contrary, as an sign that England's very enemies have sought to exploit the "the numerousness of the Leaf" in the colony.[21] By 1708 John Oldmixon claimed in *The British Empire in America* "a great Improvement" in Carolina's silk production.[22]

But no previous British American colony matched Georgia in the extent to which it focused potential investors' and settlers' attention on silk to the exclusion of other products. To demonstrate this focus, I want first to turn again to the image of silkworms on Georgia's common seal.[23] Every colony in British America at some point during its life prior to the Revolution had a common seal. Indeed, some had several seals while they were colonies of Great Britain. Of all of these seals among all the British colonies on the continent and in the Caribbean, only Georgia's contains an image of silk in any form. I am afraid I am only stating the obvious when I note that common seals serve a representative function in that they work to associate the colony with whatever images appear on that colony's seal. When we add to this the fact that images of a cornucopia appear on the opposite side of Georgia's seal, thus singling out silk among a figuratively limitless supply of products for the viewer's attention, I think it is reasonable to conclude that Georgia's seal associates the colony with silk in an unprecedented way among the colonies.

The legal power afforded a seal's status as a representation of the deliberate, expressed will of a corporation's board supplements this first-order representative function.[24] Seals literally stand in the place of the corporation's members who cannot be present whenever the goals expressed on the sealed document are to be realized. The seal's imprimatur would make things happen by providing an image that would authenticate any document produced by the corporation as legitimately the result of its collective will. The common seal would authorize the expenditure of monies for the transportation of colonists; it would prohibit the use of slaves in the colony; it would place restrictions on land tenure; and, among the various other things it would help make happen, it would confer political power on particular individuals. In this way, seals bear a striking resemblance to performative speech acts in the way they function. Like performative speech acts, seals make things happen.

They do so, it should be added, only through the implicit agreement of all parties who read the document to accept the image of the seal as a figure for the intention of a specific corporate body. Eighteenth-century British law treats corporations as fictitious persons, and the corporation's common seal acts as a stand-in or representative of that fictitious person. The seal signifies the deliberate will of an imaginary individual to transform mere writing into action in the world. In serving as the signifier for the deliberate, considered will of the entire fictitious corporate body, the seal ensures that the corporation's members do not have to be physically present to attest to the document's authenticity. The seal thus serves a function very similar to that of a signature for an individual, but with the added and quite important complication that a visual image rather than a specific order of letters operates as the authenticating mark and that this signifier is the product of the will of the corporate body rather than, as with someone's signing their own name, an act whose naming stands outside (at least in general practice) the individual's agency. We are given the names we write when we pen our signatures. We do not choose the signifying marks that identify us, in other words. In the case of corporate seals, however, the members of the corporate board choose their own signifying mark. They get to choose the image with which they want to be represented.

As a figure for that which it is not, a seal works via the logic of metonymy. Unlike most metonymic figures, though, the particular association underlying this metonymy—when one thinks of a silkworm, one should necessarily think of colonial Georgia—grows out of the Trustees' hopes and desires rather than any existing historical, economic, or cultural relation between silk and a colony that does not even exist when the seal is approved. Georgia's common seal thus represents an act of willful association in which the seal serves as a way of producing an association before it becomes a historical reality. It is in this sense that the seal is performative in a second way. For the seal not only makes money transfer hands, disallows slavery, and so forth; it also works to produce the very association it purports to represent. The seal makes real that which is—at the moment of its conception when the Trustees approve the seal, through the many times it is affixed to documents, until long after the removal of the silkworms from the seal after the American Revolution—real only in the world of discourse. We do not even need to attribute any intentionality to the Trustees in order to classify the seal as a kind of performative speech act. For regardless of whatever the Trustees intended, and even if they intended the seal to be entirely representational of a material reality they believed to exist, the seal does, in fact, produce an association of Georgia with silk in the discursive system of the period even if no silk exists in Georgia in fact.

That a British colonial project focusing so much attention on silk as the colony's signature commodity would be born in the world of 1730s London should come as no surprise, though. For the widening trade imbalance that had long helped fuel England's dogged pursuit of New World silk grew only more pronounced in the first two decades of the eighteenth century. The imbalance begins to take on noticeable proportions a century before Georgia's birth. While England struggled to produce silkworms in the British Isles or in her colonial possessions abroad, imports of both raw and thrown silk became, in the words of Linda Peck, "the most valuable of all the raw material imports throughout the middle and later seventeenth century."[25] "The value of imported silk fabrics," Peck points out, "more than doubled between 1560 and 1622," so that by 1622 "silk fabric had grown to 5.1 percent of all imports."[26] Raw silk imported for the sole purpose of being woven by English workers—or at least workers living in England if not English by birth—saw the most startling increase, moving from £118,000 in 1622 to £175,000 in 1640 to £263,000 in the 1660s to £344,000 by the end of the century. When viewed as a whole, raw silk constituted "23–29 percent of the total value of imports."[27] As one might expect, the number of silk workers in England experienced a similarly rapid growth during the century. While silk weavers had been working in England since at least the late fourteenth century, the trade was still quite small in the early years of the seventeenth century, with no more than around several hundred employed in the early 1620s. By 1666, estimates place the number at approximately 40,000.

Such local production failed to stem the tide of foreign import of silk products. Gerald B. Hertz writes that "700,0001 of fully manufactured silk goods had still been annually imported from abroad between 1685 and 1693" in spite of all of England's efforts to manufacture silk goods in England itself.[28] Since England produced virtually no homegrown silk, British writers concerned with trade and commerce frequently invoked "China's fragrant Leaf" as the prime threat posed by "foreign" products to Great Britain's economic health. Indeed, Louis Landa even goes so far as to call silk "[p]erhaps the most objectionable of all the 'foreign trumpery' . . . because of the large amount imported, both raw and wrought, and because imported silk hindered the endeavors to establish a flourishing domestic silk industry."[29] In response to such concerns, the British government prohibited the importation of thrown silk from France, India, and China, prohibitions that were relaxed only after 1713 and then only with heavy duties substituted for outright prohibition.[30]

In spite of the fact that the vast majority of silk bought by English consumers during the period 1700–1740 was in fact imported from Italy and France, silk continued to be understood by eighteenth-century English consumers as the "classic . . . luxury import from Asia to Europe."[31] We can begin to account for silk's association among eighteenth-century English-speaking peoples with China in particular and the East in general by looking at contemporaneous understandings of the etymology of the very word "China" and the history of silk production.[32] Let me examine briefly only one relevant example: Thomas Boreman's *A Compendious Account of the Whole Art of Breeding, Nursing, and Right Ordering of the Silk-Worm* (1733). Boreman dedicates his book "On the Management of the SILK-WORM" to "The Trustees for Establishing the Colony of *Georgia* in *America*."[33] In addition to a seemingly exhaustive description of the many procedures required to produce raw silk, Boreman provides a brief preface that, among other things, offers his readers a history of silk production. In a footnote to this history, Boreman claims that "The whole countery of *China* was antiently (as *Ptolemy* says) called *Serica*, from its abounding with Silk."[34] In this way, Boreman makes silk quite literally synonymous with the country of China. At least in one of the classical languages considered by eighteenth-century British elites to be a foundation of civilized thought, the two entities—silk and China—share the same name and, at least in some sense, are identical. This etymological footnote appears in the midst of Boreman's brief history of the origins of the cultivation of the silkmoth. Boreman's narrative casts silk's origins as Eastern when he writes that "it is certain that" China and Persia "had the Knowledge of Silk very early, and were the first that propagated Silk, and reap'd the Profit and Benefit of it many hundred Years before any other Country."[35]

Eighteenth-century European narratives of China's economic history account for another part of the reason why silk continued to be associated with the East long after the silk used by people in Great Britain came from elsewhere. British writers on trade and commerce in the period considered silk the key ingredient in China's development as an economic power. So while British advocates for the American production of silk were well aware of Great Britain's dependence on French and Italian silk, they asked their readers to look to China—rather than to Italy or France—as the model for the benefits silk production offer a country. If we are more like China in our silk production, these writers claimed, we will enhance Britain's own civilized status. So, for instance, in what Verner Crane calls "one of the most widely read of the commercial tracts of the century," Joshua Gee writes in *The Trade and Navigation of Great-Britain Considered* that "if Care was taken to cultivate and improve the raising of Silk in our *Plantations, Carolina, Virginia, Maryland,* and *Pennsylvania,* would produce the best of Silk."[36] But China, Gee reminds his readers, produces the best-quality silk and, therefore, its silk should serve as the silk to be emulated. When Gee begins to argue that Great Britain should devote vast resources to silk production, though, he bypasses a discussion of quality but invokes the very same Eastern image in order to convince his readers to support the efforts of British American silk producers. Look what silk has done, Gee insists, for its producers in China: "The vast Riches of *China* by this Manufacture [that is, the manufacture of silk in England's colonies]," Gee writes, "is sufficient to demonstrate the great Advantage therefore."[37]

To the historical narrative and economic advantages that tied silk conceptually to the East in general and to China in particular must be added the question of the symbolic capital conferred on silk through its association with the East. Given the dramatic rise in demand for silk we can safely assume that display of this particular fabric was viewed as a desirable supplement to one's wardrobe or room. But how was the nature of that supplement understood? What would such an association have meant to eighteenth-century British consumers and/or audiences? Would silk's Easternness have signified a kind of celebrated decadence of the kind for which the Restoration became known? Would it serve as a sign of one's cultural sophistication and taste? Products associated with the East Indies in general and with China in particular enjoyed considerable status in British society for more than one hundred years before the promotion of Georgia. The importance of porcelain, various kinds of textiles, and tea made "in the China fashion" gained such prominence before 1700 that Hugh Honour argues, "[b]y the end of the second half of the seventeenth century a vogue for orientalia was well established in nearly every part of Europe," with England being particularly found of tea.[38] Indeed, as Honour notes, "the English conception of what eastern fabrics should, ideally, look like was sufficiently distinct by the 1640s to necessitate the instruction of eastern craftsmen in making textiles in the English 'China fashion.'"[39]

But as Honour and others have taught us, the "epidemic of "Chinamania" that came to be known as "chinoiserie" that "attacked" England in the eighteenth century far eclipsed the "vogue for orientalia" of earlier years.[40] While chinoiserie attracted great interest across Europe, it enjoyed perhaps its greatest appeal in Great Britain, where it "reached remarkable heights of popularity."[41] Chinoiserie literally transformed the social and physical landscape of Great Britain. British gardens were remade and buildings erected in what was imagined to be the "Chinese" style; people redecorated their sitting rooms, drawing rooms, and bedrooms with furniture, wall hangings, and porcelains so that they could display their "Chinese" taste; audiences crowed into theatres to see plays purported to be about China or adaptations of plays by Chinese authors; and, of course, women and men draped themselves in gowns made of silk or simply added silk accessories to their wardrobes as a way of announcing their commitment to what they considered a distinctly "Chinese" aesthetic.

The Georgia promotional campaign occurs just prior to the period scholars consider to be the height of chinoiserie, the 1740s and 1750s. The classic texts of various kinds found during the chinoiserie period in Great Britain help produce what David Porter calls "a transformation in prevailing attitudes toward China" that, he argues, ultimately resulted in the "deflation of the cultural authority of the Chinese" by "transforming symbols of awe-inspiring cultural achievement into a motley collection of exotic, ornamental motifs."[42] Porter notes further that after China critics emerged during the middle years of the eighteenth century in England, "China had been transformed . . . from an unassailable seat of cultural legitimacy to a wellspring of depravity that threatened to unravel the very fabric of a well-ordered society, one enchanted viewer at a time."[43] The chinoiserie movement, Porter demonstrates, "represented an explicit rejection, in the aesthetic domain, of the very principle of substantiality that had been ascribed to China."[44]

Given the way in which the promotional material casts England in relation to the East and China in particular, though, I believe the promoters sought to capitalize on at least a significant portion of their eighteenth-century British and British American audiences' understanding of references to silk products as ways of signifying one's cultural sophistication. Since objects were often, as David Porter notes, "perceived as being 'about' the place to which, however reductively, they referred"; the use of silk in one's attire or in one's furnishings was seen as a reference to Chinese culture.[45] It is for this reason that we can see that the use of such silks by British consumers "[was] intended," as Robert Leath notes, "to blend with Chinese-inspired patterns in architecture to create a single, repetitious allusion to the Chinese taste."[46] The turn to silk as a component of "chinoiserie" was associated "[w]ithin the context of the European luxury debates," Berg argues, "not with sensuality and excess, but with ethics, harmony, and virtue."[47] Europeans who gravitated towards ideas and objects associated with China did so as a way to achieve "their own aspirations to human elegance and refinement." Through the possession of silk that was associated with China, consumers, according to Berg, "sought to access levels of civilization beyond the market" even though such objects were, in fact, creations of the market itself.[48]

We can see this attitude toward silk as an Eastern figure associated with the height of the refinement displayed by the most civilized of cultures in a widely read promotional piece, Samuel Wesley's 1736 "Georgia: A Poem." Wesley not only suggests that raw goods serve as signifiers of particular cultures whether they are literally produced or imported from that culture; he even goes so far as to suggest that in serving as signifiers of a culture regardless of their point of origin, raw goods also signify that entire culture's understanding of itself. He does this when he notes that the silk British women currently wear is something about "Which Asia boasts" and puts "Eastern Pride" on display (1. 180). We must remember as we read these lines what Wesley takes pains to point out elsewhere in the poem: the silk from which British women's gowns have been made up to this point more often comes from Italy or France than from China, and a significant proportion of that silk has been woven into its final form by workers somewhere on the British Isles. The feeling of "pride" that Wesley attributes to some mystical "East" when British women wear silk comes not from the knowledge of people in the "East" that objects grown and/or manufactured in their region are on display in Great Britain but, rather, from the fact that objects symbolically associated with the East—objects that are "Eastern" regardless of their place of production—are on display in Great Britain.

Wesley classifies what he calls "Eastern" cultures as the source of British aesthetic standards. He does this when he substitutes Georgian silks for the silks women in Great Britain have been wearing that, at least according to Wesley, carry the East's seemingly unmistakable symbolic mark. So it is, Wesley tells us, that prior to the production of raw silk in Georgia, "Asia" could "boast" and "Eastern Pride" would be on display when English women wore silk that made them beautiful. With the introduction of Georgia silk, though, "all the Beauties" of England would now "owe" their aesthetic qualities to "home-wrought Silks" of Britain's American colony (1. 170). Even when Georgia's silks replace those associated with the East adorning British bodies, the East remains the standard by which those Georgian garments are judged. For the products coming from this new colony will be considered an aesthetic success only insofar as they can be said to "emulate the Chint's alluring Dye" (1. 182). Since Wesley never suggests that Georgia will replace the East as the place with which silk is symbolically associated even when the silk itself does come from there—he never suggests, in other words, that eventually silk will become a "Western" or "American" or "British" or "Georgia" product as opposed to an "Eastern" or "Chinese" one—the poem leaves us with the impression that this explicitly Eastern aesthetic will remain the standard used to judge silk's aesthetic value each time one wears or in any way displays silk as a way of demonstrating one's civilized status. Indeed, by casting Georgia's silk as gaining its status through the continual emulation of those associated with the East, the poem sets up a structure in which any display of silk ceaselessly reproduces the East's status as the final arbiter of aesthetic value. Emulation, in this case at least, does not lead to the displacement of the values to be emulated but, rather, to their continual and seemingly never-ending reinscription as the superior set of values by which one will always be judged.

This structure of continual emulation establishes an aesthetic hierarchy that ensures the East's superiority to Great Britain on all aesthetic matters. There exists, according to Wesley at least, a subtle but unmistakable contest between Great Britain and the East for the right to clothe women in material that can be categorized as aesthetically pleasing. It is, after all, "With skillful China's richest Damask" that Great Britain must "vie" (1. 162). In this way, Wesley places Britain in an aesthetic as much as an economic competition in which the "world's" gaze on and subsequent evaluation of women's clothing serves as the ultimate arbiter of a whole culture's place within a hierarchy of civilized nations dating back in time. This is a battle Great Britain will always lose, though, so long as the East remains the standard to be emulated. For even once the "British Loom" transforms raw silk imported from Georgia into beautiful garments so that British hands assume full responsibility for the production of the most prized aesthetic goods, even when the "Beauties" of Great Britain "owe" the appeal of their garments to labor performed entirely by British subjects, even then the standards they are emulating—the standards with which they are in competition—provide the basis for judging aesthetic value (1. 179).

The subservience to Eastern standards and the fear of the consequences of circulating such a distinctly "foreign" product even more widely within the imagined social body of Great Britain led some of those connected with the promotion of Georgia to go so far as to Westernize silk's genealogy. Boreman, for one, undermined any genealogical claims that contemporaneous Chinese or Persian—or other contemporaneous Eastern—cultures might make on silk by framing his remarks on its origins with the possibility that, in fact, Noah might have been the first to "take notice" of silk since he is said to have "propagated [silkworms] in *China,* where he is supposed to have settled after the Flood."[49] In doing so, the work attempts to give credit for the introduction of silk to the East to a biblical character to whom the colonists would have claimed genealogical connection over the Chinese.

Boreman does not rest with references to Biblical figures from whom Europeans in general and English people in particular claim to be specially chosen descendants. He pulls out all the stops in his attempt to show that in spite of its Eastern associations, silk remains fundamentally tied to English people's own narratives of development. As one final piece of evidence on top of all the others, Boreman offers a plate that depicts "two Monks who first brought Silk-worms Eggs into Europe" as the visual authorization of his story of the historical movement of silkworm production from East to West. Boreman concludes his discussion of the history of silk's production in the East in China and Persia by referring specifically to the image of these Monks. In so doing, Boreman casts the production of silk in China and Persia as simply the inevitable precursor to the introduction of silk into the West. The images serve, in other words, as a visual culmination of a well-known narrative of the movement of culture Westward, an implied reference to translatio studi.

BOREMAN'S WORK takes us right up to the period in which Kirkpatrick wrote his poem, and we are now prepared to turn our attention to Kirkpatrick's verse. Given the rather obscure nature of the poem and its author, even to scholars of British American literature, we must put off our analysis of "An Address to James Oglethorpe" just a little longer so that we can provide some brief background on the poet, the context in which the work came into print, and the imagined and actual audiences for the poem. Born in Ireland, he studied at the University of Edinburgh without earning a degree and, in 1717, emigrated to South Carolina. He practiced medicine while living in Charlestown until he left for London in 1742. Kirkpatrick came to the attention of British officials when, in 1738 during an outbreak of smallpox in South Carolina, he sought to stem the epidemic by administering inoculations. This medical success prompted George Townshend, Commander of the Fleet in British America, to suggest that Kirkpatrick's medical talents could be more usefully employed in London. His *Analysis of Inoculation* was published in London in 1754, and the work earned him great renown throughout medical communities across Europe.[50] He died in 1770. Before he achieved fame as a physician, though, Kirkpatrick published several poems, at least one of which, *The Sea-Piece* (London, 1750), which David Shields calls "one of the major works of colonial American belles-lettres," suggests he hoped to become the British laureate of empire.[51] Indeed, Shields contends that *The Sea-Piece* represents "the most thoroughgoing and ambitious meditation on Britain's maritime destiny composed by any eighteenth-century poet."[52] It was, he writes, "the British American testament to the empire of the seas."[53]

"An Address to James Oglethorpe" was first published in the February 3, 1733, issue of the *South Carolina Gazette*.[54] The poem occupied approximately three-quarters of the first page of the issue, and it was followed by, among other items, notes devoted to "FOREIGN AFFAIRS," as well as notices of lists of people arriving and departing on local ships, and advertisements for salt, horses, and "Field Negroes." Its appearance in the *South Carolina Gazette* was, it seems clear, part of Georgia's promotional efforts, in this case, to enlist the support of residents of the colony in the campaign to found a British colony to their immediate south. Given that one of the purposes of Georgia would be to serve as a defense against incursions from Spanish colonies even further to the south, some South Carolinians were, to some extent at least, initially happy to offer their support.

Although it was not published in Georgia—indeed, Georgia had no press until 1763—we can be confident that at least some people in both Georgia and other colonies read the poem.[55] We can be confident of this, first of all, because the poem was reprinted one year later in the *Pennsylvania Gazette*. The *Gazette* takes note of the poem's colonial origins when it points out that it was first "published in [the] *South-Carolina Gazette*" even as it tries to indulge in a little light-hearted intracolonial rivalry by saying the poem will "supply the place of Foreign News."[56] To be sure, the pun demonstrates that the figurative possibility existed for imagining one British American colony as "foreign" to another such colony, but the fact that the poem's inclusion does not, in fact, take the place of foreign news in that week's edition of the paper but, on the contrary, reduces the amount of space devoted to such news in previous editions of the paper suggests an alternate reading. The *Gazette*'s editors' prefatory remarks indicate that by literally occupying "the place" in the paper usually reserved for news from abroad, the poem will "supply pleasure to most of [the *Gazette*'s] Readers." That is, material focused on colonial British American issues, even if from another colony, produces pleasure in colonial British American readers.

If its appearance in the *Gazette* demonstrates that the poem enjoyed at least some readership within the colonies, its appearance in the April 1733 issue of the *Gentleman's Magazine*—that is, just two months after its initial appearance in South Carolina—only increases the likelihood that the poem had readers not only in Georgia but elsewhere in British America.[57] The *Gentleman's Magazine* enjoyed a wide circulation not only in Great Britain but throughout the American colonies as well.[58] But if the poem was initially presented by a British American for an imagined audience of other British Americans, the editors of the *Gentleman's Magazine* frame the poem in such a way that only enhances its status as a specifically colonial product. Read this work, they seem to ask their readers, differently from the other works of poetry in our magazine. The magazine's organization and titling of these colonial poems encourages its readers to treat Kirkpatrick's work as a distinctly American response to specifically British leaders visiting the colonies. So, the front page of the magazine lists the poems together—unlike all the other matter listed under "Poetry" for that issue—as "Of Ld. Baltimore and Mr. Oglethorpe." The table of contents gives "A Poem to James Oglethorpe, Esq.; Georgia" as the title of the Kirkpatrick poem and "—To Ld. Baltimore in Maryland" as the title of the other poem.[59] When it comes time to provide some context for the poems themselves, the editors choose to give Kirkpatrick's work the title "An Address to James Oglethorpe, Esq.; on his settling the Colony of Georgia," but without the Latin that preceded the poem in its South Carolina version. In the right-hand column on the very same page immediately following Kirkpatrick's poem, the editors list Lewis's poem as "A Description of Maryland, extracted from a Poem, entitled, Carmen Seculare, addressed to Ld. Baltimore, Proprietor of that Province, now there," then go on to explain that it is by "Mr. Lewis, Author of the Beautiful Poem inserted in our 4th Number, entitled, A Journey from Patapsko to Annapolis."[60]

While the *Gentleman's Magazine* editors might have framed the poem in such a way as to ask their readers to read it as a specifically colonial product, the poem itself does not limit itself to what might be classified as peculiarly or distinctly or uniquely colonial issues. Indeed, the figure of silk and other products from the so-called East to which the poem draws our attention associates it with some of the most hotly debated topics of 1730s England. For when the poem was published, concerns over the importation of "luxury" items, such as but by no means limited to silk, into Great Britain had reached their peak as "the debate as to the meaning and value-laden status of luxury came into prominence."[61] Contemporaneous debates over the value of "luxury" combined with the fascination with chinoiserie that overtook Great Britain at the same time, and that contemporaries linked directly with the problems and possibilities offered by luxury items, thus place, I would argue, the Georgia pamphlets in general and Kirkpatrick's poem in particular in a different discursive context than previous works extolling the virtues of English efforts to produce American silk.[62] Kirkpatrick's poem offers a rather unusual perspective on the overlapping rhetorical battles fought over luxury items in general and over chinoiserie in particular.[63] I classify it as unusual for the following reason. This poem was written by a British American while living on the very landmass Europeans hoped would produce the luxuries that serve as the poem's focus. The poem, in other words, offers a view of the taste and refinement conferred on people by certain Eastern objects, but it offers this view from a spot on the globe where refined objects are produced rather than from a place where, at least according to eighteenth-century environmentalist theories, they can be truly appreciated or even understood.

We should be clear here. What we have seen so far in this chapter is not meant to suggest that Kirkpatrick's simple interest in and focus on silk in particular or on luxury items in general distinguishes his poem from the work of his contemporaries. As Louis Landa pointed out long ago, the lady of taste dressed in silk had become a stock figure by the 1730s. In a pair of essays investigating the image of the silkworm in British literature produced in the early eighteenth century, Landa demonstrates the many uses to which a wide array of poets and prose writers from the period, including but hardly limited to such canonical figures as Alexander Pope, Jonathan Swift, and James Thomson, "assimilated [the image of the silkworm] into their works." He further contends that the use of what Pope calls the "busy little Animal" in this literature was, first of all, "peculiarly related to the fine lady," which, in turn, "deeply embedded" the very image of silk "in a whole cluster of ideas."[64] Among the ideas Landa mentions is "the fabulous wealth of the Indies," which, in turn, is associated by British writers of the period with "thoughts of greatness and magnificence."⁶⁵

So while Kirkpatrick's focus on the figure of silk as a crucial component of the colony's value to Great Britain is a further testament to the importance of this figure in the promotion of Georgia, it does not distinguish the poem from other contemporary works. Kirkpatrick does do something none of the poets Landa mentions do, though, when, while establishing the frame to draw our attention to the colony's potential as a place for silk production, he collapses any geographical distinction between East and West. He does this when he literally substitutes the name for a region in the East for a British American colony when he refers to Georgia in the second line of his poem as "India": "While generous O-g-P's unwearied Pain / Wakes up a Muse from India's savage Plain" (l. 1–2).⁶⁶ Why cast America as the East—making it, presumably, more foreign than it has to be—rather than try to argue, as so many other contemporary writers did, that British subjects in the New World were transforming America into British soil? If Kirkpatrick wants his readers to think of Georgia as an ideal environment for the production of silk, why not cast it as China rather than India?

We find that when we investigate the possible meanings of the word "India" for Kirkpatrick's readers we see that the multiple, sometimes seemingly mutually exclusive meanings "India" would have signified in 1732 work precisely to Kirkpatrick's rhetorical advantage. First of all, we should remember that the word was more often used to refer to what was then an ill-defined region and/or regions of the world than to the current political entity that, of course, did not exist when Kirkpatrick wrote. But it is not simply that the reference for the literal location of a place known as "India" resists being identified with any precision in the real world because no such political entity existed at the time or because eighteenth-century English speakers had yet to agree on just what specific boundaries would demarcate the land known as "India." While the overwhelming usage pattern of the day associated India not with America but with regions in what British people would have called the "East" in general and most especially with the East India trade in particular, the word carries within it a history of references to America. The word "India" contains for Kirkpatrick's readers, in other words, the sublimation of West into East that occurred when Europeans "discovered" America while looking for the Indies. This extraordinary geographic error—of Europeans thinking they had found a part of one huge landmass when, in fact, they had stumbled upon an entirely separate body of land—continued to be reproduced in English until well after Kirkpatrick's poem. That is, writers quite often continued to refer to one continent,

America, with a word that designated a completely separate one well after the disjunction between signifier and signified became known.

Kirkpatrick's use of a word designating a region in the East as a way of referring to specifically American soil stands out because it defies the overwhelming usage pattern of Kirkpatrick's time. While one can still find isolated examples from the period of references to America as India, for the most part the practice had ended by the 1730s. To be sure, the colonies were often referred to as the "West Indies" or even "West Indian" and "West India," but the term "India" alone was almost exclusively reserved for references to what we would now refer to as East Asia. In going back to an older usage, Kirkpatrick can use etymology to, as it were, have his cake and eat it too. He can claim to be referring to America while, at the same time, asking his reading to subsume one space on the globe into the completely separate space that is, quite importantly, more closely associated with the products Kirkpatrick wants his readers to associate with Georgia.

Aside from benefiting from the geographic ignorance registered in the word's history, "India" provides a set of powerful associations that work like magic to advance the conceptual and commercial associations that Georgia promotional material in general sought to make real. Kirkpatrick's decision to refer to America as "India" does all this while allowing the greatest amount of associative flexibility. For, as a casual glance at the OED will demonstrate, "India" might very well in Kirkpatrick's time have been intended to make reference "allusively [to] a source of wealth," and the word served in other cases as a specific reference to silk produced in India. Referring to American soil as "India" calls forth images of great wealth and valuable commodities while mystifying the precise location of their production. "India" mystifies place because of the simple fact that the word "India" connotes all the things Kirkpatrick wants his readers to have in mind—America, wealth, silk, the East Indies, but also porcelain, wine, perfume, dates, and so forth—without pointing to a specific, identifiable, bounded place on the globe. So, although as we have already seen that China in particular was associated with silk (among a number of other products) in the British world of the 1730s, the range of commodities with which it was associated was more limited than was the case for the figure "India." Because "India" refers to the "East Indies" as well, and the "East Indies" includes China, Kirkpatrick is able to link India, China, and America through the use of a single word. In doing so, he is able to promote Georgia as a fertile spot for silk production while subtly suggesting that the colony's environment could produce a range of other valuable commodities as well.

Kirkpatrick goes on in the body of the poem to use this very same associative strategy to show Eastern products literally growing in Georgia soil. In Kirkpatrick's telling, Georgia simply and literally takes the place of the East through its production of the very same raw materials associated with the East.[67] It's not that Georgia produces raw materials *like* those found in the East. Kirkpatrick's language asks us to understand Georgia's signature products to be precisely the same as those found in the East. Nor does Kirkpatrick say that Georgia will produce silk to match the quality and quantity found elsewhere in the world. He goes even further than this. Those Georgia settlers who seek silk will find "on the well examin'd Plain . . . China's fragrant Leaf" itself (1. 92). Look no more to India for its distinctive perfumes and ointments, for "the costly Balms" previously found only in "Indian Groves" in such great quantities that their precious goods drip out of them without human labor grow, too, in Georgia's "consenting Climate" (1. 93–94). One could even quench one's thirst by drinking the very berries until now found only by wandering through "*Mecca's* Vale" (1. 100).

Eastern commercial products are not the only things of the East that one finds in Georgia. The very air itself is Eastern. Kirkpatrick accomplishes this atmospheric sleight of hand by rewriting a line from a popular British poem on women's fashion. In *Clarinda,* published in London three years before Kirkpatrick's poem appeared in the *Gazette,* James Ralph writes that "*Arabia* breathes its spicy Gale" so that British women's bodies, through the perfume made—or supposedly made—with Eastern goods, will have enticing body odor.[68] One might say that Britain's merchants breathe "Arabia's Gale" so that women might have the products they are said to desire. As Laura Brown points out, in Ralph's poem it is "as if navigation, trade, and expansion are all arranged solely for the delectation and profit of womenkind" so that women "bear responsibility" for "the systematic, bureaucratic, piratical, or mercenary dimensions of imperial expansion."[69] Kirkpatrick's subtle alteration of the line fundamentally shifts not only who breathes Arabia's air but also and even more importantly the geographic location of the air. British laborers are now breathing this Arabian air, which can only mean that somehow Arabian air exists in Georgia as well as Arabia. Or perhaps another way of putting this would be to say that, according to Kirkpatrick at least, one could speak of the air of Arabia as if it were indistinguishable from, one and the same, literally interchangeable with American air. So whereas in the Ralph version the poem suggests that British merchants' breathing of Arabian air represents a sacrifice or excessive labor done on behalf of those women who, it is claimed, crave the latest fashions, in Kirkpatrick's version British subjects consume such Arabian air "with small Pain" and, apparently, without labor.

This is a particularly important substitution given the importance of "air" to eighteenth-century notions of the environment. It would be safe to say that for those of Kirkpatrick's generation and profession, air serves as the primary indicator of an environment's habitability. As a doctor, Kirkpatrick would have known about the relationship posited between air, health, and identity. He would have learned in his readings that the quality of air differs greatly across the globe, and those same sources would have indicated that these differences could be used to account not only for the different body types to be found throughout the globe, as well as the diseases associated with specific regions, but also for the differences, at least to some extent, in cultural practices one finds in the different parts of the world. The air one breathed was often held largely responsible for the way one behaved, in other words.

Kirkpatrick challenges such theories with a simple metaphor. The phrase does not suggest that air across the globe is precisely the same; to suggest this would be to undermine the very way in which he has sought to have his readers understand America's value. Georgia is valuable to Great Britain not because the air everywhere is precisely the same, but because the air in Georgia is precisely the same as the air in Arabia. Difference still exists, but the difference between East and West has been collapsed in this instance so that West can literally be substituted for East. He challenges at least some of the reigning theories of the day by offering no suggestion that the breathing of Arabian air by British subjects poses any threat to Great Britain.

Kirkpatrick's position on the causes of identity formation differs from the standard understanding held by most other early-eighteenth-century European elites. It is entirely consistent, however, with the position on such issues put forth in other parts of this poem. Let us examine just one example. Kirkpatrick has the character of Oglethorpe say that King George "calls the Wretch of every Clime his Son" after "Wretches" "run" to the "Isle of Heroes" (65–66). In using "Clime" as a figure for nation, Oglethorpe suggests that George's powers are so great that his simple call will be able to overcome the power of environmental theory when he incorporates people from every climate on the globe into the British family. This simple act of voicing, of calling, indicates the power of the monarch's voice to transform or overcome the environmental theories.

Far from posing a threat to Britain's sense of itself as British, this Arabian Georgia actually expands the British bloodline. Georgia works to transform people from countries around the globe into happy British subjects. Indeed, Kirkpatrick goes so far as to suggest that in the opening up of Georgia to British settlement, the English bloodline gains perpetual life and literally alters genealogies. The work of Georgia's settlers, Kirkpatrick claims, will produce "an endless Race" drawn from "the Wretch of every Clime" who owe their allegiance to the British nation (1. 73; 66). Kirkpatrick uses "Race" here not in the modern biological sense. He does not suggest that Georgia will produce a new category of people who are somehow distinctly British and not British at the same time. Instead, he uses "race" here in the sense in which it was commonly used in the sixteenth and seventeenth centuries, as a figure for a family line. He makes this clear when he refers to those non-British peoples who willingly emigrate to Georgia as members of King George's immediate family. Literally every "Wretch" who comes to Georgia from abroad becomes George's own "Son."

At the same time that it perpetually expands the British race, Georgia works to limit the growth of competing races. Kirkpatrick indicates this when he uses geographic boundaries as figures for what he refers to as "racial" ones but which we would understand as "bloodlines." "Iberia's motley Race a bound shall know," Kirkpatrick has Oglethorpe announce in the poem, when Georgia's "happily increasing Band" of settlers "replenish the inviting Land" between the Savannah and Altamaha rivers (1. 49; 47; 48). Given that the poem focuses a good deal of its reader's attention on the production of the seemingly distinct category of geographic lines used to set boundaries between antagonistic political entities, the poem's use of "line" in reference to social relations only encourages the confusion of any distinction between the kinds of boundaries erected to separate geographical entities and those used to distinguish social communities.

But in spite of the challenge to such dominant environmental theories offered by the poem, Kirkpatrick remains fearful of giving up on environmentalism entirely. We see this in the way the poem consistently displaces the British American colonists—and, to some extent, British people in general—from the land in which they live. Britain might claim Georgia as its possession, British people might live on its soil, but the poem's language consistently draws a boundary between British things and American soil. This distinction begins in the origin narrative the poem offers in its opening lines. The poem comes to life when Oglethorpe's "pain . . . Wakes up a Muse from India's savage Plain." Lest we see this "pain" as American-born, the narrator quickly assigns it an English birth. For these pains were "form'd" when Oglethorpe "explor'd" the "Horrors, Dungeons" to be found in English prisons in the 1720s (1. 16; 17). Oglethorpe not only "Caught" the "Wretches Woe, and Mourners' Sighs" he found in the jails; he "makes" the pains of the "Distress'd" he found there "his own" (1. 12; 12; 10; 10).

Kirkpatrick very carefully avoids any link between these pains and American soil. Whether one construes these "pains" as emotional or bodily or some combination of the two, they can be said to awaken the Muse but they are never said to directly touch her "unform'd" ground (1. 5). Instead, Kirkpatrick suggests it is the "humane Design" developed by Oglethorpe to alleviate these pains that are said to come into contact with the explicitly non-British Muse (1. 3). For it is this "Design" that is said to have "Warm'd" the Muse and that serves to "inspire" the poem to follow (1. 3).

Oglethorpe is not alone in being distanced from the very continent that establishes his place among the greats of British history. For in the process of magically transforming Georgia into India, the structure and language of the poem simultaneously distances the poem's own readers from the land about which it speaks. Thus Kirkpatrick changes his British American readers, who are already separated geographically from their homeland, into spectators of the land on which they do live. In this way, readers in South Carolina are placed in the very same position with regard to the production of East Indian goods in Georgia as that of readers in, say, London.[70] The poem leads us to this conclusion in the following way. First, we must remember that the poem was written by a South Carolinian and published in a periodical whose circulation was limited to colonial British America. While the *Gentleman's Magazine* was read on both sides of the Atlantic, no evidence exists that anyone in the colonies imagined that colonial American papers would enjoy a readership in Great Britain. The poem's imagined audience was thus surely colonial British Americans. Second, the poem, we should remember, asks readers to adopt the same position as its speaker— that is, we are to view the scenes from the perspective of the narrative voice of the poem—who goes out of his way to avoid placing himself in any particular place on the globe, including from the perspective of "India's savage Plain." Given all this, we can reasonably conclude that the poem works to distance its original readers from the place in which they are reading. In going to such elaborate lengths to frame this very poem as speaking from the position of a colonist, the editors of the *Gentleman's Magazine* merely underscore the way in which the poem itself tries to obscure the geographic position of its speaker. In steadfastly placing the speaker in no particular place, Kirkpatrick allows his colonial reader to separate him- or herself from his or her "foreign" surroundings in America. Other colonial writers of the period adopted a strategy that called forth their place in the New World as a way of authorizing their claims about British America. In choosing to position his speaker and readers in no place, then, Kirkpatrick specifically rejects the colonial position in favor of a position no place and, in the process, distances his speaker and his readers from the very surroundings that allow for the claims that Georgia can be a British East Indies.

The colonists, it turns out, are no different from the King in their relation to American land. The monarch himself, the poem assures us, ventures no deeper than the surface of America's soil. We see this when Kirkpatrick writes, "*George's* name adorns the teeming Ground" (1. 34). An adornment, of course, beautifies, but it does so by adding a quality or set of qualities on top of an existing object. An adornment does not, in other words, penetrate the object it adorns, but merely supplements that object. In this way, Kirkpatrick asks us to understand George's name as something added on top of or as covering American soil but specifically not penetrating the very soil it serves to name. Figuring George's name as an "adornment" thus establishes a safe difference between the monarch and the land that bears his name.

In asking us to think of the naming of Georgia in this way, Kirkpatrick makes George's name bear the same relation to the American soil as that of silk to British women. I say this because "adorn" is the verb contemporaneous poets frequently choose when speaking of British women wearing silk. Samuel Wesley claims, for instance, that when Georgia's silks "adorn'd" British women those women "shall shine compleat" (1. 185). In using the very same word to characterize the relation a name bears to the land it nominates as the fabric from which an item of clothing is made bears to the person wearing that item, Kirkpatrick effectively asks us to understand an imperial act—the naming of lands whose legitimacy rests solely on the military power to defend all challengers, including the native inhabitants of the land—in terms of aesthetics. George's name enhances the value of the land in the same way a fine piece of clothing enhances the value of the person being clothed: both become more beautiful to anyone observing them. Such aesthetization of imperial acts hides the violence inherent in such acts while shifting the focus of attention to a question of beauty. Saying that George's name "adorns" the land leads us to question—if we question at all—the nature of the beauty rather than the violent processes that led to the naming in the first place.

If equating the relation that George's name bears to American soil hides imperial acts under the cover of aesthetics, it does so while subtly acknowledging a hierarchy of values. Why would American soil need to be "adorned" if it were not in some way deficient? What does America lack that makes such adornment necessary? In conferring aesthetic status on what would otherwise be a suspect or at least unimpressive object on its own, the act of granting the colony the name "Georgia" shows that the name of the British king has greater aesthetic status than the American continent. Of course, the same logic applies to Georgia silk "adorning" British women. Why, after all, do they need such "adornments" in the first place? What lack does such adornment imply, and what kind of hierarchy of values does such a system suggest? In the case of silk, the logic of supplemental adornment for British women implies that as objects these women are inferior to silk, a product long associated with the East. Georgia promotional material thus implies that British women must wear clothing associated with the East in order to make up for their own inadequacies. Just as George enhances the aesthetic value of American soil without penetrating that soil and, in the process, putting his own status at risk, British women can enjoy the aesthetic enhancement silk confers on them without risking their own status as British subjects. Silk, after all, remains on the surface; it does not penetrate the skin.[71]

Kirkpatrick challenges the very hierarchy of values that the need for George's "adornment" of the American continent exposes, even as it relies on the figure of British women as the representative for a lack of refinement on the part of the culture as a whole. For while its promoters cast Georgia as a conservative project that would serve as, in Jack Greene's words, "a mirror or counterimage that would stand as both a reaffirmation of old values and a repudiation of the baser tendencies then rampant in British life," the guiding assumptions that give meaning to the way Kirkpatrick's poem envisions the colony's success operate on a very different set of values than the conservative tenets expressed by the colony's promoters.[72] We can see Kirkpatrick's challenge to these conservative values when he offers a definition of what success would look like for the colony. At the conclusion of the poem, he gives us a vision of Georgia that will allow us "to see the Work compleat" (1. 80). Kirkpatrick's anaphoric use of "Till" to begin lines 81 and 83 poses a variety of challenges to standard eighteenth-century aesthetic and social hierarchies.

> 'Till *Georgia's* silks on *Albion's* Beauties shine,
> Or gain new Lustre from the *Royal Line;*
> 'Till from the sunny Hills the Vines display
> Their various Berries to the gilded Day;

In this passage, Kirkpatrick's use of the coordinating conjunction "Or" equates British women whose status derives solely from their aesthetic qualities with people whose birth confers on them royal status. Georgia silks serve as the sole link between these two figures of decidedly different status, at least according to conventional wisdom, and in bringing them together in this way work to break down the differences by casting them as equal indicators. Georgia's work will be complete when "either" England's beauties wear that silk or members of the royal family do.

By linking the second of these two pairs of lines with the first pair through anaphora, Kirkpatrick uses the collapse of social hierarchies enacted in the first two lines as a prelude to his erosion of the difference between the relative values afforded social and natural displays in eighteenth-century British society. For the anaphora extends the vision of the completion of Georgia's work that Kirkpatrick offers here beyond the world of elite British society into the carefully cultivated natural world British settlers hope to create in Georgia. The anaphora challenges any preconceived hierarchies the reader may have about the relative value of these two very different kinds of displays. According to Kirkpatrick, then, the simple display of American foodstuffs in their natural environment is equally valuable a signifier of Georgia's as the display of a product long associated with the aristocracy and high fashion, silk, by British women who are understood to occupy the highest social and aesthetic ranks. As a result the "display" of Georgia's "Vines" serves equally as a sign of Georgia's success as the "shine" one might see when looking at British women wearing silk from Georgia. In categorizing them in the same way, Kirkpatrick collapses any distinction between the value of women's dress as an aesthetic object that displays a culture's sophistication and the simple existence of raw materials in their natural environment. The product of British labor in America becomes equally a matter of display as the social finery of dress by British women and British royalty.

In challenging the conventional hierarchy of values that elevates royal blood over the purely aesthetic and displays of taste by fashionable women over the mere appearance of foodstuffs in their natural environment, vision serves as the fundamental arbiter of success in each instance. Our evaluations of Georgia, Kirkpatrick tells us, should be based on what the eye can see. When the products of Georgia can be classified as objects upon which one can gaze, Georgia's work will be complete. We will be able to *see* when Georgia completes its work. Georgia will be a success when "*Georgia's* silks on *Albion's* Beauties shine," when the colony's "sunny Hills the Vines display," when "pleasant Olives shine," and when "*Hesperian* Apples show" themselves to the almonds growing nearby (1. 85; 88). The work will be complete in Georgia when people in England *see* British women wearing silks made from Georgia's silkworms; when the berries growing in the colony's vineyards become visible; when the wide variety of fruits the colony's settlers will tend can be seen.

The distinctiveness of Kirkpatrick's focus in his closing lines specifically on the visibility of exchangeable goods growing in America becomes clearer when we compare it with the way Wesley closes his roughly contemporaneous poem. The two poems use such similar language that "Georgia" reads at points like an echo of the earlier poem. Where Kirkpatrick describes the region of Georgia's settlement as a "savage Plain," Wesley labels it a "naked Plain"; Georgia possesses a "teeming Ground" in the *South Carolina Gazette*, whereas Georgia itself "teems" in Wesley's work; Oglethorpe speaks of the new colonists as an "increasing Band"; Wesley has Georgia's leader cast those same colonists as a "chosen Band"; where Kirkpatrick claims that "*Albion's* Beauties . . . gain new Lustre from the *Royal Line*," Wesley writes that Georgia's silk will "add new Lustre to the Royal Maid"; Kirkpatrick uses Georgia to envision a British colonial future in which "the wealthy Lands increase," while Wesley speaks in more general terms of "new Colonies" that show King George's "Domains increase."[73] The most conceptually significant similarity occurs when Wesley, too, casts Georgia's "success" in terms of female display. Georgia's work will be "compleat," Wesley's narrator tells us, when "Admiring Strangers . . . view" British women of high social rank "adorn'd" in Britain's own "home-wrought Silks" (1. 185; 187; 185; 190). The "dazzle" and "Splendor" produced in those strangers' "Eyes" when they see the "Product" of Georgia on "each sweet Form" of British women will "aid" these women's "Conquest" of suitors that, in turn, will "increase" rather than simply maintain British political dominance throughout the "World" (1. 186; 188; 187; 195; 184; 195; 195; 205).

But whereas Kirkpatrick's poem asks us to envision the "completion" of the colonial project as the moment when the more refined aesthetic taste that Georgia silk allows British women to display makes, at the very same moment, the exchangeable goods of America visible to the world, Wesley connects the display of Georgia silk on British women to the extension of royal power. Once Georgia's silks "aid" British women in their "Conquest" of foreign suitors, Wesley writes,

> thus maintain
> The steady Tenor of your George's Reign;
> And let th' admiring World One Sovereign know,
> Of Good all studious, and without a Foe;
> With such high Worth let Him the Age adorn,
> And call forth other Nations yet unborn;
> Still by new Colonies enjoy the Stores

Of other Climates, and remoter Shores;
And see unenvy'd his Domains increase,
The work of Wisdom, and the Gifts of Peace.
(1. 197–206)

Only after British women conquer suitors through their display of silk will the rest of the World truly know King George. In this sense, Wesley suggests that the extension of George's political power outside the British Isles to "other Climates," and "remoter Shores" than the American continent emerges out of and is produced through the aesthetic displays of British women. These displays, in turn, allow George to take the position of the object viewed—in this case, the "One Sovereign" whom all the world now "admires"—that, in the previous stanza, had been occupied by British ladies who wear American silk. Women thus become crucial to English power through their display of fine goods, but only insofar as a masculine figure almost immediately co-opts the power of display for his own political and acquisitive purposes, purposes established in the name of all British peoples. In co-opting women's power of display here, the King seems to gain women's reproductive powers as well, for it is only at this point in the poem that George gives birth to new nations when he is said to "call forth other Nations yet unborn."

How different from Kirkpatrick's vision of completion. Wesley puts a more visible monarch in precisely the same structural location where Kirkpatrick places figures celebrating the visibility of exchangeable goods produced through British labor in America. In Wesley's poem, we end with a vision of the extension of British political power produced by Georgia's goods, whereas in Kirkpatrick's poem those same goods are made equal in value to the qualities they are said to gain from their association with British people of royal birth. In the ending to his poem, Kirkpatrick relegates the usefulness of Georgia's goods to the empire at large secondary to their status as objects on display. The poem draws our attention not to the political power that results from the colonization of Georgia, then, but to the value of visibility and labor in their own right, regardless of their relation to empire.

I want to be clear in what I am trying to argue here. I am not trying to suggest that we see Kirkpatrick's poem as celebrating the aesthetic qualities of a distinctly American nature in contrast to Wesley's demonstration of how the American environment can be made to serve the purposes of British expansion across the globe so that, in effect, Kirkpatrick substitutes American nature for British monarchical power. I do not believe, in fact, that Kirkpatrick celebrates anything that can be called a distinctly American nature here at all. Instead, Kirkpatrick's final lines celebrate the demonstration of the American environment's metonymic potential. He celebrates its ability to stand in for something that it is not. And he celebrates this metonymic characteristic of America as an aesthetic quality that is to be appreciated as a thing in and of itself, as adding to rather than paving the way for Britain's political aims. I believe it is no coincidence that we find this perspective in a poem written by a British American colonist for, at least originally, a British American audience, because it elevates America's aesthetic status to the level of noble bloodlines while disabling any critiques of the potential degenerating effects of the American environment on British bodies. How can, after all, America be said to drain British bodies of any claims they might have to civilized status if the environment they inhabit does not seem to penetrate the surface? So, for instance, while we are told that Georgia's laborers breathe the Mecca's air, we are not permitted to travel beneath the surface of those workers' skins to some imagined state of interiority. We remain, instead, on the outside, where the poem assumes we will be satisfied with the vision—and only the vision—of objects whose symbolic associations remain what they had, supposedly, always been regardless of their point of origin.

In asking us to value the aesthetic qualities of surfaces in and of themselves while steadfastly refusing to reveal what's beneath those beautiful exteriors and, at the same time, associating this particular set of values with British America in particular, the poem—wittingly or not—establishes a set of values that stand in stark contrast to those put forth by many of the period's elite writers when they imagine the impact of silk and other so-called luxury products on British society. The concern of British commentators over luxury items such as silk from the so-called East was not lost on Georgia's promoters. They understood that they might face opposition from those voices in eighteenth-century Great Britain who would see their colony as merely another means of making it even easier for people to acquire the luxury items these commentators believed threatened the very fabric of British society. The promoters had a number of direct and indirect responses to such concerns that do not precisely fit into the focus of my argument. Because the Kirkpatrick poem's praise of the aesthetic quality of American goods seems at least an indirect reference to these concerns, though, I want to investigate very briefly how the poem differs from a standard critique of luxury items made at the time that Georgia's promoters cite.

To do so, we need only look at the concluding paragraphs of one of the colony's very first promotional tracts, *Reasons for Establishing the Colony* *of Georgia.*⁷⁴ Written by the colony's secretary, Benjamin Martyn, *Reasons* alludes on its final page to a poem published only a few months earlier by then-famous Alexander Pope that investigates the very problems raised by the use of wealth to purchase luxury goods such as silk.⁷⁵ Martyn invokes the "Man of Ross" character from Pope's "On the Use of Riches" as a way of positioning the colony on the conservative side in contemporaneous rhetorical battles over the value of luxury items.⁷⁶ "On the Use of Riches" portrays a British society in which people of the highest rank and social standing have become more interested in the accumulation of wealth for wealth's sake, even if this means placing their own interests over those of the nation at large. Such devotion to wealth for wealth's sake on the part of Great Britain's social elite leads Pope to have a Wizard in the poem ask us to "'See Britain sunk in Lucre's sordid charms'" (1. 143). The corruption that results from the desire for wealth among those who are entrusted with the rule of a nation leads to the breakdown of the social hierarchies that allow the nation to exist, so that this same Wizard proclaims: "'Statesman and Patriot ply alike the Stocks, / Peeress and Butler share alike the Box'" (1. 140–41). How could a brief reference to a recently published poem cast the colony as conservative on matters of luxury when Martyn devotes virtually every word prior to this in his book trying to convince his readers that Georgia could serve as a place for the production of wine, silk, olive oil, and dates, items that could hardly be called necessities?⁷⁷

As it turns out, Pope's poem works perfectly for Martyn's purposes. "On the Uses of Riches" does not eschew wealth or even the display of wealth so much as advocate for its proper use and display. Pope allows those in power the "Splendor" such wealth can allow, asking only that they "balance" such displays with ones of "Charity" (1. 217–19). Similarly, Martyn asks that his readers aim only to "be Beneficent in some Degree," a state he contends "[e]very man" can attain, rather than fully or thoroughly or entirely or completely devoted to charitable acts. He doesn't ask his readers, in other words, to give all their wealth to charity or to avoid all displays of those luxury items they have been able to buy.

For Martyn as for Pope, then, wealth and luxury in and of themselves pose no fundamental threat to Great Britain. The two part company, though, when Pope casts the fundamental danger facing Britain's social structure in linguistic terms, and it is the terms in which Pope casts the fundamental problem the poem addresses that I think bear discussion in light of Kirkpatrick's poem. Pope's narrator voices the fear that drives the poem when he has two characters wonder as they die, "'Virtue! and Wealth! what are ye but a name?'" (1. 328). In equating virtue with wealth as mere signifiers, Pope's characters express their fear of the insubstantiality of the concepts that serve as the foundations for the very language that gives meaning to their lives. What if, his characters ask, no transcendental signifieds exist to which these signifiers point? What if they are only words whose meanings derive not from their correspondence to ideas, concepts, and values that exist outside and independent of language but, rather, from within the signifying system itself? This vision of the problem as a fundamentally linguistic one explains the different kinds of images Pope uses to figure wealth and virtue. Most commentators agree, for instance, that paper serves as the figure for wealth in the poem, and, as we might expect from the linguistic way Pope characterizes the problem with which the poem wrestles, we will hardly be surprised to find that the poet consistently casts paper money as being without substance or ground. Paper-credit "lend[s] Corruption lighter wings to fly!" as, like a leaf, it allows it to "scatter to and fro / Our Fates and Fortunes, as the winds shall blow" (1. 70–76).[78] Virtue, meanwhile, literally "fill'd the space" where one would normally find the "Name" on the record of the life of the Man of Ross, Pope's exemplary character.

It is precisely the same kind of insubstantiality, of surfaces without depth, that Kirkpatrick's poem celebrates as a sign not merely of the success of Georgia but, indeed, as a quality to be celebrated on its own terms. Whereas Pope casts the triumph of the metonymic, where paper money gains its value through its relation to gold in a figurative system, as a threat to the very foundations of Britain's social system, Kirkpatrick envisions the very same kind of metonymic system, in which America substitutes for the East that it is, in fact, not, as absolutely crucial to the continuing health and reproduction of that very same social system. Pope casts the move from paper money to gold and the accompanying desire for luxurious items as a threat to the very foundations of what constitutes the civilized in the first place, while Kirkpatrick's poem imagines the authority that provides the basis for any nation to claim "civilized" status as fundamentally metonymic. Civilized status depends for Kirkpatrick on displays of objects, items, behaviors, and so forth that demonstrate that status. Great Britain enters the realm of the most elite of civilized nations through the display of external surfaces, through the display of objects whose depths seem unimportant and/or irrelevant to the point at hand. We can only conclude, then, that this poem wants us to understand the things that demonstrate a nation's status among the civilized communities of the world as mere adornments whose interiorities are irrelevant. These civilizing adornments, in turn, lead the reader to see that in order to be something that it is currently not, that is, civilized, Great Britain must become something other than what it currently is. In such a system in which one's status derives from one's performance, as it were, on the world stage, what could be more valuable than a place whose significance derives from its ability to stand in for some other place that it is explicitly not?

In such a world, though, where performance counts for so much, the American environment that we have often said was celebrated by British American colonists for its distinctiveness, its differences from those they had previously known, was, at least in the case of this poem about Georgia, valued for precisely the opposite reasons. America gains its value in this promotional pitch through a structure reminiscent of metonymy. Like metonymy, according to which a word gains its meaning from its common and/or historical association with some other object, event, or concept, America derives its value from silk's association with some other place, the East in general and China in particular. In this way, Georgia's promoters value America for what might be called its "figurative" dimension rather than for some unique or peculiar quality of the place that points to its having some essence that distinguishes it in some fundamental way from other places. Georgia is valuable because it is like other places. At the same time, Georgia's value stems from its explicitly not being China or the East, since if it were, it goes without saying, Britain would have a much more difficult time reaping the extraordinary economic and cultural benefits from it that Georgia's promoters foresee.

If we think of the poem, then, as casting America's value in metonymic terms, we might see the colonial writer as writing from a location whose value derives from its likeness to other, presumably inherently or essentially more valuable locations. This way of understanding the position from which at least this particular colonial British American poet writes would seem to bear some similarities to the position of the colonial and postcolonial writer that scholars in colonial British American literary studies and eighteenth-century British literary studies have recently begun to investigate.[79] In the way this colonial or postcolonial scenario is most often presented, the colonial or postcolonial writer is cast as writing from a set of values and conceptions that are borrowed—or perhaps even imposed upon him or her—from his now-forsaken homeland. Thus, we tend to cast British American colonial writers as endlessly pining after British scenes, British places, and British forms even as a radically different continent exists at their very fingertips.

This scenario certainly applies to some extent in the case of the promoters of Georgia, but I think America's metonymic status as a suitable substitute for the East raises some provocative issues. For in this case, at least, the more prized location is pointedly not the colonial writer's homeland. Instead, the East occupies the position in this structure of the place to be emulated, of the transcendent signified that seems to provide the ultimate source of value. To be sure, the value of the East on which these works draw comes from Great Britain in particular and from Europe more broadly, but this imported value system does not place Britain at the top of the cultural hierarchy. In fact, Georgia's promoters cast the East—what commentators in the twenty-first century often refer to as the "third world" or, more recently, "developing world"—as superior to Great Britain in some rather fundamental areas including, it would seem, as the very picture of a thoroughly civilized, sophisticated society. In serving as a key figure in remaking Great Britain into what it is not, then, this poem quite pointedly and explicitly asks us to imagine America's value in relation to what it classifies as "Chinese" and/or "Eastern" standards and objects rather than in terms of either the distinctive products to be found in the American environment or some resemblance to the mother country of Great Britain. Instead, the poem uses figures it links to the East to ask readers to judge its success by its ability to display its resemblance to things which are not unique to it.

CHAPTER 3

Humanity's Eastern Home in Benjamin Franklin's Oriental Tales

*I*n a famous 1784 letter to his daughter, Benjamin Franklin lays out his criticism of the newly formed "Society of Cincinnati." The letter owes its fame in the twenty-first century to Franklin's remarks extolling the virtues of the turkey as the symbol for America over the bird chosen by the Society, the bald eagle. Franklin begins his letter not with a discussion of birds, though, but by lamenting the Society's hereditary membership requirements. While admittance to the Society would be restricted initially to those who had served in the Continental Army or Navy, membership in the future would be granted only to the eldest sons of any original member upon that member's death. Franklin criticizes the Society's criteria for entry as being "in direct Opposition to the solemnly declared Sense of their Country."[1] Not only was the system contrary to the expressed will of the new country for which the society's members had supposedly fought, but, even more damaging, it relied on the methods for advancement used by America's enemies abroad. Franklin makes the "un-Americanness" of the system explicit by telling his daughter that the hereditary system of membership used by the Society imitates systems of rank used in "Europe" that "the united Wisdom of our Nation" had specifically decided, through the Articles of Confederation, had no place in America.

Franklin quite carefully avoids denouncing hereditary systems in and of themselves, though. Instead, he suggests an alternative model that would be "more useful to the State." We should model ourselves, Franklin tells his daughter, less on the Europeans than on the Chinese, who are, he says, "the most ancient, and from long Experience the wisest of Nations."[2] Franklin thus reaches for the figure of China as a way of imagining the future of the infant American nation. Even more interesting, Franklin establishes a triad according to which European and Chinese institutions stand as contrasting models for a third nation, America, a triad that places China above Europe in the hierarchy of nations. Look not to Europe for ways to keep the future nation healthy, Franklin implores his daughter, but to Asia for the systems that will produce a thriving new communal being.[3]

On closer inspection, Franklin's turn to China as a model for behavior should hardly surprise us. For while Franklin may have altered his views on a wide range of issues over the eighty-four years of his life, including a dramatic shift from cheerleader of the British Empire to champion of a revolution against that very empire, he remained remarkably consistent over seven decades of both public and private writings, not simply in demonstrating an interest in but also in showing great respect for Chinese culture, philosophy, and institutions. He was, as Owen Aldridge has pointed out, "the first and foremost American Sinophile."[4] Franklin's great friend Benjamin Vaughan recalled that the noted natural philosopher was "very fond of reading about China" and quoted Franklin saying late in life that "if he were a young man he should like to go to China."[5] Franklin published selections from translations of Confucius in the *Pennsylvania Gazette* in the 1730s, and he sprinkled his personal letters and published writings with philosophical tenets drawn from Confucianism. He pointed his readers to what he described as specifically Chinese methods he hoped Europeans and British Americans might adopt for, among other things, windmills, compiling censuses, determining fair compensation for physicians, making English spelling more phonetic, producing silk from silkworms, finding ginseng in the wild, using stoves to improve one's health, shipbuilding, rowing boats, making compasses, discouraging borrowing by establishing high interest rates, and solving mathematical problems.[6]

His interest in using as models for behavior in the West practices and philosophies associated with the East extended beyond China to objects and philosophies linked to other Oriental places and peoples. In this chapter, I concentrate on just one of the Eastern forms Franklin thought would be useful in the West: the Oriental tale. Franklin wrote three such tales, all in the final decade of his life.[7] "A Turkish Apologue" and "An Arabian Tale" were written sometime in the late 1770s and/or early 1780s, while Franklin was in France. "Sidi Mehemet Ibrahim" was written less than ten years later in 1789, long after his return to Philadelphia, while he lay stricken in his bed with the illness that would lead to his death.[8]

In order to understand Franklin's Oriental tales, we need to have some basic understanding of the history of the genre in Britain's American colonies, for this history would have helped give meaning to Franklin's tales in the first place. To do this, we need to fill a gap in the scholarship on American literature before 1800, for, despite the genre's enormous popularity in both the colonies and Europe, scholars in the field have paid it relatively little attention. When we consider Franklin's tales, though, we will need to know whether Franklin was turning to a genre that was an old favorite among American readers, or whether it was a newly discovered import. Just how common, in other words, were Oriental tales to American readers, and how long had they been a staple of American magazines? And while the genre's popularity among readers would have been reason enough for magazine editors to publish as many Oriental tales as they could in an effort to stay afloat in a market that saw one periodical after another disappear after only a few issues, we will need to consider, as well, the distinctive value Oriental tales conferred on their readers that contributed to their appeal for both magazine publishers and readers in the first place. The chapter thus begins with an all-too-brief history of the genre in the British American colonies and early nation, laying out, first, the genre's growing popularity up and down the Atlantic seaboard and, second, exploring the value attached to the Oriental tale on top of mere popularity. Our consideration of the genre's value will lead us to examine the way these tales were valuable not in spite of but perhaps in part because of the threat they posed to readers. For reading the Oriental tale might, or so it seemed to those in the eighteenth century, turn its readers Turk.

Once we understand the history, value, and threat the tale posed, we can turn our attention to an analysis of Franklin's tales. Franklin, we will see, uses form to shield his readers from the threat posed by Oriental tales. A close examination of Franklin's Oriental tales shows that once he has contained the threat these tales pose for their Western readers, he uses the genre to interrogate some of the most fundamental philosophical problems of the Revolutionary era. The Oriental tale provides a geographic space for Franklin to interrogate what Dorinda Outram identifies as "a key word in the 'Enlightenment'—reason."[9] Franklin uses one of the most popular genres of his era to cast Eastern geographic space as the site that restores reason to its rightful place, allows it to be seen for what it really is, and, in the process, offers us a glimpse of what Franklin casts as the truly human. He uses the ideas, images, and conceptions linked to the category of the "East" by the symbolic spatial economy of Revolutionary America, that is, to define the "human" itself, and, in so doing, Franklin suggests that we can see the human in its truest, most essential form on display in the imagined geographic space of the East. In establishing the terms of true humanity, Franklin provides the conceptual foundation for the praise of individuality his *Autobiography* would ultimately be known for promoting.

ORIENTAL TALES appeared so frequently in eighteenth-century British American periodicals that Frank Luther Mott classifies them as one of the "three kinds" of fiction that dominated early American magazines.[10] Tales of the East appeared in periodicals up and down the coast, in places as diverse as Baltimore, Boston, Fredericktown, New Haven, New York, Newark, Boston, Philadelphia, and Woodbridge, New Jersey. They appeared as far north as Bennington, Vermont, in *The Monthly Miscellany; or, Vermont Magazine*, and as far south as Charlestown, South Carolina, in the *South-Carolina Gazette*. Magazines that survived only a year in a market that brought ruin to virtually all early American periodicals, magazines such as *American Magazine* and *The Rural Magazine*, carried Eastern tales, as did those periodicals that found some way to stay in print for many years, such as *Massachusetts Magazine* and Matthew Carey's *American Museum*.[11] Those who fancied themselves among America's social elite read Oriental tales, as did those closer to the bottom of America's social ladder who were fortunate enough to be literate. Women read tales of the East; men read them, too. If we use Edward Pitcher's list of works of fiction published in America before 1800 as our guide, one in ten tales published in American magazines prior to 1800 could be classified as an Oriental tale, far exceeding any other generic category.[12]

Just which Oriental tale should be considered the first published in the British American colonies—and who authored that tale—remains a matter of dispute.[13] While the identity of the first Oriental tale published in British America continues to elude scholars, we do know the first story in the genre to attain considerable and sustained popularity among readers in provincial North America: Giovanni Marana's *Letters Writ by a Turkish Spy* (first published in London in 1684).[14] James Franklin, Benjamin's older brother, considered *Turkish Spy* so valuable that he listed it as "one of the books kept in the office of the paper for the use of writers," along with the works of Shakespeare and various issues of the *Spectator*.[15] The appeal of *Turkish Spy* seems to have transcended the political, economic, and cultural differences that divided the colonies of British America. In the staple colony of Virginia, for instance, the elder William Byrd, who died in 1704, requested that his son in London send "all but the first volume of *The Turkish Spy*" back home to Virginia, and another member of the Virginia Council, Edmund Berkeley, who died in 1718, counted the first and fourth volumes of the series among his collection.[16] Over a hundred years after the *Turkish Spy*'s first European publication, *New York Magazine* in 1794 called it "a book which has delighted us in our childhood, and to which we can still recur with pleasure."[17] The magazine did more than simply note the appeal of the work across an individual's life; it attributed the magic worked on readers throughout their lives to the literary quality of the work. According to *New York Magazine*, in other words, *Turkish Spy* was not only popular but also superior in quality to *any* of the many other works in the epistolary form it inspired, with the exception of "the charming Letters of Montesquieu."[18]

Whenever and whatever counts as the "first" published and first popular Oriental tale in Britain's American colonies, these tales retained their appeal to American audiences throughout the eighteenth century before exploding in popularity in the British American colonies in the century's concluding decades. The Revolutionary period of the 1770s saw what Mark Kamrath describes as "a nearly two-decade-long fascination" that "occupies an immense amount of textual and ideological space" in American magazines.[19] In the last fifteen years of the eighteenth century alone, magazines in the new nation "carried," according to Mukhtar Ali Isani, "well over a hundred Oriental stories," a figure that, of course, tells only part of the story in that it does not include newspapers, books, or works imported from Europe. The many tales set in the East that appeared in print were not simply translations of European origin or reprints from British periodicals. Isani estimates that "nearly *two-thirds*" of the tales of the East published from 1785–1800 "appear to be of American authorship."[20]

Estimates of the extent of American interest in the Oriental tale depend, of course, on just how one defines the genre. What qualified a piece of writing, after all, to be classified as an Oriental tale by an eighteenth-century reader? What features of the work would provide the cues those readers would use to label a work an Oriental tale? Imagined geographic space serves as the primary factor used to define the Oriental and/or Eastern tale for the eighteenth- and early-nineteenth-century American reader. The terms "Oriental tale," "Eastern tale," and "tale from [or of] the East" were used synonymously to indicate any tale—generally but not always fictional—purported to relate to the East, as the East was defined by eighteenth- and early-nineteenth-century American readers. What we have seen about the East in previous chapters remains true in Franklin's time. A much larger section of the globe counted as "Oriental" and "Eastern" for eighteenth-century British American readers. Oriental tales are thus, at least when Franklin writes and continuing on through much of the nineteenth century, tales either from or about the "Orient" or the "East," tales purported to take place in the East or to be narrated by someone from the East.

As for the stylistic and/or formal features that allow a work to count as an Oriental tale, eighteenth-century commentators and modern literary scholars rarely provide explicit, detailed explanations. The lack of precise definitions by eighteenth-century analysts should hardly surprise us, given the genre's modern origins. Why debate the definition of a literary form born, unlike the classical genres, out of the crudities of the modern marketplace, those in the eighteenth century might have wondered. When they do offer brief descriptions of the genre, their ideas of what distinguished this peculiar "style" grow out of the way they understood the East. The Orient, these commentators say, lends itself to parable and fable. The "metaphorical" quality that eighteenth-century writers claim characterizes the Oriental tale can be found most clearly in the realm of plot rather than language. So, the language of an Oriental tale is not to be taken at face value; in order to understand these tales, we must look beyond what we are explicitly told to what we are *not* told. Second, not unlike the genre of Romance, what happens in these tales can exceed the bounds of the physical world; these tales do not, in other words, aim to be literal transcriptions of the actual world but, rather, try to present scenes in which what happens can only be imagined. Such allegorical plots work well in an Oriental tale, we are told, because of the peculiar nature of the imagined geographic space of the Orient. The space itself is understood as unreal in the sense that it is cast as relatively unknown, a place where the physical laws known to exist in the West might not operate everywhere at all times.

This was the understanding of the Oriental tale that appeared in some of the very spaces used to demonstrate American culture's civilized status while at the same time those very spaces worked to produce the civilization it claimed to be merely putting on display. I am referring here to the appearance of these tales in British American magazines of the period. As material objects, of course, these tales are printed with ink no different from that used to display the other stories in the magazines, newspapers, and other printed material of the period. Like every other piece of printed matter, tales of the East appear as simply ink on paper. But the editors, printers, and authors responsible for devoting the ink to an Oriental tale could very easily have chosen to expend it on a wide range of other topics. Given the very low survival rate of American periodicals during this period and the difficulties printers faced just to stay in business, those who had a financial interest in what occupied the space of the page must have thought that spilling ink on matters of the Orient would allow them to recoup their investment. They must, in other words, have placed great faith in the genre's ability to generate more money in magazine sales than the cost of the ink, paper, and so forth that it took to print them in the first place.

How do we explain this value? What value, in other words, did these tales add to an otherwise blank space of the printed page that other figures of speech might not have added? What was it about this genre that would have produced greater surplus value than other kinds of tales? Or, at least, what value did the genre have that would have led those who invested in magazines to believe they would not only recoup their investment but make a tidy profit as well? Part of their value to those responsible for deciding what went on the page surely had to do with the symbolic status of Oriental goods in general in the late eighteenth century. The display and consumption of such goods signified an elevated social status in Revolutionary British America, a status that helped allow British Americans to feel on a par socially with their supposed betters in Europe in general and in England in particular. As Pierre Bourdieu puts it, "Taste classifies, and it classifies the classifier."[21] Demonstrating their own taste by drinking Chinese tea out of cups made in the Oriental style while sitting in rooms surrounded by porcelain objects displayed on walls covered with silk, Americans sought to identify themselves as persons of distinction. In this way, John Wei Tchen argues, "'things' Chinese had become" by the period of the American Revolution "one of the forms of currency" used by British Americans "for gaining cultural 'distinction.'"[22] The Oriental tale served as yet another "thing" through which provincial Americans could demonstrate—and help produce—their status as members of the metropolitan community. After all, though an extraordinarily popular genre, these tales had gained literary and cultural distinction when the leading members of England's cultural elite—including but not limited to figures regarded with great respect in the British American colonies such as Joseph Addison, Oliver Goldsmith, Lady Montague, Alexander Pope, and Samuel Johnson—went to great extremes to announce that they, in fact, read or wrote or planned to write in the genre. Oriental tales thus signified a cosmopolitanism and worldliness to American readers that could be transferred onto those who read them, or at least onto those who claimed to have read them.

By including Oriental tales, then, a periodical could claim the same kind of cultural value that Revolutionary-era British Americans conferred upon tea, porcelain, and other so-called Oriental goods. In this way, Eastern figures of speech redefined a physical space cast by its promoters as distinctly if not definitively American—the space on the page, that is, of American printed matter—as cultured, as civilized, and, at the same time, as civilizing. The practice of devoting so much space on the paper used for print in British America to figures of the East suggests an attempt by those responsible for the contents of those pages to transform American into Eastern space because, in fact, the Oriental symbolic space carried greater cultural value than other places on the globe in the eighteenth century. Printers, editors, and authors used these tales' symbolic status as signs of civilized culture. They did so in an attempt to transform as if by magic the supposedly degenerate cultural status of American print culture into one that would be considered, if not equal to Europe's, at least good enough to avoid the mockery American cultural products usually received when read abroad.

Circulated among British American readers throughout the colonies and early nation, Oriental tales brought the East into domestic and public spaces of British America. The Oriental tale, Ros Ballaster reminds us, was a "fabricated import, a hybrid construction similar to other commodities in demand and imported from the Orient in the period similar to Indian muslin or Chinese porcelain."[23] The Oriental tale, like porcelain, silk, and tea, integrated the Orient into the everyday lives of supposedly provincial Americans. It was not just that these tales were now being read in coffeehouses and private homes by more and more British Americans, making the East a crucial part of some of the very spaces in which Americans tried to demonstrate their civility. Oriental tales did not halt their incursion after they had been allowed into physical spaces that played crucial roles in forging British Americans' definitions of themselves. Once let into the new nation's homes and public houses, the Oriental tale, through its formal structures, set its sights on the imaginations of its readers and, thus, their very ways of organizing the world around them. Sometimes tales of the East put their readers into imaginary dialogue directly with people from the East; other times these tales took their readers literally inside the most intimate areas of the consciousness of Oriental characters. In asking readers to imagine themselves as occupying bodily spaces against which British American audiences had long been taught to define themselves, the Oriental tale jeopardized its audience's sense of who they were and the values with which they associated themselves. If civilized, literary society claimed that Oriental tales such as Franklin's offered its readers such powerful visions of the human that they were an ideal place to turn to in order to understand the most fundamental aspects of humanity, what was to stop the readers of this genre from trying to adopt the manners and even identities of the people these stories portrayed? What was to stop readers of Franklin's tales to, as it were, turn Turk when confronted by the philosophical sophistication offered by the East? To answer these questions, we need to turn now to an analysis of Franklin's Oriental tales.

WE BEGIN OUR examination with the very last of Franklin's published writings: "Sidi Mehemet Ibrahim on the Slave Trade" (1790). I have chosen to begin with a tale published at the end of Franklin's life because this particular story provides the best entryway into the problems and concerns shared by each of the tales Franklin wrote. Before we analyze the story itself, though, we need to first consider its generic status. For while I have asked us to consider the text as one of Franklin's Oriental tales, the letter has never been classified by critics as an instance of the genre. Instead, critics who have discussed "Sidi Mehemet Ibrahim on the Slave Trade" have generally considered it alongside narratives of Americans captured by Barbary pirates.[24] These narratives, often referred to as Barbary captivity narratives, began appearing in American periodicals in approximately 1785 and remained popular until around 1815. They grew out of the conflict between the new nation and the Barbary states once British protection was no longer afforded American vessels operating in Barbary waters, resulting in the taking of numerous American ships and the capture of their crews and passengers.[25]

It is true that Franklin's tale grows out of and is, in fact, a direct response to events surrounding these conflicts. In 1790, after James Jackson gave a speech in Congress wondering whether Franklin's signature on an antislavery petition demonstrated the venerable old patriot's senility, Franklin responded from his deathbed—albeit anonymously—with "Sidi Mehemet Ibrahim on the Slave Trade." In co-opting the voice of an Algerian in defense of the enslavement of captured Americans in Africa, Franklin hoped to discredit the arguments advanced by slavery's opponents by showing them to be identical to arguments that had been discredited throughout the colonies. To do this, Franklin turned to the genre of the Oriental tale, not to a form of captivity narrative that had not yet become recognizable. Written at the beginning of the crisis before the explosion of stories that helped define a particular Barbary subset within the genre of captivity narratives in general, Franklin's letter resembles not so much those later narratives to which it is most often compared by scholars as it does the Oriental tale with which Franklin was intimately familiar. Franklin's piece, after all, takes the form of a letter from an informant, one of the characteristic forms of the Oriental tale and one that is relatively unknown among Barbary captivity narratives. When examined through the lens of this genre rather than, say, as an early instance of the Barbary captivity narrative, the story works to imagine for its readers the category of humans united by the inability to reason.

Published in *The Federal Gazette* of Philadelphia in the March 25, 1790, issue, this story, precisely like Franklin's moralistic Oriental tales, must be translated for its "real" meaning to be understood. The tale works through a version of allegory in the form of irony by saying one thing but meaning something else. Franklin adopts the guise of the letter-writer—a standard form for the Oriental tale throughout the century—responding to what he has read in the *Gazette*. Jackson's speech urging Congress to avoid "meddling with the Affair of Slavery, or attempting to mend the Condition of the Slaves," reminds Franklin's persona of a speech made by "a member of the Divan of Algiers" named Sidi Mehemet Ibrahim in 1687. After these initial framing remarks, the rest of the letter consists entirely of a "translation" of what Franklin's readers would have immediately recognized as a completely fictional speech. How would they have so easily recognized that it was entirely made up? For one thing, the speech mimics the arguments made by Jackson in particular and by American supporters of enslaving those of African descent in ways that do not apply and were known by readers not to apply to American citizens held for ransom in Algiers. No one claimed, as Sidi Mehemet Ibrahim does, that Algerian pirates had enslaved over 50,000 Christians, and the absurdity of the idea that so many Christians were living against their will in Africa over 100 years ago would have clued Franklin's readers in within the very first lines of Ibrahim's speech. Instead, Franklin simply has Ibrahim offer the most common arguments of those who favored slavery in America. They claimed it would be financial suicide for those in the South who depended on slave labor while, at the same time, it would unleash onto the streets of Algiers a foreign people who would be unable to assimilate and who wouldn't want to go home. They would refuse to leave Algiers, Ibrahim insists, because far from being oppressed as slaves they knew they were far better off in Africa than they had been and would be in their own home countries. And, as if these economic and practical reasons were not enough to convince his listeners, Ibrahim closes by claiming that, in fact, the holy book to which Algerians look for moral guidance, the *Koran*, authorizes rather than forbids slavery by those of its faith. It is as if Ibrahim has a checklist of the Southerners' arguments for slavery from which he plagiarizes.

The frame not only specifically calls our attention to the "Reasonings" found in the speech but also tells us that the fact that the reasons given by the American congressman and the African divan are precisely the same proves the way "Interests" "operate" on "Intellects" "with surprising similarity in all Countries." We see that, read in the ironic tone in which it asks to be interpreted, the letter wants us to understand that what the congressman has called "reason" is nothing other than "interest," and that, far from being peculiar to this individual spokesman, such a substitution of human vanity for disinterested thinking provides the link between the human species across the globe, regardless of whatever classifications we might make that distinguish one people from another.

THE EROSION OF those boundaries that puts the philosophy of a white, pro-slavery American congressman into the mouth of a member of Alger's government appears in different form in Franklin's "A Turkish Apologue." In the opening paragraph of this story, Abdéllamar, the fable's protagonist, engages in an interior monologue that places us inside Abdéllamar's very mind in order to hear him speak "within himself."[26] In order to hear Abdéllamar's dialogue with himself, the reader must, if only for a moment, imagine him- or herself as inhabiting a space that eighteenth-century theories of the self would have cast as accessible to one's self and only to one's self. One might say, that is, that the reader must imagine him- or herself in the very place where the self imagines it is most itself, where, that is, the masks the self adopts when engaging with the outside world are laid aside, creating, in effect, a realm of the pure, unmixed self. What's more, the reader would have to imagine him- or herself inhabiting this space in such a way as to be undetectable to that self. Given that the reader enters this realm of the pure self without disrupting the sense that this realm has been compromised by "external" forces, I think it is safe to say that the reader at this moment transforms him- or herself into the very self he or she now inhabits. When reading "A Turkish Apologue," Franklin asks us to become—or at least pass for—Turks.

In taking us not only beneath the skin of the protagonist in this way but, indeed, into a space closed off to all but the self and God—or so eighteenth-century readers would have imagined—the tale thus leads us imaginatively into what would otherwise be an "Eastern" space considered dangerous by Franklin's imagined audience. Franklin leaves no doubt about the geographic spaces with which we should associate this character.

Indeed, he goes a little overboard in pointing out the status of this character as a person from the East when he refers to Turkey in the title, then announces the character's unmistakably "Eastern" name in the fable's opening sentence, and, as if all this did not demonstrate to Franklin's satisfaction just where on the map we should place Abdéllamar, devotes the second sentence to the entirely irrelevant information that Abdéllamar "had studied all the fine Arabian Writers." In repeatedly locating his reader in the East, Franklin takes us into a space that early modern Western readers had long been taught to define themselves explicitly against. When eighteenth-century readers turn Turk in order to listen in on Abdéllamar's conversation with himself, they threaten their own status as Westerners by inhabiting the most intimate mental spaces of a consciousness that stands for the alien and alienizing influence of Christianity's archrival, Islam.[27]

Given the enormous popularity of the Oriental tale, the transmigration the reader undergoes in "A Turkish Apologue" represents something much more than a unique rhetorical ploy devised by Franklin. Indeed, it might be seen as the defining paradigm for one of the most popular genres of eighteenth-century fiction in British America as well as across the ocean in Europe. How does Franklin shield his readers against this threat to their very status as members of Western civilization? Against the threat of turning Turk when imagining themselves at the very core of a Turkish person's being, Franklin offers form. Allegory protects Franklin's readers from becoming the very thing against which Christians in the West had long defined themselves and their community. The peculiar qualities of allegory allow readers to be so close to another consciousness that they could be mistaken for that other without threat of losing their distinctiveness from that other. The tale's reader can, through allegory, be two things at the very same time. Through the use of allegory Franklin can immerse his readers in the very qualities associated with the East by the symbolic spatial economy without having that immersion threaten to redefine the reader as Eastern.

We can see how this works by examining the titles of Franklin's most generically conventional Oriental tales, "A Turkish Apologue" and "An Arabian Tale." What, after all, is specifically "Turkish" about "A Turkish Apologue"? Is there any quality, characteristic, or element that might have been thought distinctively "Arabian" to be found in "An Arabian Tale"? These are not tales that, in any sense, are fundamentally *about* the people or places their titles name. Indeed, by calling one an "apologue" and the other a "tale," Franklin uses the titles to limit the way these works should be read. For eighteenth-century audiences, both "tale" and "apologue" would have signaled the presence of allegory. Tales and apologues were, at least in eighteenth-century American periodicals, most often allegorical narratives. In this sense, the titles ask readers to see these tales as being quite specifically about something they do not directly claim to be. The inclusion of words that signify both categories of people and/or locations on the globe alongside such markers of allegory suggest that we should not expect anything distinctively Turkish or Arabian but, on the contrary, something that will be about something other than the people and places it names.

But this does not mean that by titling the tales as he does and setting them in Turkey and Arabia Franklin evacuates these locations of the meanings and associations that these people and places would have had in the late-eighteenth-century symbolic spatial economy. Quite the contrary. Arabia, Arabians, Turks, and Turkey would serve the needs of an allegorical narrative precisely because of the aesthetic associations these figures would have produced among readers at the time. As I noted above, allegory and parable were styles cast as distinctively if not exclusively "of the East." One need look no further than the work of Hugh Blair, surely the most influential writer on rhetoric and style in the Revolutionary and early national periods.[28] Though his goal is to demonstrate that writing which his contemporaries label "oriental" is not, in fact, distinctive to any particular region, Blair provides a useful window into the qualities eighteenth-century thinkers associated with what he calls the "oriental style." Blair claims that a "strong hyperbolical manner" characterized by "concise and glowing" language that employs "bold and extravagant figures of speech" had "been long" seen as the "peculiar" signatures of what was called a specifically "oriental manner" of writing.[29] We needn't look far in American magazines of the period to see an instance of the very tendency Blair identifies. *Massachusetts Magazine* in 1789 claims that the very "style of the eastern nations is figurative and metaphorical." In order to document his claim, the anonymous writer of this piece asserts that "eastern . . . sages . . . deliver many of their moral lessons in parables and fables" (76–77).

Franklin takes his reader to this land where the words we read never—indeed, cannot, by the laws of allegory—directly reveal the truth to define the human. The same figure serves Franklin's purposes in each story, for Franklin uses each of his Oriental tales to define the human by mystifying the category of reason. In both works, the protagonist's reference to "reason" prompts a response from a "superior being" that, in turn, brings about the story's denouement. Appeals to reason, in other words, bring about the narrative's conclusion, the moral of the story, which in each case seems to be that human reason is not really reason at all.

In the case of "An Arabian Tale," we learn of the limits of human reason when Albumazar, the story's protagonist, asks Belubel, the genie who keeps him company in his place of retirement atop "the lofty mountain of Calabut," to "inform" and "enlighten" him.[30] What leads Albumazar to prostrate himself before this genie? His "reason" cannot resolve a theological conundrum. Albumazar has found himself unable to "account" for the "existence of evil in the world" that stands in stark contrast to "wisdom and goodness of the Most High" in spite of "all the efforts of [Albumazar's] reason" to reconcile the two.

Belubel uses the invocation of "reason" as an opportunity to define the human. He does this, first, by completely ignoring Albumazar's question. He never provides an answer for how evil can exist in a world created by a thoroughly wise and good God. He never even bothers to try to answer the conceptual problem the protagonist describes. Instead, he redirects Albumazar's—and the reader's—attention to the category of "reason" and, in doing so, implies if does not directly state that what humans call "reason" is anything but. The "quality . . . thou callest reason," Belubel tells his supplicant, is reason in name only. It is what humans "call" reason, not reason in its true form.

Once reason has been exposed as merely a label with no content, Belubel goes on to claim that humans have turned reason on its head. He does this when he tells Albumazar that reason "would rather be a matter of humiliation" than pride if the "good magician" only "knewest its origin and its weakness." "Men," Belubel patiently explains to an Albumazar, who has now cast himself as the genie's eager pupil, are precisely those beings who "canst yet have no conception" of the "powers and faculties" of those creatures above them in the great chain of being that leads, ultimately, to God himself.

The gratuitous insertion of Belubel's definition of the human in "An Arabian Tale" suggests the work that Franklin expects the symbolic space of the East to perform. The East, this rhetorical gesture suggests, serves as a space for the definition of the human. How else to explain Belubel's rush to provide a definition of the human as a corrective to one that was never offered? When Belubel takes aim at the way humans use reason to establish their very "value," he denounces a claim about how humans understand their own self-worth that is made in the story only by Belubel himself. Albumazar never says their capacity to reason establishes the value of the human species. Only Belubel makes this claim. Offering his definition out of the blue, as it were, signals a defensiveness about that very definition that implies, even if it does not explicitly name, the existence of other, competing ways of defining what it means to be human.

The gratuitous inclusion of a definition of the human suggests, further, a lack of self-knowledge on the part of humans in the first place. After all, why would a human need a definition of what it meant to be himself? Who else would know better what a human is than a human? To define the human in such a way implies other possibilities, other ways of understanding human nature. Take Belubel's reading of Albumazar's call to "reason." His reading seems to assume that the human capacity for reason—or what we humans call reason—provides the foundation for the value of the human species in the first place. He never says this directly, but then he doesn't have to. The way the story uses his assumption about what constitutes the true foundation of human value, without indicating any need to explain the basis of his assumption, in order to move the dialogue forward suggests a generic logic operating beneath the explicit logic of the characters in the story. Belubel offers a definition of the human not because it is called for by Albumazar's appeal to reason, but, instead, because it is called for by the genre of the Oriental tale. The eighteenth-century British American reader would expect to find supernatural beings interacting with humans as if it were only natural in the imagined geographic space of the East in the Oriental tale; so, too, would he or she only expect to find a definition of what it means to be human in that space.

Belubel's redefinition of the human as without true reason substitutes narrative for reason. Here, Belubel seems to say to Albumazar and, in effect, to the reader as well, let me tell you a story that will help you understand why humans are incapable of finding the solution to the dilemma you describe through their reason. Any understanding of the story Belubel tells, though, depends on the powers of reason for it to be convincing. The story resolves the conflict through what David Lovejoy has called "a rationalistic anti-intellectualism."[31] The genie asks Albumazar to "see" something that literally cannot be seen. He uses "see" metaphorically to demonstrate the limits of reason, and, in so doing, depends on the human ability to draw what can only be described as reasonable inferences from nonempirical evidence. After all, one can only "contemplate," as Belubel says, the "gradual diminution of faculties and powers" in the "scale of beings from an elephant down to an oyster" that the genie elsewhere says one "seest." How often does one have the scale of beings presented to one's vision at all, much less in the order of their respective places in the scale of beings? Where does one "see" the "faculties and powers" of each of these creatures on display?

One does not "see" the intelligence and/or faculties of the elephant or the oyster, but rather one sees these creatures in action and, in watching them, deduces their powers and faculties from their actions so that, in effect, their actions become a signifier of those powers and actions. The "small step" that separates the "powers and faculties" of these creatures exists only in the imagination of the onlooker. It cannot, as Belubel says, be "seen." These gaps in status are thus not visible to the naked eye; they exist only as conceptual deductions applied to the creatures in a relational scheme where the placement of one species in the hierarchy of species depends entirely on a distance between those two species that exists only in the imagination, only in the world of signifiers. It demonstrates the limits of human reason by recourse to that which is invisible to the human eye and which is, in fact, available only through the mental activity of imagining some figures who are not visible to the human eye who exceed the human capacity to reason.[32]

Now that we have seen how Franklin turns our attention to the East as a way of exposing the problems with human reason, we are ready to see how he recuperates the very category that his tales of the East have asked us to question. We can see how this works by turning to Franklin's second Oriental tale, "A Turkish Apologue." In this story, Franklin has God himself identify "reason" as misnamed. Reason, God tells an anonymous Angel, is simply "Vanity" wrongly labeled. We learn this when we hear God instruct this Angel to "Take from [Abdéllamar] all his Appetites . . . and all his Passions, except his Vanity, which he calls his Reason." In order to understand the significance of this categorization of reason, we need to remember that the very genre of the apologue transforms characters into representative figures. As a form of allegory, the apologue asks us to read characters and ideas not as representations of particular individuals or ideas but as figures for the conceptual category (or categories) of which that individual or idea is merely a small part. So, just as the story's generic conventions ask us to read Abdéllamar not simply as a particular man but as a figure for the human condition in general, so, too, do those same generic conventions ask us to understand "Reason" not simply as an instance of misnaming but as a figure for the human capacity to misname in general. It is not simply that humans misunderstand the true nature of reason but, rather, that reason serves as the very figure for humans' misunderstanding in general, a misunderstanding that is represented as a misnaming.

The problem Franklin presents us with in this story, then, consciously or unconsciously, turns out to be a linguistic problem, a problem of signifier being mismatched with the signified to which it should, rightly, be attached. One thing is called something that we now know it is not. In this way, the story suggests a fundamental misunderstanding of the world—a disjunction between the labels we attach to the world and the essential qualities that define those things we name. When the signified becomes detached from the signifier in this way, all those who use this particular signifying system can be said to be unable to understand truly the world in which they live and, indeed, their own actions and motivations.

We must remember that in suggesting that what humans label "reason" is, in fact, "vanity," Franklin takes aim at one of the defining categories of his era. For what eighteenth-century reader—in France, England, or the Confederation of American States—would not think of the call to "reason" that had swept Europe throughout the eighteenth century? The very category called upon by countless eighteenth-century writers to challenge conventional wisdom, even to establish a new form of government and, along with it, a radically different system of social organization, was, Franklin tells us, not what we thought it was.

Such a theme might have led Franklin to a thorough critique of the Enlightenment and, along with it, the American Revolution. Instead, "A Turkish Apologue" aims to have quite the opposite effect. Franklin uses his tale of the East as a way of preserving the category of reason. By having God say that humans have mistaken their vanity for reason, the story puts the identification of the improper signifier into the voice of the very figure who is responsible for establishing a relationship between a word and its meaning. God, after all, is the transcendental signifier, the namer of all things. God thus implicitly acknowledges the existence of the category of reason. He simply insists that humans do not possess it.

Why reserve the category of "reason" for the realm of heaven? The apologue removes reason from the realm of the human in order to save reason from contamination by what Mary Douglas has called the "social pollution" symbolized by the "vulnerable points" exposed when the body's borders are transgressed.[33] This becomes clear when we examine God's response to the interior monologue that opens the narrative. When God is "offended" upon hearing Abdéllamar question why the Almighty has "given [Abdéllamar] the Passions and Appetites of Animal Nature" that only "debase" him, he takes away those very characteristics Abdéllamar hopes to "subdue." The death of Abdéllamar from starvation at the close of the narrative shows that these very "appetites" allow him—and, of course, all humans—to survive. In this way, the story demonstrates how these supposedly "animal" aspects are absolutely essential to the very existence of the human. They may be shared with the "animals," but humans would not be humans without them and, as a result, animal aspects define the human as well.

The story never renounces the "animal" nature of these appetites, nor does it challenge in any way the language of "debasement," "defilement," and "disgust" that Abdéllamar associates with those appetites. The story, in effect, concedes the "animal" nature of the human. It is the rejection of the "animal" nature of the human that the story challenges. In so doing, "A Turkish Apologue" subtly reinforces a binary opposition between body and intellect, an opposition that operates to, among other things, limit the claims of human reason by exposing it to the potentially corrupting influence of bodily desire. It is no coincidence that Franklin names only two obstacles to Abdéllamar's devotion to "profound philosophic Speculation": eating and sex. Eating and sex put the purity of reason at risk by allowing exterior objects to penetrate the body's boundaries. The narrator calls attention to this when he has Abdéllamar suggest that his status as "a reasonable Being" might be "defile[d]" by the simple act of "putting Bits of the Flesh of a dead Beast into my Mouth." So as not to leave any doubt about what is most appalling here, the narrator makes sure to conclude by stating the obvious: "and swallow them."

While the mere thought of eating "disgusts" Abdéllamar, sexual intercourse threatens to unman him. Here, too, Franklin specifically and pointedly poses bodily pleasure as a threat to Abdéllamar's status as "a reasonable Being," and here, too, Franklin casts the threat as one to the body's very boundaries by having Abdéllamar wonder why he should "mix" with another in this way? To show us that sexual intercourse between any two individuals, no matter how sanctioned by love or authority, no matter their social status, can escape the debasements the protagonist associates with the body, Franklin goes to great lengths to connect the woman with whom Abdéllamar might have sex to the very symbols of what would count in the eighteenth century for female purity. For Franklin does more than simply label the potential bride a "Virgin" who, he assures us, is as "fair as the Morning" itself and "fresh as a Rosebud." This is a woman, the narrator insists, whose virginity rivals that of the "Houries of Paradise," who have their virginity restored every day even after they have "despoiled" themselves through sexual activity the previous night. Sexuality does more than simply disgust our philosopher, as eating did. Sexual intercourse threatens the very humanity of Abdéllamar, who speaks of having sex with his potential Bride as having to "perform the Functions of a Brute." Sex threatens to unman the narrator by transforming him into the very definition of the nonhuman, the "Brute." Sexuality, the performance of the male role in heterosexual activities, one of the very acts, it would seem, that would demonstrate manliness in eighteenth-century British American culture, puts him at risk of losing his very identity as a man.

The binary that casts true reason as threatened by the most basic of human bodily functions, the story suggests, keeps the family alive. The very category of "reason," indeed, even the very binary that sets body and mind in opposition to one another, casts all things pertaining to the body as forms of debasement, and so seeing these qualities as bodily and therefore debased becomes inextricably linked to the maintenance of the social system the story depicts. To suggest that sensual pleasure represents something other than debasement puts the borders of the body, and the borders of society, at risk. We see this in the way the story registers failure by casting the real tragedy of Abdéllamar's death as the way it prevents his parents from being able to "continue to live in the Offspring of their beloved Son." In imagining himself as pure intellect, Abdéllamar kills not only himself but, and more importantly, his family's line and that line's social advancement. The story closes not by focusing our attention on the protagonist's death, but by calling attention to the precise ways in which that character's actions have hurt his parents. The final paragraph relates in detail how his parents' "fond Hopes . . . of seeing Abdellamar [*sic*] promoted to the most Honourable Offices, for which he seem'd so fit" are dashed. Abdéllamar's actions have done more than merely "cut off" his parents' "flattering Expectations" for him, though. Misnaming reason for vanity ends his parents' hope of "finding themselves continuing to live in the Offspring of their beloved Son." Abdéllamar's mislabeling of vanity prevents his parents from living on through their descendents. The tragedy of "A Turkish Apologue," then, is not that an individual dies as a result of his linguistic mistake; the tragedy is that such a mistake does a disservice to his parents and literally kills off a family line.

In asking us to mourn not Abdéllamar's death but rather the deleterious effects of his death on his family's fortunes, Franklin uses the East to examine not only the true nature of the human in its individual form—separate, solitary, distinct—but also, through the protagonist's misunderstanding of the relation between mind and body, the effects of this misunderstanding on the social body. Franklin turns our attention East, in other words, to show us, first, the value of reason in helping produce healthy individuals and, then and only then, to demonstrate the threat to social reproduction if we fail to heed these warnings.

When Franklin turns our attention to the East, then, both before and after the Revolution, he does so in order to offer a vision of the category that eradicates rather than erects borders. The "human" that Franklin conjures up for us in Turkey, Arabia, and Algiers is not only a human lacking in national identity but also one whose chief characteristic challenges the very discourse of his age. Franklin's "human" might be called a "cosmopolitan" human in the sense that this human type extends across the globe, but it is cosmopolitan only insofar as it recognizes its intellectual limitations. Looking East, Franklin asks us to see a human who knows no geographic boundaries but who is defined, instead, by the internal limits of his (and the gender is quite important) mind. It is this vision of the human—gendered male but without racial specificity—that provides the conceptual foundation for Franklin's vision of the self-made man for which he would become famous. This is a man who makes his own way in the world, but he does so not without keeping an ironic distance from reason's claims and not without going into great detail about the dynamics of social reproduction.

CHAPTER 4

Edgar Allan Poe's Oriental America

One could hardly find more unlikely allies among nineteenth-century canonical American writers than Ralph Waldo Emerson and Edgar Allan Poe. Poe gained much of his notoriety in the period from his merciless attacks on those groups he repeatedly insisted had seized control of the United States' still-embryonic literary culture. Groups such as the "Frogpondians"—whom we now know as the Transcendentalists—were simply "word compounders and quibble concoctors" who hid their attempts to destroy the careers of many a writer in America behind a "Cloud Land of Metaphysics."[1] Emerson reciprocated his literary colleague's disdain by referring to Poe as "that jingle man."[2] While they loathed one another's literary productions and the aesthetic theories on which those productions relied, they found common cause when it came to the figure of the Arab. For instance, Emerson's intellectual and conceptual ties to what he considered an Oriental approach to the world were so deep that they led him in one journal entry to say of himself, "I am an Arabian within."[3] Poe's own conceptual affiliations with what he imagined to be Oriental ideas led him not only to title his first collection of stories *Tales of the Grotesque and Arabesque*, but also to include what L. Moffitt Cecil calls "significant allusions or imagery drawn" from what Poe would have considered the Arab world in virtually every one of the stories in that collection.[4]

More specifically, Poe and Emerson agreed on the place of one Oriental tale in the canon of world literature: *The Arabian Nights*, or what we now refer to as *The Book of One-Thousand-and-One Nights*. Emerson and Poe each considered it to be not only a work of great quality but also required reading for all who aspired to be civilized, cultivated, and tasteful. Emerson lists the work among those few "world-books" to stand as "the true recorder & embodiment" of its time; indeed, he calls it one of the "best books" of its kind.[5] He goes so far as to say that he hopes one of his own proposed works will be read as a "supplement" to the work of his "Arabian friend" who composed the *Nights*.[6] Poe offers less frequent praise, but those comments he does make leave little doubt about his admiration for the work.[7] In *Pinakidia* 27, for instance, Poe uses the consensus among American literati of the literary quality of the *Nights* in one of his assaults on a rival American critic. In this case, Poe responds to the question "Who does not turn with absolute contempt from the rings and gems, and filters, and caves and genii of Eastern Tales as from the trinkets of a toyshop, and the trumpery of a raree-show?" posed by James Montgomery in his *Lectures on Literature*, by simply saying: "What man of genius but must answer 'Not I.'"[8] As if to drive the point home that Montgomery lacks the taste to distinguish true literature, Poe adds a parenthetical exclamation mark after the word "literature" when citing the title of the work from which the passage is taken.[9]

Much has changed, of course, in the symbolic spatial economy from the appearance of Bradstreet's poems in the seventeenth century to the battles over America's literary future waged by writers such as Emerson and Poe prior to the Civil War. While Bradstreet composed her poetry before Orientalism, Emerson and Poe wrote in what some consider one of its most virulent phases. When Bradstreet turned her gaze to the East, she saw countries that dominated the world economy and at least one religion, Islam, at war with the faith to which she had devoted her life. By the time Poe and Emerson turned to Arabia for their model of literary achievement, Europe had reached, at least in its own and America's view of the world, the pinnacle of world power economically, politically, militarily, spiritually, and culturally. It had changed so much, in fact, that John Pickering could use the occasion of his address to the initial meeting of the American Oriental Society in 1843 to imply that America might be wise to adopt some of Europe's Eastern imperial ambitions.[10] The Eastern imaginary operating during the years Poe and Emerson were alive would also have led them to differentiate more precisely the people and places that made up the region. Antebellum America "distinguished the image of the Arab from the image of the Turk or the Persian and from the conglomerate image of the Islamic oriental," as Jacob Rama Berman has written, in ways that would have been inconceivable to Bradstreet.[11]

In spite of the vast differences in the way Arabia would have signified in the symbolic spatial economies of the seventeenth and nineteenth centuries, the Eastern imaginary remained for Poe and Emerson, as it did for Bradstreet, a place that absorbed vast regions of the globe into a single category whose cultures and communities were thought similar enough to be grouped together. Indeed, the East had in some ways expanded by the time Poe and Emerson entered the scene. Pickering, for instance, includes not only the entire "Eastern continent," including Arabia, Egypt, and India, in his definition of what constitutes the Oriental but also "the region of the globe which has been called Polynesia."[12] What strikes me as particularly remarkable, though, when we look back to Bradstreet as we move into the nineteenth century is the fact that authors at the epicenter of America's literary history continue to turn, in spite of the many differences that have emerged in the place the East occupies in the symbolic spatial economy, to the East as a way to demonstrate America's civilized status.

I want to use the agreement, then, on the value of *The Arabian Nights* by two prominent American writers at the very period when a nationalist literary movement gained unprecedented support as a way of drawing our attention to the work of at least one canonical nineteenth-century American writer who used what he called "Eastern tales" to establish the United States' status as a civilized nation.[13] Both sides in the rhetorical wars waged over literary nationalism operate on the assumption that America's literary prowess would demonstrate America's place in the pantheon of civilized culture. Debates over how best to enable the production of "great" literature in America in this period were ultimately debates about how to prove—to Europeans and to Americans themselves—that American culture was as civilized as any European or ancient culture. Poe's "The Thousand-and-Second Tale of Scheherazade" intervenes in these debates by asking its readers to side with a theory of aesthetics directly at odds with the aesthetic theories of those critics who advocate a "nationalist" literature.

In order to show how Poe makes the case for a civilized and civilizing aesthetics in "The Thousand-and-Second Tale of Scheherazade," we first need to understand just what Poe and his readers thought of the tale he used as the basis for his Orientalizing of American literature. In order to understand just why Poe might have chosen this narrative rather than some other, as well as what his particular revisions of this particular narrative might mean, we need to understand both what people understood to be the basic elements of the plot of *The Arabian Nights* as well as the meanings and implications they attached to the story cycle. Thus, we begin our examination of the story with a brief history of the reception of this collection of tales in antebellum America. Our investigation of the life of *The Arabian Nights* reveals that, in addition to its being one of the most popular tales in the new United States, reviewers considered its stories to be exemplary models of the very romance aesthetic Poe fiercely advocated in the pages of just about any American magazine that would have him. "The Thousand-and-Second Tale of Scheherazade" aims to promote the romance aesthetic with which *The Arabian Nights* was associated so that American letters could be considered truly civilized. Poe clues us in to the real aims of the story in its first few paragraphs, where he links his discovery of the tale to people, issues, and books associated with the contemporaneous debate over the future of American letters. In the body of the narrative, Poe's frequent deviations from the plot of standard translations of *The Arabian Nights* allow him to make the King to whom Scheherazade tells her stories the butt of an unrelenting satire aimed at the more "realist" aesthetic theories espoused by proponents of a national literature. In a bitter reversal of the story that readers would have found—and what one still finds today—in their own copies of *Arabian Nights*, Scheherazade's stories lead the King to kill rather than save her. In the process, Poe turns her into a figure for the modern author, an author put to death by a character who serves as a representative of the very people in America who claim they want to assist in the birth of a truly national literature. Poe thus transforms a specifically American scene of writing into an Eastern one, with a female as its representative storyteller.

In casting the King as the villain and killing off the character with whom we most sympathize in the story, Poe aims to manage both negative and positive images of the East in mid-nineteenth-century America. He tries, that is, to draw on Americans' vision of Oriental monarchs as inevitably autocratic, despotic, and cruel in a story that uses an Eastern work that, by the time Poe wrote, had come to stand as the very model for the romance aesthetic in literature. By the middle of the nineteenth century, though, allegory isn't enough, as it was for Franklin, to shield American readers from the threat of going native. Or at least it is not enough for Poe. To ward off the threat of a feminized, Orientalized America, the very vision Poe offers in the story as the solution to America's literary problems, Poe stages the execution of Scheherazade. In this way, he encourages his reader to understand the specifically female, Oriental body she inhabits in the story as distinctly, definitively Other while retaining the reader's commitment to a romance aesthetic.

❧

BY THE TIME Poe published "The Thousand-and-Second Tale of Scheherazade" in *Godey's Magazine and Lady's Book* in February of 1845, readers on both sides of the Atlantic had demonstrated a seemingly inexhaustible interest in what was then known as *The Arabian Nights Entertainments*.[14] The story of the work's reception by readers in Great Britain and the United States begins with the French Orientalist Antoine Galland's translation into French of stories in Arabic, Persian, and Turkish that he had come across in his travels in the East.[15] The first volume of stories appeared in 1704 as *Mille et une nuit,* and volumes of new material continued to be issued until volume 11 in 1717, when Galland had been dead for two years. Galland appears to have thrown the edition together rather hastily and without much thought toward the commercial or scholarly potential of the work or, it seems, about whether the stories truly had their origins in the East. None of this seems to have had any bearing on the work's sales, though, for *Nights* became an instant bestseller throughout Europe. The fact that pirated editions appeared almost immediately after Galland's French version was issued indicates the enormity of its initial popularity. An English translation was produced in the first decade of the eighteenth century, though precisely when it appeared is an issue of some debate, but by 1715 a Grub Street edition of the *Nights* advertised itself as the "Third Edition" of the tales in English.[16] The stories remained so popular in England throughout the eighteenth and nineteenth centuries that by 1793 at least eighteen different editions of the *Nights* in English had been issued in England alone, and, according to Peter Caracciolo, "the rate of publication (whether reprint or new translation) was to double" in the first thirty years of the nineteenth century.[17]

As these publication figures imply, the popularity of the *Nights* only increased in nineteenth-century England; they increased to such an extent, in fact, that the book could be said to "penetrate every stratum of the reading public."[18] No hyperbole seemed too excessive to describe the appeal of the *Nights*. One reviewer, for instance, asks his readers, "Who is there that remembers not with delight the time when he first read the *Arabian Nights?*—who that recurs not occasionally to their pages with renewed pleasure?" In a review of six new editions of the tales in 1839, Leigh Hunt calls the *Nights* "the most popular book in the world."[19] The *Nights'* plots, characters, and settings seeped so thoroughly into English popular culture that authors who made reference to the text "felt," according to Muhsin Jassim Ali, "sure that their readers were so familiar with the tales that they had no need to check a 'scholarly companion' to the *Arabian Nights*."[20] Commentators cast a thorough understanding of the *Nights* as *the* sign of a cultivated literary taste and judgment. So it is that the editor of a nineteenth-century

English translation of the *Nights* contends that "Not to be acquainted with the 'Arabian Nights,' argues a literary apathy, the imputation of which no one, we think, would be willing to bear."[21] It should come as no surprise, then, that the list of English authors who made use of the tales in any number of ways constitutes a kind of Who's Who in English letters of the period, regardless of genre or ideology. Samuel Coleridge, Lord Byron, Charles Dickens, Sir Walter Scott, and Lord Tennyson were among those English authors who made significant reference to or in some way incorporated aspects of the tales into their writings.[22]

American readers were no different in their regard for the *Nights* from their counterparts across the Atlantic, indicating that members of America's literary culture could at least agree on the value of a set of tales of distinctly foreign origin even if they fought about the nature and value of promoting a specifically national literature.[23] Interest in the *Nights* was part of a larger interest shown by nineteenth-century American readers in materials related to what we would call the Middle East.[24] Travel narratives, fictional tales, and a range of other writings gained wide readership in the United States, and they produced an especially keen interest among the small but growing members of America's literary culture in the 1830s and 1840s—precisely the time Poe was writing. Of all the works related to the East that were published or read in the United States in the nineteenth century, *Nights* was without question the most widely discussed.[25] Speaking of what she calls the "virtually inexhaustible reservoir from which nineteenth-century writers in Europe and America drew their knowledge of the Near East," Dorothee Metlitsky Finkelstein contends that all this writing "ranks second to the great classic of all times: *The Arabian Nights.*"[26] American readers possessed just as intimate a familiarity with the *Nights* as American writers did. Or at least writers for mid-century magazines thought so. Reviewing a new edition of the *Nights* in the December 1847 issue of *The American Review*, G. W. Peck cast the *Nights* in terms of sentimental relations when he says that he doesn't need to restate the plots of the stories in detail because, after all, the tales were a "common friend" to all his readers.

Magazine editors considered material related to the *Nights* to be a potential boon to sales. American magazines of the period faced intense competition for readers in order to maintain their very livelihood. The competition proved so fierce and the market for such magazines so small that only the *North American Review* managed to survive—and it did so only barely—for any sustained period before 1833, and very few from 1833 to 1860. In this context, Charles Fenno Hoffman's decisions as editor of the *Literary World*, the first important periodical in America devoted solely to a discussion of current books, suggests that he, at least, considered the *Nights* to be of supreme interest to American readers. Hoffman commissioned a series on the origins of the tales and their importance to literature in general. The series ran for five issues in the spring of 1848, covering ten pages; the last segment examined *Nights*' "Influence on General Literature."[27] The importance attached to the *Nights* at least by America's self-proclaimed arbiters of literary taste can be gauged, I think, by the unprecedented focus—at least over the course of the magazine's five-year existence—over a series of issues on the history and significance of a single literary work.

American reviewers argued that the *Nights*' importance derived from its affecting portrayal of what they cast as a universal human condition.[28] For these reviewers, Scheherazade's stories not only reveal the peculiar features of Arabian society but also, and more importantly, use those peculiar features of a particular society to portray traits that readers in any civilized society will recognize as distinctly and definitively human.[29] More than one reviewer, in fact, compares the tales favorably to Shakespeare's plays by focusing precisely on the way these stories are said to succeed at demonstrating a kind of universal human nature. The stories depend for this effect, of course, on the ability and willingness of American readers to recognize themselves when they read tales set in the seemingly and unfailingly "un-American" settings of the Arab world. In this sense, at least, the stories ask readers to imagine themselves as Arabs as a way of imagining themselves as humans.[30]

In casting the stories as repositories of fundamental truths about a human nature shared by those in Persia and Providence, reviewers cast the *Nights* as not merely a valuable work of literature but as an exemplary work able to serve as a model for what constitutes superior fiction in the first place. In praising Scheherazade's tales in this way, reviewers could then use the *Nights* in debates over the nature of what they considered—following writers in Germany and Great Britain—to be literature's most elemental forms. The figure of the "romance" and the quality of "fancy" figured most prominently and frequently in these debates, and it is no surprise that *Nights* is read in relation to theories of these two categories. One reviewer argues, for instance, that "all true lovers of romance must rejoice" in the publication of a new edition of the *Nights*. He contends that the stories' "greatest charm" is that they are "creations of the pure fancy," a fancy that, he says, "runs on and on at its own sweet will, precisely as it does in dreams."[31] The stories of Sinbad serve as prime examples of this quality for they offer "the nearest approach to absolute dreaming" he has seen in literature as a whole.[32]

The frequent invocations of "fancy" and "romance" in these reviews link the *Nights* to debates about the current state and potential future of American literature in particular.[33] Writers such as Nathaniel Hawthorne and William Gilmore Simms argued against those who claimed that American authors would produce literature of great quality only if they aimed to represent in what we would call a "realist" fashion the social, environmental, and political world peculiar to the United States. Simms and Hawthorne in particular wielded the figure of "romance" in opposition to such propositions. In his now famous "Preface" to *The House of the Seven Gables*, Hawthorne distinguishes his "Romance" from the category of the "Novel" by claiming, first of all, that the "Romance" stands "as a work of art," a status that obliges it to portray "the truth of the human heart" without the necessity, under which novels labor, of "a very minute fidelity, not merely to the possible, but to the probable and ordinary."[34] Simms casts the difference between "romance" and "realism" in starkly moral terms when he has the narrator of "Grayling; or, 'Murder Will Out'" open the tale with a meditation on storytelling in mid-nineteenth-century America. The narrator bemoans the "evil" effect that "modern reasoning" has had on those who tell "romantic" stories. The "materialists" who insist on the "monstrous matter-of-fact" in their fiction "have it all their own way" in America, the narrator contends. Simms's narrator claims that this emphasis on science has produced a generation of "story-tellers" whose works "are so resolute to deal in the real, the actual only," as opposed to the storytellers of "preceding ages" whose "love of the marvelous belongs . . . to all those who love and cultivate either of the fine arts." The devaluation of the romantic in favor of the realist not only resulted in "derision" for literary classics such as *Faust* but, even more troubling, brought about the very loss "of those wholesome moral restraints which might have kept many of us virtuous, where the laws could not."[35] Fiction in the form of romance, it would seem, helps regulate the behavior of those who read it.

These reviews—and "The Thousand-and-Second Tale of Scheherazade"—appeared in print when debates over the nature and even the necessity for a distinctly "American" national literature reached, according to Benjamin Spencer, its "crest," as well as over how specific categories such as "fancy" and "romance" would or should characterize that literature raged among the small circle of literati up and down the Atlantic seaboard.[36] Periodicals in Philadelphia, New York, and Richmond, to name only a few, hoped to generate sales with essays devoted to the issues surrounding the development—or lack thereof—of a uniquely American literature. They published articles defending copyright laws that allowed publishers the opportunity to present their readership with the very best material from around the world without having to pay the high royalties fees to authors that would, or so the publishers claimed, result in the publication of "cheap" rather than "quality" works. Articles also appeared bemoaning the lack of an international copyright law, the absence of which, these authors contended, made it impossible for American authors to earn a living when forced to compete with pirated copies of works culled from the world over. The battle over international copyright grew so fierce that Cornelius Mathews would claim in a much-reprinted speech to the American authors club that "There is at this moment, waging in our midst, a great war between a foreign and a native literature." Evert Duyckinck writes in his "Literary Prospects of 1845"—which appears in the very same month as "The Thousand-and-Second Tale of Scheherazade"—of the "*taboo* of the American author in the booksellers' stores" (150).[37]

Poe opposed the focus on a specifically American literature from the time he entered the American literary scene in the 1830s. In his "Exordium to Critical Notices," first published in the January 1842 issue of *Graham's Magazine,* Poe contrasts his own view of literary nationalism with those of most literary critics in America in the early 1840s for whom, Poe writes, "the watchword now was, 'a national literature.'"[38] Poe mocks his critical colleagues' devotion to a strictly "national literature" by saying "as if any true literature could be national—as if the world at large were not the proper stage for the literary histrio."[39] Poe contends that "our reviews urged the propriety—our booksellers the necessity, of strictly 'American' themes."[40] He accuses reviewers of "liking, or pretending to like, a stupid book the better because (sure enough) its stupidity was of our own growth, and discussed our own affairs."[41] Poe uses "The Thousand-and-Second Tale of Scheherazade" to satirize the American literary scene by calling attention to the drawbacks of a specific form of literary nationalism that trades specifically on fears of the "foreign."[42] To counter such fears of un-American things, Poe uses a unanimously praised collection of unambiguously "foreign" material and challenges the very goal of a distinctly *American* American literature whose distinctiveness emerges in relation to European literature.

Poe wastes no time linking this story of Arabian nights with American literary culture. Indeed, the very first paragraph locates the story specifically in American literary culture and, in the process, also identifies the narrator's national identity. He does this in the opening paragraph by, first, making sure we understand the "American" and "European" literary communities as two distinct entities. The narrator accomplishes this when he qualifies his claim that a work he has found during his "Oriental researches" is, first, "scarcely known at all," then, "is little known 'EVEN' in Europe," and, finally, "has never been quoted, to my knowledge, by any American."[43] The narrator's sentence provides a telescoping of fields of knowledge: he begins by telling us what is known about the book by people anywhere, moves next to inform us of its status in Europe, then finishes by noting what is known about it in America. By ending with its status in American letters and, then, going on to comment on the one work of American writing that might, in fact, have cited the text, the narrator establishes his own position as an American critic as he separates himself—and the American literary scene in general—from European literary culture.

In the very process of insisting on the separation of American and European literary cultures, the narrator simultaneously presents these two worlds in a hierarchical relation to one another. In concluding with America, the narrator focuses our attention on the American literary scene in particular, but he focuses our attention on that scene *only* in relation to Europe and the world at large. Why even mention Europe if the story takes aim at the American literary scene? By making Europe the object of the comparison, the narrator grants Europe a privileged position within literary, and specifically Oriental, studies. With the simple use of the adverb "even," then, Poe's narrator casts Europe as the site of superior literary knowledge. We have a fictitious source found by an American that demonstrates the wrong-headedness of the literary establishment about a common and central feature of literary history. It is as if, in the stereotypical fashion of postcolonial writers, the narrator continues to evaluate his own community by the standards of those whose political authority, at least, was long ago rejected.

But Poe undercuts the privileged position in an imagined transatlantic cultural hierarchy his narrator affords Europe by collapsing the very distinction between these two worlds he has himself helped to establish. Both Europe and America, while they may have different acquaintances with the *Isitöornot*, have been operating under the very same misapprehension. Regardless of how much they knew about this obscure work, both literary communities have behaved as if they knew the full story of Scheherazade when, in fact, they did not. The narrative thus opens with the narrator exposing the pretensions of both literary worlds with regard to one of the most popular and well-known works of literature.

The first paragraph thus establishes a literary cultural hierarchy only to equalize both parties in that hierarchy by pointing out that a single American researcher alone knows the "true" story of one of the world's most famous narratives. In beginning the story in this way, Poe substitutes a fiercely individualistic American literary nationalism for the conventional understanding of the transatlantic literary establishment he has here exposed as a fraud. That is, the narrator neatly turns the slur on American literary culture against both European critics and the American literary establishment when he, an American, finds a book that completely alters our picture of what was regarded as one of the most impressive collections of Oriental tales.

In ridiculing the literary establishments of both Europe and America in this way, Poe calls attention to the oddities of such a way of organizing knowledge in the first place. His telescoping of knowledge—from anyone, to Europeans, to Americans—demonstrates the contradictions such a category of "national knowledge" produces. What, the paragraph implicitly asks, does "national knowledge" have to do with "literary knowledge" in the first place? We see this in the narrator's characterization of the "originality" of the *Isitöornot*. It is simultaneously an original and a reprint; it manages at the same time to be both a new work and an old one. We have, then, a rather curious originality called to our attention whose structure calls to mind a similar structure in debates over an American national literature. For what does it mean for something to be valuable only because it has not been quoted by someone of a particular nationality? What, in other words, does the category of the national have to do with the category of knowledge in general? Doesn't knowledge, at least as it is imagined in its ideal state, transcend national boundaries?

On the off chance his readers have failed to pick up on this structural parallel, Poe refers in this paragraph to a recent, well-known work that calls forth precisely the same problems as the *Isitöornot*, Rufus Griswold's "Curiosities of American Literature." Griswold's volume, the narrator tells us, may be the only other book printed in America that makes reference to the *Isitöornot*. "Curiosities of American Literature" was first published in 1844 as an appendix to an American edition of Isaac Disraeli's enormously popular *Curiosities of Literature*. The *Curiosities* was a series of miscellaneous brief essays and anecdotes on world literature that were "published in countless editions, authorized and pirated throughout the English-speaking world."[44] Disraeli's *Curiosities* aims to "stimulate the literary curiosity" of those who simply lack the time or the training to learn the most important facts about literary history that would allow them to understand the "great works" of literature of any period. Griswold's introduction to his appendix invokes precisely the same cultural hierarchy as the narrator of "The Thousand-and-Second Tale of Scheherazade" to authorize his addition of specifically American national curiosities to Disraeli's explicitly nonnational collection of anecdotes. "In this country," Griswold writes, "the materials for such a work [as Disraeli's *Curiosities*] are not abundant, and the reader will not expect to find in the following pages articles intrinsically as interesting as those given by an author unequaled in this department, whose field was the world." Griswold begins, in other words, by apologizing for the inferiority of American literature when compared with the literature produced by the rest of the world. He offers no defense of America's literary products, but, instead, he contends that the value of the "new" materials he has added comes from the distinctive perspective they offer: "an American impression." "Impressions," of course, reward a particular point of view for its point of view regardless of its intrinsic value.

The effort to "Americanize" a work that offers no single national impression dramatizes the American literary scene of Poe's time. Griswold's supplication at the very opening of his appendix to the gods of other national literatures only makes explicit what the very appearance of yet another edition of Disraeli's book in and of itself already concedes: American readers look to traditions outside America to satisfy their literary desires. An edition that includes curiosities of admittedly "lesser" American literature not only fails to address issues of quality but also, and perhaps more intriguingly, seems designed more to find yet another way to profit from the pirating of foreign literary goods rather than helping create a market for American writers regardless of their subject matter. Even those positively disposed toward Griswold's appendix acknowledged this. As the anonymous reviewer of this edition of the *Curiosities* points out in the May 1844 issue of *Knickerbocker, or New York Monthly Magazine*, Griswold's addition of a specifically American set of anecdotes will make his edition "the only one for the future in the American market" (490). The reviewer goes on to note that American literature "is now grafted on a work which will secure its life" (492). Opponents of such piracy who argued that it worked against the production of a native American literature noticed the irony as well. As Joel T. Headley would point out in "The Prose Writers of America," the same man "who denounces . . . our Congress for not protecting the works of authors, has himself taken D'Israeli's [sic] *Curiosities of Literature*, and tacking on a few 'American Curiosities,' so as to usurp the English edition in the American market, issued it with his name on the title page."[45]

Poe produced a remarkably similar set of anecdotes and brief essays that stand in stark contrast to Griswold's "Curiosities of American Literature" and tell us something about the critique he makes here of Griswold's "Curiosities." The difference between the two suggests that Poe's reference to the "Curiosities" is designed to call attention to the problems for those interested in producing literature in the United States—if not precisely "American" literature—of approaches such as Griswold's. When he was running—if not, in name, at least in practice—the *Southern Literary Messenger* in the 1830s, Poe, too, produced a series of anecdotes modeled on Disraeli's *Curiosities*. He did so again in the 1840s when he published his "Marginalia," very short pieces that purported to be his marginal comments in books he was then reading. Unlike Griswold's work, however, Poe's anecdotes cover more than simply the American literary scene. These anecdotes work to train readers in how to value literature as a category seemingly divorced from political categories rather than to promote American literature specifically. In so doing, the pieces worked to produce—in not so subtle a fashion—a literary culture in America whose standards would be Poe's standards. Poe's own work, then, stands in contrast to the "Curiosities" to which he refers in the opening paragraph of "The Thousand-and-Second Tale of Scheherazade."

It's not simply that the very reference to Griswold's "Curiosities" in "The Thousand-and-Second Story of Scheherazade" mocks the peculiarly national nature of Griswold's volume. The reference to "Curiosities" also makes absolutely no sense in context—and its absurdity would have been quite clear to readers of *Godey's* magazine. In suggesting that perhaps only the author of the "Curiosities" might have quoted from the *Isitöornot*, the narrator suggests the impossible. Griswold's "Curiosities" are "gleaned from many rare and curious old books relating to our country or written by our countrymen"—they are, in other words, interesting and/or otherwise important stories told about America or by Americans. In this sense, a story from the *Arabian Nights Entertainments* would have no place in "Curiosities of American Literature." What seems like supplication to the comprehensiveness and coverage of Griswold's "Curiosities" amounts, instead, to a critique of it for its sole focus on national matters—and matters that are hardly "ancient" as the "Curiosities" suggests about the roots of American literature. The joke here seems to be that attempts to promote a national literature risk blinding us to the stories right before us that might be non-national in character.[46]

Once the opening paragraphs have established the nation's literary scene as the real source of the satire, Poe turns our attention toward the problem of aesthetic theory that, as we mentioned earlier in our discussion of Hawthorne and Simms, took center stage in mid-nineteenth-century debates over the nature and form of American literature. Given Poe's ties to the gothic and romance traditions, we should hardly be surprised that he uses the story to mock those who stand for what Simms would have classified as a more "realistic" literature as America's defining style. To get his reader to take his side on such aesthetic matters, Poe must first deflate his readers' sense that the modern world is superior to all previous ages, ages that are associated by Poe's readers with the romantic vision of art that Poe advocates.

We can begin to understand how Poe accomplishes this by examining one of the contrasts he draws between the stories told by his Scheherazade and her more famous predecessor. If the *Nights* contained stories with unexpected twists and turns of plot, the tales of Poe's Scheherazade form predictable patterns that offer little in the way of surprise or suspense. She focuses in the *Isitöornot* on stories of Sinbad's adventures that she had not already told. In each of these stories, most of which last no more than a paragraph or two, what Sinbad describes as magic turn out to be natural phenomena or common man-made, and self-consciously modern, items. So, Sinbad tells us about a series of voyages at sea on the back of a "vast monster" moving "with inconceivable swiftness." A "vast number of animals" remarkably like men lived on the back of the "'hideous' monster." After having been bound and taken prisoner, Sinbad consents to travel the world with the crew. On their travels, Sinbad visits an array of modern marvels unknown—or at least unmentioned—in ancient times. These include "an island . . . built in the middle of the sea by a colony of little things like caterpillars" (a coral reef built by worms); a land "where the forests were of solid stone" (a petrified forest); "a land in which the nature of things seemed reversed" (a South American lake where trees appeared to be growing underwater following an earthquake); the "native land" of the ship's captain, inhabited by the "most powerful magicians," whose magic included a "huge horse whose bones were iron and whose blood was boiling water" (a train operating in the United States) and a "mighty thing that was neither man nor beast" whose "fingers . . . it employed with such incredible speed and dexterity that it would have had no trouble in writing out twenty thousand copies of the Koran in an hour" (a printing press).

The implicit contrasts these descriptions establish between the modern and ancient worlds are part of an elaborate rhetorical ruse designed by Poe to undermine for careful readers the very distinction between ancient and modern perspectives. Before we see how Poe ultimately unravels the very contrasts between historical periods on which the story's humor seems to depend, let me explain the historical comparison Sinbad's descriptions seem to produce. First of all, if Poe hopes to elicit laughter with this story—and it appears quite clear that he does hope for just such a response—such a reaction depends upon his readers drawing comparisons as they read between the original *Arabian Nights* and Poe's adaptation. We are supposed to laugh, at least in part, because of the discrepancy between the two. Given the extraordinary popularity of the *Nights* and its ubiquitous references in nineteenth-century American popular culture, one would think that Poe's readers could not help but compare the modern "wonders" Sinbad finds in "The Thousand-and-Second Tale of Scheherazade" to the marvels he discovers in the old world of the infinitely more famous *Nights*. Poe's Sinbad fares quite badly in such a comparison. Indeed, he looks quite ridiculous, and so, too, then, does the ancient world he represents.

Second, the dramatic irony between the readers' and the characters' understanding of what Sinbad describes seems to mock the ancient world for its lack of simplicity as it trumpets the modern readers' greater sophistication. For the objects that Sinbad presents as fantastic, that the King and Scheherazade's sister take to be beyond the power of magic to produce, are, in fact, simply natural objects of the modern world. We laugh at their inferior knowledge because we understand the narrative in a way that they do not and, through this laughter, the modern reader—and modernity itself—demonstrates its superiority to the ancient world. Sinbad validates this chronological hierarchy when he labels as "magicians" people whom we know to be normal humans engaging in acts that are so commonplace in the modern world, so mundane and expected, that readers would hardly notice them in their day-to-day lives. Sinbad even fails to recognize the categorical distinction between human beings and those objects we have created and over which we have dominion when he mistakes modern technology for living creatures.

The simplistic, even primitive nature of Sinbad's character in Poe's story invites nineteenth-century American readers to make yet one more comparison between historical periods that seems to confirm modernity's sense of its superiority to all that came before. In mistaking commonplace objects of the modern world for magic, Sinbad takes on the role of the innocent and ignorant ancient dazzled by the remarkable achievements of modern society. In being blind to the categorical distinctions between the human and that which the human has created to serve his or her needs, Sinbad suggests the reader's superiority and, as representative of the world of a no-longer-present Arabia, the inferiority of the ancient in relation to the modern world. Sinbad's awe at what he sees, his amazement and wonder at the marvels of the modern, even lays the responsibility for his subservience to the modern world on his own shoulders. The simple primitive authorizes his own subjugation by recognizing that he and the world from which he comes is, in his own judgment, not as worthy, not as accomplished, as the world he is only visiting.

In fact, our laughter when Sinbad mistakes the mundane for the magical merely diverts us from the real target at which the story takes aim. It gives the reader precisely what he wants to hear—that is, a story reminding the modern of its own superiority to all that came before—even as other elements of the story eliminate the very distinction between the modern and the ancient on which such laughter depends. We need look no further than the footnotes provided by Poe to see how he undermines key aspects of the distinctions—and the hierarchy that seems to go along with those distinctions—on which much of the story's humor seems to depend. Far from providing a basis for distinguishing between Scheherazade's primary narratee and the modern reader, the footnotes establish an equivalency between the King and the modern reader. Cast in the voice of the author "Poe" rather than the voice of any of the multiple narrators of "The Thousand-and-Second Tale of Scheherazade," the notes decode Sinbad's descriptions of what he sees on his adventures. They tell us what he really sees when he travels to the modern world rather than what he says he sees. The very need for such notes suggests that the modern reader might mistake these tales for fantasies, too, for it goes without saying that neither Sinbad, the King, the King's sister, nor Scheherazade has access to Poe's notes. I suppose one might say that access to the notes is yet one more distinction between the modern reader and the ancient characters about whom he is reading. Such a comparison hardly shows modernity in a positive light, though. Indeed, this distinction only subtly mocks the very magazine-reader who might arrogantly mistake his modern perspective as superior to those of the characters in the story, the King and Sinbad, at whom he is supposed to laugh. Were it not for the intervention of a third, more knowledgeable party, might not the reader be just as much the object of scorn as a King who puts a storyteller to death for no better reason than that she tells stories that seem untrue?

In linking the King and the modern reader through their ignorance, the footnotes redirect the source of the satire from the realism of the stories to the aesthetic theories by which those stories are judged. We will examine in more detail precisely what about Scheherazade's stories leads the King to order her execution, but for the moment we need only acknowledge that the story leads us to laugh at his order because we know something he doesn't: that the stories are, contrary to what the King asserts, true. We cannot say, though, that we would have spared Scheherazade because what she said was true, for this mocks the King for lacking the very information the story felt the modern reader needed as well. We, too, needed Scheherazade's stories to be verified. If the modern reader wants to retain some sense of distance between himself and a King who arbitrarily executes his subjects for no more than telling tall tales, that modern reader must imagine that he or she, in the same situation, would not have killed Scheherazade. We, the readers, know that she should not be killed, not only because the stories are, in fact, true but also and more importantly because it doesn't matter whether the stories are true or false. Since we know the stories are true, the footnotes put us in the position of saying we would spare Scheherazade even if the stories were not true. If we want to laugh at him for killing the storyteller, we are left with no other reason to laugh than that he places too much emphasis on the stories' historicity and overlooks their value as entertainment. In order for readers to laugh at the King they must establish a different value system—they must side with Scheherazade's aesthetic of storytelling over the King's.

Poe goes to great lengths preparing his reader to be ready to reject the King's aesthetic long before he invites us to laugh at that King when he kills Scheherazade for the simple sin of creativity at the story's conclusion. He creates a story-within-a-story that focuses our attention on the King's reaction to what he hears as he listens to Scheherazade by making the King's opinions on this matter an integral part of the narrative. The story-within-a-story of the King's response shows the monarch to be a very bad audience who, in kingly fashion, sees no need to temper his remarks with courtesy, respect, or politeness. The King's behavior, then, his responses to the stories offered him by a master of narrative, instructs us beyond a shadow of a doubt that we, in order to be good readers ourselves, must distance ourselves from the King's aesthetic at all costs. This story-within-a-story allows Poe to concentrate his readers' attention on the competing aesthetic theories that animate the King's reaction to what he hears even before the King uses those very theories as the basis for sentencing Scheherazade to death. While the King begins by noting his interest, virtually his entire dialogue consists of brief expressions of disapproval. He says, for instance, that he finds these "latter adventures of Sinbad" to be "exceedingly entertaining and strange" (M 1159). He says that he finds her story of the man-beast's travels over the ocean "very singular" and has "doubts" about whether, as Scheherazade asserts, the stories are "quite true" (M 1159). He begins to say "Hum" after each story or detail that he finds implausible, but Scheherazade explicitly ignores him. Indeed, the story describes her as "paying no attention to his remarks" (M 1160). He continues to signify his doubts by saying "Hum," then "Fiddle de dee," "Oh fy," "Pooh," until he exclaims, after hearing one of her tales, "That, now, I believe . . . because I have read something of the kind before, in a book" (M 1165). He moves on to "Nonsense" (M 1165), "Fall al," "Ridiculous" (M 1167), "Absurd" (M 1167), and, finally, before he orders her to stop, "Preposterous" (M 1169).

The story stages at least one point on which the reader, the King, and Scheherazade might agree, though. Poe has the reader, Scheherazade, and the King agree that women's beauty serves as the foundation not only for aesthetic theory but also and more importantly as a way of demonstrating a culture's taste and civilized status. In the "nation of necromancers" (M 1167) that concludes Scheherazade's tale, Scheherazade claims that the "wives and daughters of these eminent conjurers represent everything that is accomplished and refined; and would be every thing that is interesting and beautiful" (M 1169)—would be, that is, were it not for an "evil genii" who "has put it into the heads of these accomplished ladies that the thing which we describe as personal beauty, consists altogether in the protuberance of the region which lies not very far below the small of the back" (M 1169). Scheherazade does not endorse the fashion. On the contrary, she explicitly mocks the fashion. Her critique of women's fashion represents the first time in "The Thousand-and-Second Story of Scheherazade" that Poe has Scheherazade offer an opinion on any of the stories Sinbad has told. When Scheherazade says that "the days have long gone by since it was possible to distinguish a woman from a dromedary," the King orders her to stop (M 1169). While it is surely the combined effect of his incredulity at the absurdity of the stories he has heard, he draws the line at this way of understanding women's beauty. The presumption to pass off as true a story that claims a culture would define beauty in terms of the breakdown of the distinction between beautiful women and pack animals prompts the King to murder Scheherazade.

The King finds such transformations of women's bodies necessarily to be a "lie"—implying, in so doing, that no nation would willingly allow women's bodies to be so transformed as a sign of beauty that they would be indistinguishable from animals. In this sense, a notion of beauty that depends on women's bodies provides the foundation for the King's distinction between the "real" and the "romantic." In this way, the "beauty" of women's bodies—not the beauty of a specific woman but the beauty of women's bodies as a categorical object—represents the foundation of what constitutes the "real" against which a story's veracity can be judged. How does one know if a story is true or not? Look to what the story says about the way a nation understands the beauty of women.

Poe's nineteenth-century American reader knows that such a fashion exists in the United States. Indeed, Poe believes knowledge of this style of dress would be so widespread that he offers no footnote to explain Scheherazade's story of a style that his remarks here and in other stories indicate he considered quite ridiculous. In knowing that such a fashion does exist in the United States, the reader knows, too, that the King is wrong—cultures do define women's beauty so that it is indistinguishable from that of pack animals. Readers can be expected to distance themselves through their laughter from any aesthetic theory so sure of itself that it requires the execution of those who violate its tenets. In having the King murder Scheherazade when we know that her stories do, in fact, follow the aesthetic theory the King uses to legitimate his murderous actions, Poe shows the theory to be fundamentally flawed by showing the King's aesthetic principles in action. Such a theory, the story shows by having the King order his wife's hanging because he mistakenly believes her story does not faithfully represent the world as it is, requires that readers know everything about the material world as it is at all times. Since omnipotent readers do not exist—and, indeed, the very idea borders on the blasphemous—such a theory cannot be trusted to guide our judgments on literary matters.

But the problems raised by the King's principles do not end here. For the King's aesthetic theory constitutes a subtle attack on aesthetic production itself by denying the very possibility that storytellers can produce beauty that does not yet exist in the world. In short, the theory completely ignores the imaginative power of the storyteller to offer us the "truth" beneath the surface that defines the world as we see it. The stories Scheherazade tells her husband here do just that and, thus, highlight this flaw in the King's aesthetic theory. The very footnotes that obliterate the distinction between modern and ancient audiences simultaneously elevate the imaginative power of the storyteller. The fact that Scheherazade's renderings of the mundane phenomena of modern life could be mistaken for fantasy suggests the power of the storyteller who can make even the world of nature and technology appear magical. For while Sinbad is said to witness the events Scheherazade narrates, modern audiences encounter the modern wonders-that-are-not-wonders through Scheherazade's descriptions of them. Sinbad fails to understand what he sees in front of him, the story suggests; modern readers might not recognize everyday objects that define their world when they encounter them through a narrator's description of them. They might mistake, that is, descriptions of perfectly natural phenomena for creations born out of the imagination of a master storyteller. The need for such notes testifies to Scheherazade's skills as a storyteller in that they acknowledge her ability to transform the trivialities of the material world into a world of magic, wonder, and limitless possibility. She turns, in other words, realism into romance.

If Poe gets us to laugh at the King's execution of Scheherazade as a way of mocking the aesthetic theories that give rise to the murder, he uses our admiration of Scheherazade as a storyteller able to transform the real into the romantic in order to show us the virtues of the aesthetic principles with which the story associates her. In Poe's version of the story Scheherazade becomes the very embodiment of the aesthetic. She represents beauty in the community, and any threat to her life constitutes a threat to the aesthetic. We see this in the liberties Poe takes with his source material when Scheherazade tells us why she puts her life on the line by marrying a King who has had each of his previous wives executed. Scheherazade volunteers for such a dangerous match in order to "redeem the land from the depopulating tax upon its beauty" (M 1152). No such language exists in the frame story of the translation Poe most likely read, by Edward William Lane, nor can any language of a tax on beauty be found in *any* English translation of any period.[47] Each of the previous translations that Poe might have encountered focuses the readers' attention on the infidelity of women in general rather than on women's beauty in particular being taxed or reduced. Taxes, in fact, never come up. So, for instance, the most popular American edition of the *Nights* until the late 1840s, a translation by Jonathan Scott first published in the United States in Philadelphia in 1830, has the brothers agree that "there is no wickedness equal to that of women."[48] The sultan is convinced that "no woman was chaste."[49] Once convinced of this, he vows that "in order to prevent the disloyalty of such as he should afterwards marry" he plans "to wed one every night and have her strangled the next morning."[50] He is "sure" that his brother "will follow my example" when he returns to his home.[51]

To be sure, at some point during their narratives, each of the translations to which Poe had access associates women with the beautiful, and, in so doing, each links women in some way and at some point with aesthetics. But none of these translations at any point links the King's murder of women to aesthetic terms, and certainly no language casts these murders as a threat to the aesthetics of the community as a whole. In the case of Scheherazade, for instance, beauty becomes a supplemental quality. The bulk of the description of Scheherazade focuses on her accomplishments. She "possessed courage, wit, and penetration, infinitely above her sex. She had read much, and had so admirable a memory that she never forgot anything she had read. She had successfully applied herself to philosophy, medicine, history, and the liberal arts; and her poetry excelled the compositions of the best writers of the time."[52] It is only as a final quality that beauty is mentioned—"Besides this, she was a perfect beauty, and all her accomplishments were crowned by solid virtue."[53] Her physical features do play a role in her relation with the King, for when the sultan first sees her "he found her face so beautiful, that he was perfectly charmed."[54] But when the narrative concludes, she does not mention, as Poe's Scheherazade does, that "this odious tax is so happily repealed" (M 1154).

Since Poe's Scheherazade stands as the very embodiment of the aesthetic in a story that, first of all, asks us to read it in relation to debates over the nation's literary culture and, second, provides us with a model to reject in the King, her character seems the most obvious place to look for just what principles Poe wants American literary culture to support. Scheherazade's aesthetic theory promotes, for lack of a better phrase, art for art's sake. We can see this most clearly when we compare her motives for telling the King stories in Poe's short story with those offered in the translations to which he had access. Stories are valued in "The Thousand-and-Second Story of Scheherazade" for, and only for, their aesthetic quality, whereas in the translations to which Poe had access, a story's aesthetic qualities are merely a means to perform social work. In contrast to Poe's focus on aesthetics, the translations available to Poe cast Scheherazade's storytelling as a way of restoring familial relations in the kingdom. Each of these translations without exception has Scheherazade cast her motives for putting her own life in jeopardy as a way to restore sympathetic familial relations within the nation. The unnamed narrator of Scott's translation, for instance, describes the effect of the King's murderous marriage ritual in terms of the grief of countless fathers who are "inconsolable [at] the loss of [their] daughter[s]" and "tender mothers dreading lest their daughters should share the same fate." The King's treatment of these young women so thoroughly permeates the community that the country is filled with "the cries of distress and apprehension."[55] Scheherazade hopes the successful completion of her plan will "stop the barbarity which the sultan exercises upon the families of this city."[56] This sentimental reaction to the King's murderous behavior poses a threat, the narrative tells us, to the kingdom itself. Happy families are thus linked to a healthy, stable, political order.[57] The stories in the translations thus produce two related effects: they save Scheherazade's life and, at the same time, relieve the communities' families of their emotional pain.

In casting Scheherazade's stories as saving the lives of women while simultaneously healing a grieving nation of families, the storyteller in the *Nights* performs a distinct and particular social function that Poe's Scheherazade pointedly does not. Poe removes all such language from his version of *The Arabian Nights*, or at the very least it must have seemed he had quite consciously done so to any careful nineteenth-century American reader of the tales. His Scheherazade tells her tales for her own purposes, not to restore her country's health or even to save her own life. She tells her stories in Poe's tale, that is, without the threat of death hanging over her and, perhaps even more importantly, without the accompanying threat to the community's women, for the stories are told after she has "finally triumphed" and "the tariff upon beauty [is] repealed" (M 1154). With her life no longer in danger and Arabia's women safe from the King's wrath, Poe must provide another motive for Scheherazade to keep talking. Scheherazade's Poe justifies the production of still more narrative by recourse to something in the stories themselves. She has not, she tells us, provided us with "the full conclusion of the history of Sinbad the sailor" (M1154). In this way, the narrative is produced to satisfy what the author casts as an aesthetic quality defined by the stories themselves: wholeness. She must keep telling us stories because this particular cycle of stories has a beginning and an end that exist independently of the author or audience. She cannot be fully satisfied unless Sinbad's story is told to its conclusion.

Poe makes sure we know that the author's satisfaction matters infinitely more in "The Thousand-and-Second Tale of Scheherazade" than does the satisfaction of her audience. We see this when Poe yet again parades for all to see his perversion of the traditional frame story that accompanied every translation of the *Nights*. If Scheherazade offers tales in *Nights* tuned specifically to satisfy her audience so that she—and the other women who would follow in her wake should she fail—could stave off death, Poe's Scheherazade couldn't care less about her listeners' responses. To be sure, she says her stories will "entertain" her audience, but they will do so, we learn as the story progresses, only on her terms. If they fail to entertain, well, Scheherazade seems to believe this says more about the listener than about the tales themselves. Again and again, she brushes aside the ridicule we saw the King heap upon her tales. So, for instance, after he classifies her stories as "preposterous," she "continue[s] . . . without being in any manner disturbed by these frequent and most ungentlemanly interruptions on the part of her husband" (M 1169).

When Poe shifts the storyteller's concerns away from her audience toward the stories themselves, Scheherazade's plight comes to bear a remarkable resemblance to the nineteenth-century author in America as Poe imagined that figure. She reminds us of Poe's vision of the author, first of all, in her unwavering fidelity to a story's "true" and "complete" form, even if a commitment to the story's "inherent" qualities conflict with the desires of her audience. Poe even grants her belief in the formal qualities of literature a form of punitive power usually reserved for God. For the act of refusing to allow Scheherazade to tell her stories in full, he "reaped for him[self] a most righteous reward," a phrase that echoes Biblical verse in which God himself metes out such rewards on the basis of righteous—or, in the case of the King, decidedly unrighteous—behavior.

Scheherazade's resemblance to Poe's notions of those ideas, issues, and principles for which an author should stand are nowhere more evident, though, than in her final thoughts "during the tightening of the bowstring." Poe uses these thoughts to send the reader away with a notion of a thoroughly individuated author, an author, that is, who bears the hallmark of a modern individual: a distinctive voice who can be silenced only by the grave (M 1170). After all, how else to understand Scheherazade's characterization of the stories the King will be denied once the bowstring performs its office as "inconceivable" if she is merely telling stories of natural phenomena? Why would she say that "depriving him of many inconceivable adventures" will be the King's "reward" for her murder if these are stories that can be told by anyone? Couldn't someone else tell the stories? Indeed, the fact that the unnamed narrator of the story has pointed out to us that these stories are not Scheherazade's inventions but are, in fact, merely historical anecdotes only highlights the abilities of this particular storyteller. She transforms the "natural" into stories others would be unable to imagine, and she writes these stories that are so vivid they transform the mundane into the miraculous for herself and only for herself rather than as a way to restore communal health. What could be further from the Scheherazade of the *Nights*, who tells generic stories not simply as a way of saving her life but on behalf of her entire community, than a storyteller who persists in telling her own stories her own way regardless of the consequences to herself and without thinking of, as though it were not worthy of her consideration, the impact those stories might have on the community at large? If the *Nights* call our attention to the power of stories in a community, then, "The Thousand-and-Second Tale of Scheherazade" presents us with a teller of tales who cares more about maintaining the purity of her own vision of storytelling in spite of the risks and who does so while individuated from rather than indivisible from those around her.

By the time he kills off in the story's final sentence the very figure who represents America's hope for literary achievement, then, Poe has used the contrast between the aesthetic associated with the King and the one represented by his storyteller to demonstrate what is at stake in debates over the direction of American literary culture. To put it perhaps too bluntly, the story shows that those who advocate for a nationalist literary aesthetic risk killing the very source of true aesthetic production. But the issues raised by the story's ending refuse to be resolved in so neat a fashion. His imagined "solution," so to speak, to the problems faced by those concerned with the production of literature in the United States raises at least as many questions as it answers. Would white, male American readers be entirely comfortable that the answer to their country's literary deficiencies was to be found in an Arabian woman from ancient history?

Indeed, Poe's transformation of the traditional story so that Scheherazade's stories no longer spare her from execution but actually become responsible for her death threaten to dethrone her from her very position as the figurative solution to America's literary woes. On the one hand, as we saw above, Poe sacrifices his image of the proper aesthetic so that he can illustrate in the most dramatic fashion possible the cost of an errant aesthetic theory. But Poe's most extreme inversion of the plot of *Arabian Nights* also and at the same time puts his audience—and Poe himself, for that matter—at a safe distance from what must have seemed, simply by virtue of her being an Arabian woman, to Poe's readers to be a very dangerous figure. The death sentence he metes out to the very character with whom we are supposed to side shields his readers from the danger of becoming too Oriental. The corpse's abject status allows Poe to keep his largely male, probably exclusively white audience a safe distance from the story's figure for the truly civilized aesthetic. No longer does Poe ask his readers to consider themselves part of Scheherazade's community, a community united by a shared aesthetic theory currently under siege. When Scheherazade dies, Poe asks his readers to imagine themselves as fundamentally different from the story's title character. She has crossed the ultimate divide. Readers of Poe's story are alive; the character of Scheherazade is dead. In placing Scheherazade at arm's length by killing her in the story's final lines, though, Poe protects his readers from the threat she poses without having to sacrifice the aesthetic principles she represents. Readers can, in other words, still side with her on the proper direction of American literary culture even after—especially after—they no longer have to imagine her as besting figures of patriarchal authority.

Or at least this seems to be Poe's hope. The hostility toward female figures indicated in the way Poe stages Scheherazade's death suggests that her dying is not quite enough to ward off the threat she poses. Readers of Poe will hardly be surprised to find in his work such thinly veiled hostility toward women. After all, in one of his most well-known prose works,

"The Philosophy of Composition," when recounting how he wrote what was and would remain his most popular poem, "The Raven," he tells us "the death ... of a beautiful woman is, unquestionably, the most poetical topic in the world."[58] Poe takes this hostility to a new level with his portrayal of Scheherazade. He transforms a figure of female empowerment—a figure who gains her power by recourse to the aesthetic, a figure who uses the aesthetic as a way to put a stop to violence against women by the most powerful male figure in the nation—into one who ends up being a figure for powerlessness itself. Far from being actively engaged in working against a patriarchy that specifically targets women's bodies, Poe's Scheherazade passively accepts her fate—and she does so in the name of the very aesthetic that had been the source of her strength and the means she used to subvert the will of the state in its campaign of violence against women.

The hostility with which the story treats its protagonist demonstrates a deep, unresolved ambivalence at the very heart of Poe's effort to solve America's literary problem by turning to the East, an ambivalence that, in some respects, mirrors the contradictory way in which American readers and writers understood the East dating back even before Bradstreet. On the one hand, Poe draws on the image of Eastern rule as despotic, tyrannical, and irrational, images that by the time Poe wrote had become clichés in the countless Oriental tales Americans consumed, to ensure that his readers will have no sympathy for Scheherazade's royal husband, Poe's figure for the aesthetic theories he railed against in his magazine reviews and essays. At the same time, he calls on the image of the Orient, and specifically the tale he revises, *The Arabian Nights,* as the space of storytelling in its purest form, a space of sophisticated cultural products that bear the mark of centuries of civilization to which the United States—and Europe—can only aspire. In drawing on this second element of the Oriental imaginary, Poe asks his readers to imagine themselves as if they were Orientals as a way of civilizing American culture. If Western political ideas and racial character are understood as superior, the romance theory on which the *Nights* depends presents a model superior to what Western cultures—not limited to America but also including Europe—have produced. It offers a space, in other words, that effectively equalizes America with its former colonial masters by positioning both Europe and the United States as cultural inferiors to Arabia's literary masters. In suggesting that this superior, Eastern model of literature could serve as a model for the United States—were it not, that is, for those who foolishly advocate an unacceptable aesthetic theory—the story offers a way of imagining America's entry into the status of civilized cultures, a way that imagines American culture as superior to Europe through the adoption of what it casts as a more Oriental aesthetic theory. In so doing, the story suggests that the American cultural scene must become more Oriental if it is to be civilized. But, at the same time, it needs to be sure that it doesn't become too Oriental. America needs the romance aesthetic associated with the East for it to be a truly civilized culture, Poe suggests, but America needs just as badly to be safeguarded against the dangers posed by the very feminized Orientalism on which entry into the pantheon of civilized nations depends. In the final analysis, "The Thousand-and-Second Tale of Scheherazade" offers no resolution to this contrary view of the role of the East in helping America become more civilized; it is satisfied merely to illustrate the contradiction with which its readers must wrestle.

EPILOGUE

This study's primary goal has been to call attention to the vast archive of figures of the East in early American literature. *Oriental Shadows* represents merely a starting point for future work rather than a comprehensive description or comprehensive analysis of the meanings, implications, and significance of figures of the East in early American writing. Much more work is needed not simply because this book's focus on a very limited number of works by just four authors has left an enormous amount of material untouched. It is not, in other words, simply that this study leaves huge gaps in the story of British American writers' use of figures of the East that must be filled in by future scholars. Numerous conceptual questions, problems, and issues remain insufficiently explored in the preceding pages.

I have not, for instance, considered in any detail the way the despotic, luxurious, and hypersexual becomes associated with the East during this period, a set of associations that are quite different for colonial British American writers and readers from those of their counterparts in Great Britain.[1] Focusing on these topics might change the way we understand the crucial role played by the imperialist imaginings found in the writings of many eighteenth-century British American colonists, who were active participants in the British empire simply because they lived at the very edge of that empire, as well as in works by citizens of the new nation, whose involvement in a newly formed political culture in which expansion across a continent filled with people—of American, African, and European descent—served as a defining though controversial issue of collective identity.[2] And surely the presence of the East in early American writing deserves greater examination than this book has offered in order to investigate the role that figures of the East play in the emergence, development, and/or production of modern American categories of race that come into being during the same years this study covers. Whether we believe that modern notions of race were born in the seventeenth or the eighteenth century or believe, instead, that these notions existed in practice if not in name even before modern forms of imagining collectivity emerged, figures of the East surely played their role in the production of a category of collective identity, race, whose foundational logic required that each racial group differentiate itself from every other racial group across a spectrum of difference rather than within a binary system. Someone was black not only because they were not white but also because they were not Asian or Native American or Polynesian. The crucial role figures of the East played for the writers covered in this book, and the way these figures tied Eastern people, places, and things to the very category of the civilized, suggests a role for these figures in the production of a system of classifying identity that continues, in some sense, to structure American culture.[3]

And what role did the peoples of the East themselves play in the often contradictory concepts, images, and ideas associated with these regions by the British American writers of the period this study covers? To be sure, British American colonists and members of the new nation had precious little contact with people across the Pacific. Recent research, though, has shown that they had far more contact than we have heretofore believed and, in any case, sustained contact is surely not the only way that people on one side of the globe influence the way people on another side figure them.[4] Historical events, literary texts, and economic exchanges name only a few of the myriad of possible forces that might produce ripple effects strong enough to alter a discursive system in some distant land whose people have never met. My focus on the implications and associations called forth by figures in a single text has limited my ability to examine these particular kinds of ripple effects, but this does not mean that I think they do not exist or are unimportant.

Each of these issues constitutes an important matter about which much more worked is needed. The most important questions this study prompts for literary scholars, though, concern what effect a greater attention to the presence of the East in early American writing might have on the story we tell of American literature. What does the history of American literature look like once we have incorporated the figures of the East that litter the archives into our story of the literature of this nation? What difference does it make to the story of the beginnings of a distinctly American literature when we are aware that this very literature was born, at least in part, of a sense of inadequacy, an inadequacy that grew out of a triangular structure in which New England, Virginia, Bermuda, Georgia, and other American locales would always be judged inferior not only to Europe but also, and more profoundly, given that it was the very landmass America was supposed to be, to an East that Americans could never be? What previously obscured themes, concepts, problems, and formations come into our line of sight when we recognize that a careful attention to early American writings shows that they cast their value as much in terms of those goods, ideas, and forms they considered a part of the Eastern world, a world they understood primarily as mediated by their so-called betters in Europe? What might we learn about the rhetorical battles over that for which America would stand, battles in which literature played a crucial role, once we pay more attention to the role of the East as a foundational fiction, one whose meanings and discursive power grew out of a mix of American writers' admiration of, fear of, and desire for what the East had to offer?

These questions are, of course, completely in step with recent scholarship that examines American literature in relation to intersections and connections that extend beyond the nation proper. Scholars have sought to read early American literature in relation to a variety of paradigms that challenge the strictly nationalist trajectory that traditionally dominated the field. Transatlantic, hemispheric, and global approaches have each been singled out by scholars as the best way to illuminate American literature, especially early American literature.[5] Some scholars are now arguing as well that greater attention needs to be paid to the eighteenth-century Pacific. *Oriental Shadows* grows out of these efforts to show the inadequacy of seeing American literature, and especially early American literature, as a pure product of American soil whose development and many conflicting traditions, figures, and forms can be satisfactorily understood without recourse to material drawn from outside America's own tradition. I began researching the literature that would eventually provide the focus of the four chapters that make up *Oriental Shadows* from a Transatlantic perspective, but my research on figures of the East in the literature of the period led me to see the severe limitations such an approach has for understanding of the literature and culture of the period. To be sure, the shadows of the Orient were cast as much from Europe as from the Orient itself, so that the value American writers granted the New World when linking a burgeoning American culture to civilizations in the East grew largely out of the value those figures accrued in European discursive systems rather than in ones in Asia. Nonetheless, too great a focus on the Atlantic has a tendency to reinscribe a vision of the world that places Europe and the United States at the very center of the globe. The works examined in *Oriental Shadows* have been not simply marked by signs attesting to America's provincial position within European structures of power but also (and ironically) have pointed out Europe's fear of its own provincial status, at least during much of the period studied, in relation to Asian and Southeast Asian economic power and cultural traditions. For Europe to acquire its status in Western discourse as the site for "civilized" cultural production and "legitimate" economic power, the East had to be displaced. The writers examined in the preceding chapters contributed to the emergence of a new discursive system with Europe at its center. In constructing another tradition within American literature, one in which figures of the East bind Bradstreet and Poe in a shared attempt to imagine their own sense of their collective identity in relation to Europe, *Oriental Shadows* thus hopes to help illuminate one small but significant discursive element in the emergence of a modern symbolic spatial economy. This new world of symbolic associations would relegate the East to the dustbin of history and, in the process, open up a set of questions, problems, and issues related to early America's role in the formation of discursive systems that help provide the conceptual foundations which, in part at least, guide our interactions with each other and the material world.

NOTES

INTRODUCTION

1. E. Emerson 45.
2. *Complete Works of Captain John Smith* 3:199.
3. Heimert and Delbanco 130; Caldwell 28.
4. "In Honour of That High and Mighty Princess Queen Elizabeth of Happy Memory," line 90, Hensley 195.
5. From *Edward Taylor's Gods Determinations and Preparatory Meditations*, "99. Meditation. Isa. 24.23. He shall walk before his Ancient gloriously." Line 25, pages 386–88; "143. Meditation. Can. 6.10. Who is she that looks forth as the morning," 470–72. For a brief discussion devoted specifically to Taylor and the East, see Isani, "Edward Taylor and the Turks."
6. Bosco, "A Song of Emptiness, To fill up the Empty Pages following. Vanity of Vanities," lines 48–52, page 84. For the most complete discussion of the publication and reception history of *The Day of Doom*, see Bosco, "Introduction" and "Michael Wigglesworth."
7. Nathaniel Hawthorne, *The Scarlet Letter*, in *The Centenary Edition of the Works of Nathaniel Hawthorne*, 1:83. Luedtke offers the most thorough analysis of Hawthorne's interest in the Orient. Jee Yoon Lee provides a compelling analysis of the passage I cite here in particular.
8. The most thorough discussion of the search for a Northwest Passage by European powers remains Williams's *Voyages of Delusion*. One of the writers I cover in this study, Benjamin Franklin, showed particular interest in the possibility of the passage's discovery. Williams mentions Franklin only in passing (212, 263, and 276). Chaplin mentions Franklin's interest in the Northwest Passage in *The First Scientific American*, 146–47. Solis-Cohen provides a thorough discussion of Franklin's interest. Mapp offers a particularly useful and convincing discussion of how efforts to find a Northwest Passage relied on a profound ignorance about the geography of North America. Mapp's analysis has quite provocative implications for the study of symbolic spatial economies of the period.
9. Bushman provides perhaps the classic study on the various ways—including but not limited to decorating, dressing, speaking, and reading—by which Americans sought to demonstrate their refinement, a refinement based largely on European models.

10. In studies of related topics outside of literary studies, see, for instance, Bushman's study of efforts by British American colonists to produce and display their own gentility; Bowen provides a more focused discussion of the ways in which elite members of British American colonial society sought to live up to the "gentlemanly ideal"; see Bowen 125–46. For a more extended discussion of attempts to display their ability to live as gentlemen, see Rozbicki; Tchen's study also provides great insight into efforts of British Americans in the period to demonstrate their gentility.

11. India, of course, is a particularly problematic signifier during the period this study covers. To take just one example of the problems this word raises, the word "India" in English did not correspond to a clearly defined region on the globe in the earliest years this study examines. See Raman's discussion in the opening pages of *Framing "India"* 1–3.

12. Meriton's *A Geographical Description of the World* (London: 1671) provides one instance of the way Greece presented a classificatory problem. In the list of parts of the world in the opening section of the book, Greece is included in the section on "Asia." The introductory section to the portion of the book devoted to Europe, though, discusses Greece as a part of Europe (123).

13. Lee makes a similar point in discussing *The Scarlet Letter* on page 949.

14. Lewis and Wigen 54.

15. Inden 49–50 and Hegel 173.

16. On the other hand, Berman argues that it was during the early years of the nineteenth century that one finds "the formation of an American antebellum discourse on Arabs, one that distinguished the image of the Arab from the image of the Turk or the Persian and from the conglomerate image of the Islamic oriental—and then elaborated the stakes inherent in these distinctions" (3–4).

17. The relative dominance of communities in what we term the "East" versus what we now call the "West" or, more precisely, "Europe" in the early modern period is a source of some controversy. The so-called California school of historians, for instance, argues that Asia's powerful role in the world economy in the early modern period has been drastically understated in traditional histories of the period. For a powerful and important discussion of these controversies that argues that "we cannot understand pre-1800 global conjunctures in terms of a Europe-centered world system; we have, instead, a polycentric world with no dominant center," see Pomeranz, *The Great Divergence,* 4. Gunder Frank, on the other hand, sees Asian communities as the dominant economic powers in the world prior to 1800. He writes, for instance, of "the predominant position of Asia in the world economy" prior to the nineteenth century, and he contends that "Christopher Columbus and after him many Europeans up until Adam Smith knew" that "the entire world economic order was—literally—Sinocentric" (11 and 117). Hobson makes an even more forceful case for Asia's economic superiority in comparison to Europe before 1800. Hobson provides a discussion, as well, of the historiographical tradition that helped produce a conception of a mutually exclusive and historically separate "East" and "West" in twentieth-century studies of world economic development. See esp. 1–28.

18. Brotton is hardly alone in pointing this out. See, for instance, Shankar Raman on the shift from medieval to early modern conceptions of the world, particularly as they relate to the notions of "East" and "West," in *Framing "India."* For a broader discussion of the history and significance of ways of imagining the world in terms of East and West, see Lewis and Wigen.

19. Brotton 28.
20. Ibid., 97.
21. Ibid., 34.
22. See Foerster, *The Reinterpretation of American Literature*, for the most concise series of arguments by these scholars of the 1920s. In addition to having a chapter devoted to "The Frontier," written by Jay B. Hubbell, the four "factors" Foerster lists as "most important" in the development of American literature "may be comprised," he claims, "under two heads: European culture and the American environment" (26).
23. For a discussion of the role geographical considerations have structured some important works of scholarship on American literature, see C. Porter. For a discussion of the possibilities the new cultural geography holds for scholars of American literature, see S. Blair. For a broader discussion of the study of American literature in relation to geography, see Brückner and Hsu. For a discussion of the spatial at work in the distinction between the domestic and foreign as it plays out specifically in nineteenth-century works, see Kaplan, *Anarchy of Empire* 23–50. For a critique of the restrictive effects of the continent as a defining trope in the field, see Dimock, "Hemispheric Islam," "Planet and America," and *Through Other Continents*.
24. Bauer 11–12; Brückner 6.
25. A number of theorists of space, as well as literary critics writing about geographic space, have also had a profound impact on my thinking about spatial matters in this book, though I rarely engage direct with these writings in the body of my analyses. Among those works that were the most influential, I would list Aravamuden, *Tropicopolitans;* Bauer; Brückner; de Certeau; Foucault, "Of Other Spaces"; Lefebvre; Raman, "Re-viewing the World: Cartography and the Production of Colonialist Space" in *Framing "India"* 89–154; and Soja.
26. Versluis 13.
27. Other relevant book-length studies of the Orient in American literature before 1860 include Luedtke and Yu. Isani's dissertation remains one of the most thorough and illuminating studies of pre-Revolutionary writing on the Orient. See also Isani's "Mather and the Orient" and "Edward Taylor and the Turks." Among the notable essays that either offer broad overviews of American literature of the period and the Orient or provide more specialized examinations of particular issues within the broad topic, Kamrath provides an illuminating analysis of the Oriental tale before 1800 that focuses on an important American magazine. Hayes offers an informative discussion of the importance to the *Koran* in various of Thomas Jefferson's more famous intellectual projects. If one uses the definition of the Orient or East that I use here—that is, the operative definitions of the eighteenth century and the early nineteenth century—one might also include analyses of the Barbary captivity narrative in American culture. If one looks to the discipline of history, Tchen's stands out as an excellent examination of the notion that "[t]he use of Chinese things, ideas, and people in the United States, in various imagined and real forms, has been instrumental in forming this nation's cultural identity" (xv).
28. Warner 61.
29. Ibid.
30. Miller provides no footnote in *Errand to the Wilderness* to indicate just what scholarly works he has in mind.
31. Ibid., 187.
32. Ibid., 186.

33. William Spengemann has, perhaps, produced the most extensive writings on the problem of continuity in American literary studies in the last twenty years. See *A Mirror for Americanists* and *A New World of Words*. R. C. de Prospo has also written some provocative material on the problem of continuity in "Marginalizing Early American Literature" and *Theism in the Discourse of Jonathan Edwards* 9–56.

34. For Anderson's argument regarding the use of the dead in nationalist movements, see "Memory and Forgetting," in *Imagined Communities,* esp. 198.

35. While I focus here on Ballaster's work on tales involving the Orient in British literature of the period, other scholars working on the same material operate on the same assumption when discussing the relation between this material and empire. Aravamuden, for instance, offers some of the most revealing analysis of the Oriental tale, and he, too, approaches these tales with the same assumptions about a British readership.

36. I am referring here to the sense of inferiority often expressed—sometimes implicitly, sometimes explicitly—by provincial and/or postcolonial writers. For an analysis of American literature of this period as a postcolonial literature, see Hulme; Kaplan; Madsen; Schueller; Schueller and Watts; Schmidt and Singh; Warner, "What's Colonial About Colonial America?"; and Watts, *Writing and Postcolonialism* and *An American Colony*.

37. Buell uses the term "cultural dependence" on page 415 of "American Literary Emergence"; he casts American literature as "the first postcolonial literature" on page 434 of the same essay.

38. Lefebvre 42.

39. Ibid., 46.

40. My decision to focus exclusively on works written in English by British American colonists and by writers of European descent in the new nation requires some explanation. As to the question of language, my decision to analyze only works written in English grows out of my sense that such a focus would allow me to make comparisons between texts from different historical moments without having to wrestle with the conceptual problems that translations necessarily produce. Much valuable work has been done that examines work in different languages during the period this study covers. My own training, research, and interests, though, led me to concentrate on works in English produced in Britain's North American colonies that would go on to stage a revolution. I hope, in fact, that my analysis of this particular category of figures will prompt other scholars either to investigate similar categories in other literatures or to examine comparisons between languages.

CHAPTER 1

1. Eberwein 140. As evidence for her claim that Alexander dominates "The Four Monarchies," Eberwein points out that Bradstreet gives Alexander "24 pages of text in contrast to 19 for all his successors in the Macedonian line, 15 for the Assyrian monarchy that ran much longer, 26 for the Persian, and a pitiful 3 for the Roman" (134).

2. One other reason why "The Four Monarchies" has received little critical analysis is also worth noting: "The Four Monarchies" is bad poetry. Virtually every literary critic for at least the 150 years considers "The Four Monarchies" to be an aesthetic failure. For

instance, Elizabeth Wade White calls it "tedious" (237), while Wendy Martin characterizes the lines as "doggedly written and mechanically rhymed" (48). McElrath and Rabb say one "can easily sympathize with [Bradstreet's] exhaustion, perhaps boredom" (xxx). While "The Four Monarchies" has received little critical attention, some scholars have examined it. See, for instance, Eberwein; Tamara Harvey 37–40; Maragou; Rosenmeier 61–70; Stanford, *Anne Bradstreet* 65–70; Emily Stripes Watts 10–13; White 228–38.

3. Critics before me have also noted that Bradstreet's poetry favors things of the Old World over those of the New. In her introduction to a modern edition of Bradstreet, Jeannine Hensley points out that although Bradstreet "shared the frontier experiences, she ignored most of the signs of a New World to write of the lore of the Old World and of hope for the next. She praised God and ignored the Indians; she eulogized her husband and ignored colonial politics" (xxiii).

4. "The Prologue" 33; "A Dialogue Between Old England and New" 284 and 282. For reasons explained in note 15, I have chosen to use *Several Poems* as the authoritative Bradstreet text.

5. "The Four Monarchies" 901 and 685.

6. Ibid., 1295, 1494, and 1488.

7. Ibid., 2169–70.

8. Ibid., 2287.

9. "In Honour of that High and Mighty Princess Queen Elizabeth of Happy Memory" 90; "Four Monarchies" 2512.

10. Spengemann provides his most focused investigation into the concern with what he calls "American Things" in "American Things/Literary Things: The Problem of American Literary History," *A Mirror for Americanists* 143–65.

11. Bradstreet's interest in the East has received little scholarly attention, but her interest in Alexander has not escaped scholars' notice. Helen Maragou provides a thorough and informative discussion of Bradstreet's representation of Alexander in "The Portrait of Alexander the Great in Anne Bradstreet's 'The Third Monarchy.'" For analyses of representation of Alexander in literature in English before Bradstreet wrote "The Four Monarchies," see Barbour; and Gilles. For analyses of Alexander in English literature in the latter part of the seventeenth century, see Orr. Ng provides a very useful and insightful reading of the figure of Alexander in the early modern period more broadly.

12. Goffman provides an overview of the relationship between the Ottoman Empire and Europe during the seventeenth century. For a much more concise overview of the Ottoman Empire's composition and influence at the end of the seventeenth century, see Treasure 601–20. For an analysis of the views of the West toward the Ottoman Empire during this period from which I have learned a good deal, see Woodhead.

13. I take the phrase "before Orientalism" from the title of Richard Barbour's work, from which the analysis in this chapter greatly profited.

14. Vitkus 8.

15. It is not entirely clear just how much control Bradstreet had over the poems in *The Tenth Muse* or in *Several Poems*. John Woodbridge, her brother-in-law, had the poems published in London without Bradstreet's knowledge or consent, though just how much or little she knew about or acceded to their publication we do not know. We know little, too, about the circumstances surrounding the publication of *Several Poems*, though it is clear that John Rodgers edited the book. Just what differences between the 1650 and

the 1678 editions are Bradstreet's doing and which are Rodgers's is unclear. We do have evidence, however, that Bradstreet revised the poems after 1650 and that these revisions appear in the Boston edition. McElrath Jr. and Robb consider the 1650 edition the authoritative one in their *Complete Works*. As Schweitzer points out, "[T]his represents a conservative choice that prefers versions of Bradstreet's published poems, which we know to have been published without her supervision, over versions of the poems that we have some evidence to indicate she revised to some extent" (*The Work* 261n8). For this reason, I have chosen to use *Several Poems* rather than *The Tenth Muse* when citing lines of poetry. See Hensley, "Anne Bradstreet's Wreath of Thyme"; McElrath Jr. and Robb, "Introduction" xi–xlii; and Schweitzer.

16. Maragou provides the most extensive analysis of the various sources Bradstreet used, in addition to Raleigh's history, to help her write "The Four Monarchies."

17. Other Bradstreet poems in which figures of the East play a significant role include "A Dialogue Between Old England and New," "In Honour of Queen Elizabeth," "David's Lamentation," and "To My Dear and Loving Husband."

18. "The Four Monarchies" 3408, 3416, and 3414. Further references to this poem are made parenthetically.

19. John Shields provides a thorough and illuminating discussion of the significance of the theory that the cultural center of civilization moves west in *The American Aeneas* (3–37). Shields argues that this theory should be labeled "translatio cultus" rather than, as it has been traditionally known, "translatio studii."

20. Bradstreet's interest in Alexander can also be seen in the way she adapted her source material. Maragou, for instance, argues that Bradstreet's history of the world diverges most sharply from its sources in its portrayal of Alexander. "Bradstreet's approach to Alexander" represents, Maragou writes, "a clear departure from Raleigh's *History*" and shows "a striking divergence" from the character of Alexander found in "the histories of Plutarch and Curtius" (78; 75).

21. Maragou and Eberwein also read the poem as demonstrating Bradstreet's interest in Alexander in particular. Maragou speaks of Bradstreet's "fascination" with the Greek leader (76), while Eberwein notes "Bradstreet's disproportionate concentration on Alexander" in "The Four Monarchies" (136). Harvey, too, provides an illuminating discussion of the significance of the figure of Alexander in support of her argument that Bradstreet mounts a feminist critique in her poetry. See T. Harvey 37–40.

22. Eberwein offers a very different reading of these lines. See "Civil War" 134–35.

23. Eberwein does argue, though, that the poem shows Bradstreet's views on the Civil War in England in particular and on monarchy in general.

24. Rosenmeier 95. For alternate readings of Bradstreet's Sidney elegies, see Rosenmeier; Round 177–78; Stanford, "Anne Bradstreet's Portrait" and *Anne Bradstreet*, esp. 12–17; T. Sweet 157–61; and N. Wright 243–52. Oser does not discuss Bradstreet's Sidney poems but does read her poetry in relation to the work of Sidney's own writing, as well as that of Edmund Spenser. Schweitzer offers a very different reading than I do of the differences between the two versions on page 298–303 in "Anne Bradstreet Wrestles. . . ." Cavitch's reading touches on issues of identity that are related to what I discuss in this chapter. He reads the poem as showing how "Bradstreet seems to feel the thread of her Englishness slipping away," and he goes on to argue that Bradstreet, in this elegy, "finds [that] the link between mourning, writing poetry, and being English in America is dif-

ficult to maintain for a poet writing in America" (57).

25. McElrath Jr. and Robb 116.

26. Ibid., 81 and 137.

27. Falco 120. For a discussion of the many elegies about Sidney as well as the use of Alexander the Great in those elegies, see Falco, esp. 52–94.

28. "An Elegie," *Several Poems* 95. Falco discusses these conventions at length. Further references to this poem are made parenthetically, except when it is necessary to refer to the version published in *The Tenth Muse*. References to this version of the poem appear in the notes.

29. The date is listed in *The Tenth Muse* immediately after the poem's title with the line "By A.B. 1638."

30. Stanford provides an illuminating discussion on the elegy from which Bradstreet drew her inspiration, Sylvester's elegy on Sidney.

31. The most comprehensive discussion of the case for a familial link between Bradstreet and Sidney can be found in White 12–17. Stanford provides further evidence in "Anne Bradstreet's Portrait of Sir Philip Sidney" 97–100.

32. White, for instance, argues that the revisions show that Bradstreet recognized the poem's flaws in "taste" (148). In "Anne Bradstreet's Portrait of Sir Philip Sidney," Stanford argues that the revisions show that Bradstreet "bowed to decorum" though she never "retracted" her "claim to kinship" with Sidney (98). In her later literary biography of Bradstreet, *Anne Bradstreet: The Worldly Puritan,* Stanford finds evidence to suggest that more than mere decorum was at issue in these changes. She contends that the "change was not made merely . . . for reasons of decorum, but because of outright criticism" (120). In making this argument, Stanford traces the argument that decorum was responsible for the changes to Augustine Jones, the nineteenth-century biographer of Bradstreet's father, Thomas Dudley.

33. White 158. Simon Bradstreet's service to the colony was much more extensive than I have listed here. For instance, he also served on the Massachusetts Bay Company for more than thirty years, including a stint as secretary. From 1638 to 1643, he played a key role on the committee that worked to form "The United Colonies of New England," a confederation of Massachusetts, Plymouth, Connecticut, and New Haven. And, after serving as deputy governor, he became governor in 1686 and then, when Andros was overthrown, was acting governor of the colony until May of 1692, when William Phipps took over.

34. Miller, *The American Puritans* 109; Mitchell 311.

35. Cotton Mather 137.

CHAPTER 2

1. *Gentleman's Magazine* 2 (July 1732): 874.

2. The Earl of Egmont's diary entry for the meeting (pages 285–86 of Volume 1 of Perceval, *Manuscripts of the Earl of Egmont*) contains no discussion of the approval of the seal.

3. I have found no contemporaneous records that describe any discussions over what images to use for the colony's common seal. In *Creating Georgia,* Baine provides

a transcript of a meeting among the Trustees of Bray's Associates at which "Oglethorpe reported, that he had receiv'd Proposals from several Persons for making a Common Seal, one ask'd an hundred Pounds, another sixty, another thirty, and another eight, and Mr. Oglethorpe was desir'd to agree for that of eight" (114). This is an especially provocative note in that it leads one to wonder just who made these proposals and what they might have looked like. Alas, the minutes provide no further details.

4. Martyn, *Some Account of the Designs* 3.

5. Silk was not the only product associated with the East, and with China in particular, that Georgians tried to produce. Some English experts believed the American soil contained clay of the very type used to make Chinaware. The men, Edward Heylyn and Thomas Frye, to whom the "first Bow patent" granted in England was issued—that is, the first patent given for making Chinaware in England rather than having it imported—had 20 tons of clay shipped from the Carolinas to London in 1743–44, though what precisely became of this clay has never been determined. For a discussion of English efforts to use American soil in the production of English attempts at replicating Chinaware, see Emerson, Chen, and Gates, *Porcelain Stories* 160. For a discussion of the history of the attempts by colonial Georgians to promote the use of Georgian soil in the European production of porcelain, see Barber.

6. W. Calvin Smith offers perhaps the most provocative way of describing the appeal of silk to the Trustees when he attributes its "vitality to the magic, mystery, and romance connected with the word 'silk' itself." He goes on to describe silk as a "magic word" to eighteenth-century Georgia promoters and colonists. See Smith 25 and 34.

7. See the introduction and pages 31–33 for further discussion of the changing notions of the "East" in British and British American writing of the period.

8. I have focused my attention in this chapter on the British and British American perspectives on the commodities associated with what they considered to be the "East." Many analyses are available now of this trade from the perspective of these "Eastern" countries. For a brief analysis of the way in which this trade was understood in just one of these communities, see Vainker, "Luxuries or Not?" and *Chinese Silk*. For a more detailed economic analysis that covers a broad section of what we now call Southeast Asia, see Chaudhuri.

9. For a history of the movement that came to be known as "chinoiserie," see Appleton for a study focused specifically on England. For a more recent treatment of chinoiserie in England, see Porter, especially chapter 3, "Chinoiserie and the Aesthetics of Illegitimacy" (133–92). For treatments that extend beyond England to include all of Europe, see Honour; Jacobson; and Vainker, *Chinese Silk*. Willis provides the most detailed, imaginative recreation of the way in which Asian commodities became an integral part of everyday domestic life in Great Britain. He begins his essay on European consumption of Asian products in the period by imagining a "fine summer morning in 1730" when a "prosperous London merchant flings back the chintz quilt, very old-fashioned but a beloved family heirloom, straightens his muslin night-shirt and puts on his Chinese silk dressing-gown as the maid enters with the tea, milk, and sugar." Immediately following this scene, "the newly bought matched blue and white china tea service is smashed" (133).

10. Tailfer 26.

11. In contrast to my argument that the emphasis on silk—not to mention other products to be discussed later in the chapter—in promotional documents led to the

colony's association with the East, some commentators on Georgia have used Martyn's remark that the colonies will produce goods from the "Southern Countries" as a way of categorizing how the promotional material cast the products geographically (See Greene, *Forty Years* 281). I find this a provocative phrase for Martyn to have used, but I believe the evidence indicates that it is quite the exception rather than the rule. Indeed, whereas I can find only one use of this phrase in all of the promotional literature related to Georgia, the promotional documents are littered with instances in which the very same goods that Martyn casts as "Southern" originate somewhere in what they refer to as the "East." Martyn himself, in fact, points his readers toward the East more often in those tracts he authored when discussing the original places of production of the goods he says will be made available by the colonization of Georgia. Oglethorpe, too, links Georgia with what he refers to as the "East Indies," and its products with what he calls "Asia." See, for instance, Oglethorpe 18, 20, and 54.

12. I do not aim in this chapter to provide a history of the early years of the Georgia colony, regardless of whether one considers those early years to be the colony's first ten, twenty, thirty, or forty years. I did consult a number of histories of the colony in my research. I relied in particular on material in the following: Coleman's *Colonial Georgia*; Greene; Ready, "Philanthropy and the Origins of Georgia"; and Reese, *Colonial Georgia*. Crane provides a thorough background to the years leading up to colonization, *Southern Frontier* (303–25). I have also learned much from the first two chapters of Stewart's *"What Nature Sufers to Groe."* For an informative discussion that looks at the importance of the London business community in the initial stages of the colony's promotion, see Meroney. For more specifically literary histories, see R. Davis 59–64 and 1503–5; and Shields, "Literature of the Colonial South" 183–84, "Eighteenth-Century Literary Culture" 444–66, and *Oracles* 45–55.

13. For analyses of the significance of environmentalist theories of identity as they relate to early American literature and/or culture, see Bauer; Canup; Chaplin, *Subject Matter*; Eden; Egan, *Authorizing Experience* and "The 'Long'd-for Aera' of An 'Other Race'"; Finch; Kupperman, "Fear of Hot Climates" and "The Puzzle of the American Climate"; and Parrish. For the perspective on these issues from scholars of British literature, see Feerick; Floyd-Wilson; and Wheeler. For an analysis that does not rely on climatological theory in examining the way early Southern colonists were said to behave but that nonetheless provides a potentially useful perspective, see Bertelson 88–96.

14. The poem appeared in the *Gazette* without a title. For the sake of convenience, I refer to the poem by the title under which it appears in the *Gentleman's Magazine*. I have also listed the date as 1732 even though, according to modern calendars, the poem was published in what we would term "1733." Since England did not adopt the Gregorian calendar until 1751, though, I have chosen to list the date as it would have been known by Kirkpatrick and his contemporaries in England.

15. The poem was published in three different periodicals in the eighteenth century. It was published first in the *South-Carolina Gazette* and again two months later in the *Gentleman's Magazine*, and finally it was reprinted from the *Gazette* in the April 4, 1734, issue of the *Pennsylvania Gazette*. See Lemay, items 245, 256, and 300 from *A Calendar*. The only difference I can see in the three printings of the poem has to do with the way each is framed. The *South-Carolina Gazette* version prefaces the poem with a brief passage from Horace's Epistle II. We do not know whether the editor of the *South-Carolina*

Gazette inserted the epigram or whether Kirkpatrick requested that it be included. The choice of Horace is hardly surprising, though, given the poet's popularity among eighteenth-century British writers. See Goad. I discuss the way in which the other two printed versions of the poem are framed in the body of this chapter. See Shields's discussion of Kirkpatrick's poetry in *Civil Tongues* 292–95.

16. My discussion in this paragraph thus focuses exclusively on British attempts to cultivate silk in the colonies, omitting entirely the even longer and no less important history of attempts by other European nations to produce silk in their American colonies.

17. Gray puts it most provocatively: "In selecting silk as the most desirable commercial product, the promoters of the Georgia Company either were unaware of or disregarded the numerous unsuccessful attempts that had been made in the older Southern Colonies" (186). I do not mean to suggest, however, that the colony enjoyed no success in producing silk. Georgia experienced a short but nonetheless noticeable boom in silk production in the early 1750s. See Smith, "Utopia's Last Chance?"

18. For a discussion of attempts to produce silk in British America, see Brockett 26–34; Chaplin, *An Anxious Pursuit*, esp. 158–64; Craven; Hertz; and Gray 1:184–87. Gray provides an especially clear, concise summary of Georgia's activities in particular (186–87). He notes that "[f]or twenty years every encouragement was employed to stimulate the industry" (186). More recent discussions of attempts to produce silk in Georgia in particular include Coleman, *Colonial Georgia* 113–16; Greene; McKinstry; and Stewart, *"What Nature Suffers to Groe,"* esp. 53–86.

19. Hariot 7.

20. For a thorough discussion of the history of attempts to produce silk in colonial Virginia, see Hatch.

21. Ashe, 8.

22. Oldmixon 378.

23. For very brief discussions of the common seal of Georgia, see Greene, *Forty Years* 294; Preble 630–31; and Reese, *Colonial Georgia* 137n2.

24. For a discussion of the legal significance of common seals in the corporate law applicable to the British American colonies, see Joseph Davis 34–35.

25. Peck 85.

26. Ibid., 14 and 85.

27. Ibid., 85.

28. Hertz 710.

29. Landa, "Pope's Belinda" 226.

30. For more detailed statistics on English imports and exports during the period, see Schumpeter, "Table XII: Values of the Principal English Exports of Woolen Goods for the Years 1697–1771, 1775, and 1780"(35–38); "Table XIV: Quantities of the Principal English Exports of all Textile Goods for the Years 1697 to 1771, 1775, and 1780" (44–47); "Table XV: Values of Selected Imports into England and Wales for the Years 1700 to 1771, 1775, and 1780" (48–51); "Table XVI: Quantities of Selected Imports into England and Wales for the Years 1700 to 1771, 1775, and 1780" (52–55); "Table XVIII: Quantities of Imports, Re-exports, and Retained Imports of Selected Commodities for England and Wales from 1700–1808" (60–62); and "Table XXXV: Exports of Wrought Silk by Geographical Division, 1700–1800" (67). For a discussion of silk imports from Asia to Great Britain from 1700 to 1760, see Chaudhuri 343–58. For a synthesis of scholarship on trade

between Great Britain and Asia during the period, see Marshall. For a different perspective, see Pomeranz.

31. Berg, *Luxury and Pleasure* 50. Berg and Eger contend that "Eastern or oriental imports were part of the classical, western definition of luxury." They go on to note, "From Pliny onwards, arguments made against eastern luxury items were based on a fear of financial ruin in the West, as silver and gold flowed east to purchase the treasures of the Indies" (Berg and Eger 8). Just how much silk was imported from China during the period? As Berg notes, "Silk, pepper, spices, and textiles made up three-quarters of total imports before 1740; towards the end of the period tea and coffee were among the prominent imports" (Berg, *Luxury and Pleasure* 56).

32. For a fascinating discussion of the origin of the name "China" in English, see Liu, *The Clash of Empires* 75–81. See also Liu, "Robinson Crusoe's Earthenware Pot," for a discussion of the use of the word "China" in English in the seventeenth and eighteenth centuries. One way to see the instability of the meaning of the word "China" as it pertained to specific geographic matters is to look at how the word was used on maps of the period; see Szczesniak.

33. Baine argues that Oglethorpe "evidently subsidized the appearance" of *A Compendious Account*, and he contends that Boreman's book should be read as "the final promotional pamphlet" in the initial promotional campaign (105–6). Baine notes as well that "the trustees evidently stored copies and distributed them to the colonists" as late as 1747 (106).

34. Boreman 11. Boreman did not invent this etymology. Indeed, a number of his contemporaries make similar references to "Serica" as the ancient name of China. For a very brief discussion of the significance of the history of the word "Serica," see Honour 30 and Berg, "Asian Luxuries" 228.

35. Boreman 10.
36. Crane, "The Promotion Literature" 284. Gee 96.
37. Gee, 96.
38. Honour 50 and 52.
39. Ibid., 50.
40. Ibid., 125.
41. D. Porter 134.
42. Ibid., 136–37.
43. Ibid., 166.
44. Ibid., 135.
45. Ibid., 137.
46. Leath 56. British American colonists, like their counterparts in Europe, sought to incorporate products marked as "Chinese" into their daily lives as a way to display their sophistication and taste. See Barber; Denker; and Leath.
47. Berg 50–51.
48. Ibid., 50–51.
49. Boreman 10.
50. For a discussion of Kirkpatrick's medical career, see Waring.
51. Shields, "Dr. James Kirkpatrick" 39.
52. Shields, *Oracles* 25–26.
53. Ibid., 26

54. The poem has drawn virtually no attention from literary critics in recent years, and the author to whom we ascribe the poem perhaps only slightly more. Shields writes, for instance, that Kirkpatrick's writing has, like this poem, "languished in [a] limbo of neglect" ("Dr. James Kirkpatrick" 39). While an untold number of poems from the British American colonies remain equally if not more neglected than this one, the deafening silence from critics in relation to Kirkpatrick's work is surprising given that the praise I quote above is by a scholar of such respect and influence as Shields. A. Franklin Parks is the only scholar I can find to have examined Kirkpatrick's poetry at any length recently. He does not list "An Address . . ." among Kirkpatrick's work. Parrish also mentions Kirkpatrick's *The Sea-Piece* and "The Non-Pareil," 207–9. No entry exists for Kirkpatrick in the *Dictionary of Literary Biography*. As for the poem I discuss in particular, Cohen provides a very brief analysis in "Two Colonial Poems" (131); Shields provides brief analyses of the work in "Literature of the Colonial South" (183–84) and in *Oracles* (47; 51–52). R. B. Davis mentions the appearance of "An Address . . ." in the *Gentleman's Magazine* and the *South-Carolina Gazette,* but he does not analyze the poem. Boys also mentions the poem without offering an analysis, and he lists only its appearance in the *Gentleman's Magazine* (23).

55. While no one in colonial Georgia recorded any explicit response to the poem in the 1730s, the Malcontents cite some of the very passages analyzed in this chapter in *A True and Historical Narrative*. Their remarks suggest, further, that they, at least, believed the poem had an audience up and down the Eastern Seaboard as well as on both sides of the Atlantic.

56. *The Pennsylvania Gazette,* April 4, 1734.

57. Lemay considers it "unlikely" that the *Gazette* "could have been the source" for the poem published in April 1733 of the *Gentleman's Magazine* (*Men of Letters* 43). I am not so much concerned with the problem of where the magazine got the copy of the poem it published as I am with the way in which they framed that poem—regardless of its source—as a specifically colonial product.

58. See Hall 417.

59. *Gentleman's Magazine* 3 (April 1733): 209.

60. The magazine does not identify the author of the poem, though we now know it to have been written by the Maryland poet and schoolmaster Richard Lewis. In fact, Lewis published a number of poems in English periodicals, and his authorship might very well have been recognized by readers at the time in spite of not being specifically identified.

61. Berry 126. For his extended discussion of "luxury" in the eighteenth century, see 126–76.

62. I do not mean to suggest here that earlier discussions ignored the issue of luxury but, rather, that the issue of luxury was represented very differently in these earlier debates and operated on and was organized in relation to a different set of assumptions.

63. For a discussion of chinoiserie in America specifically, see Denker; C. Frank; Leath. For a discussion of interest in what might be called "the China taste" in the latter half of the eighteenth century, see Blaszczyk and Tchen, especially xv–59.

64. Landa, "Pope's Belinda . . ." 234.

65. Ibid.

66. In contrast to my reading of the word "India" as a reference to the East, Shields

reads the line "savage India" as a playful twist on its Eastern referent that aims to call our attention to Oglethorpe's sympathetic relationship with the local Indians. For a thorough discussion of the history of the colony's relationship with local native populations, see J. Sweet.

67. Shields offers a different reading of the closing lines of the poem. He reads these lines as an "exercise in wishful projection." What is "revealed" in these lines, he argues, "is the global consciousness that mercantilism had engendered." Rather than seeing Georgia here figured as a substitute for the East, he argues that it has been "transmuted into the world in the poet's imaginings." As in his reading of "savage India" as referring to the land of the American Indians, Shields argues that "Indian Groves" refers to the local orchards. Once these orchards have been "cleared," Shields continues, they "will . . . mix the cultivars of the several continents" (*Oracles* 51–52). He makes a similar reading in "Literature of the Colonial South" 183–84.

68. Ralph 37–38.

69. Laura Brown 118.

70. This is one reason, I would suggest, that the poem could be printed on both sides of the Atlantic without any changes being made.

71. I think it is important to add that such in a figurative system, women not only, as Laura Brown points out, bear responsibility for the imperial acts that result in the importation of silk into Great Britain but also bear the burden of an entire culture's imagined deficiencies. I say this because the logic of this figurative system depends on British women being deficient in and of themselves, and because British women are here not merely figures for their gender within the nation but, in fact, figures for the nation as a whole. So while it is true that the system grants women representative status by placing the figure of the woman as the sign for British culture writ large, it does so by casting largely male acts of violence as the products of what it casts as specifically feminine desire while holding this very desire responsible for the ills of an entire nation.

72. Greene, "Travails," *Imperatives* 116.

73. Oglethorpe 1. 2, Wesley, *Georgia*, "Tomochachi,"1. 24; Oglethorpe 1. 34, Wesley, "Georgia," 1. 157; Oglethorpe 1. 47, Wesley, "Georgia," 1. 83; Oglethorpe 1. 79–80, Wesley, *Georgia*, "Georgia," 1. 196; Oglethorpe 1. 95, Wesley, "Georgia," 1. 203 and 205.

74. *Reasons* appeared in at least three separate printings. Six hundred copies were printed in March 1733, followed by six hundred more in April as a petition for additional funds in support of the colony was making the rounds of Parliament with the stipulation by the Trustees that "one of them be deliver'd to Every Member of Both Houses of Parliament." A second edition with further changes and additions appeared later in the same year. For a discussion of the various issues, see Crane, "Promotion Literature" 289–90.

75. The reference to Pope occurs in each of the three printings of *Reasons*. As for why Martyn chose Pope's poem from among the many possible works on luxury he might have cited, his relationship with Pope might have influenced his choice. We know that Pope and Martyn were, at best, acquaintances. The two worked together, for instance, to raise funds for a monument to Shakespeare in 1737–38, but there is even speculation that they co-authored Martyn's play *Timoleon*, performed in January 1730 to some acclaim and published in the same year. For a discussion of Martyn's life, see Alexrod; and Reese, "Benjamin Martyn. . . ." Since at least the nineteenth century, the consensus among critics has been that Pope did not contribute to *Timoleon*. See, for instance, Griffith, who includes

Timoleon in his bibliography of Pope's writings but notes, "Probably nothing here by Pope" (292). In the most distinguished biography of Pope to date, though, Mack chooses to qualify but not dispute Pope's claim to co-authorship when he writes that Martyn "is thought to have received contributions by Pope." See Mack 925.

76. "The Uses of Riches" was first published in London in 1732. For a discussion of the history of the poem's printing, see Griffith 215–16 and Mack 522. For a modern edition of the first printing of the poem that reproduces the original spelling and punctuation, see Wasserman. Given their relationship, it might be that he had access to Pope's poem even before it was published, since Pope might have completed it a year before having it published. See Mack 522.

77. Many previous commentators on Georgia have remarked on what seems to be the discrepancy between the colony's philanthropic goals of helping those in debt and its focus on producing the very luxury items that, some would say, had led to an increase in such debtors in British society in the first place. Shields, for instance, says the "irony of the philanthropic myth was that the commodities the colonists would be producing in Georgia were in many cases the luxuries that fueled temptation in the Old World" (*Oracles* 51). To take another example, Greene reads the colony's philanthropic effort as a sign of the feelings of "guilt" on the part of elite members of society whose efforts to acquire more wealth and luxury items might have, they felt, also contributed to the growth of Great Britain's indigent poor (*Imperatives* 119–20).

78. Nicholson makes a similar case for the way in which Pope figures paper money. In Pope's poem, Nicholson argues, paper forms of payment "substituted a material insubstantiality for the dimensions of the commodities they thereby circulated" (144). The "shift," he continues, "from perdurable quantities of metal specie to the promissory note of paper money signifies a powerful threat to once-solid foundations for trade and commerce," which, in turn, "constitutes a clear and present danger to wealth-sustaining landed property and its associated virtue" (144–45).

79. For discussions of the relevance of postcolonial theory to the study of early American literature specifically, see Hulme; Schmidt and Singh; Schueller and Watts; and Watts, *Writing and Postcolonialism* and *An American Colony*.

CHAPTER 3

1. *Benjamin Franklin: Writings* 1084.
2. Ibid., 1084–85.
3. Franklin's reference to China in a letter that has become rather well known to historians has itself received relatively little attention. Olson connects the rhetorical strategies that Franklin employs in the opening of the letter to criticize the membership requirements of the Order of Cincinnati with Franklin's objection to the bald eagle as the symbol for the Great Seal, but he does not mention the reference to China.
4. *Dragon and Eagle* 25.
5. Quoted in ibid.
6. See Aldridge for the most detailed treatment of each of these interests. Tchen, too, provides a brief discussion of Franklin's interest in using Chinese practices as models for American behavior (17).

I have not included in this list Franklin's references to the British Empire and, later, the Confederation as "China Vase[s]" that I mentioned in the introduction. The figure of the China Vase in these instances differs from those on which this chapter focuses. Indeed, I suspect that an examination of Franklin's use of this phrase deserves its own, independent analysis, one that would begin by investigating just what "China Vase" refers to. After all, the term was used at the time to denote Chinaware produced not simply in China or even in Europe, and it appeared at precisely the time when British Americans began in earnest their own attempts to produce Chinaware in the colonies. These attempts allowed the phrase "China Vase" to resonate in ways that called to mind issues of the value of tasteful goods in the colonies in relation to the production of those same goods abroad. Franklin himself was intimately involved in these efforts. Frelinghuysen provides a brief discussion of Franklin's involvement (8–9). Beurdeley provides a brief description of early U.S. interest in porcelain (130–34), which includes a brief history of the society of Cincinnati's commissioning of an emblem on a china service, to be made in China, in the society's honor (134). Barber provides an excellent collection of selections from eighteenth-century newspapers, primarily advertisements and announcements, in *Pottery and Porcelain;* these collections demonstrate the extent of American interest in Chinaware. Mudge offers a thorough discussion of the importation of porcelain in eighteenth-century British America, while Frelinghuysen thoroughly explores attempts to produce porcelain in the eighteenth-century British colonies and the new United States. Klamkin shows that in the final years of the eighteenth century and the early years of the century following, Americans demonstrated a great interest in having their china adorned with patriotic displays.

7. "The Ephemera," published as a bagatelle on Franklin's press in Passy in 1778, might also qualify as an Oriental tale. The didactic goals of the story about a man coming to understand the vanity of human political achievements when he overhears a conversation among flies parallel those of the standard form of the Oriental tale of the time, but the lack of references to the Orient or to "Oriental" characters has excluded it from the genre. E. W. Pitcher has demonstrated, though, that the story might have started as an Oriental tale. Pitcher has identified a work, "The Walk of Al Raschid, the Arabian Philosopher," published in the *New York Weekly Museum,* xv, No 29 [whole No. 768] (July 16, 1803), that bears such similarities to "The Ephemera" that it must be considered either an "Orientalized" plagiarism of Franklin's work or a "translation of an original used by Franklin for his work" (236). If "The Walk of Al Raschid" represents a translation or reprint of an unknown source for Franklin's essay, this would seem to indicate that Franklin's story might very well represent his attempt to, as it were, de-Orientalize his story.

8. None of the works has been the subject of much scholarly analysis. "Sidi Mehemet Ibrahim" has drawn the most attention, no doubt because of its focus on slavery. Allison provides a brief analysis of the tale (103–6), and Baepler discusses the story in his introduction to *White Slaves, African Masters* (8). Also see Marr 142–43; Peskin 85–86; Schueller 48–49; Waldstreicher 238. "An Arabian Tale" was the subject of an essay in *PMLA* in 1942; see Pitt. Berman mentions the tale (5), as does Schueller (26). "A Turkish Apologue" has never received sustained literary analysis.

9. Outram 1. For a discussion of "reason" in *The Enlightenment in America* in particular, see May.

10. Mott 42.

11. Mott provides the most extensive discussion of each of these magazines in *A History of American Magazines*. See Kirsch for a discussion of *Massachusetts Magazine*, and R. H. Brown for a discussion of *American Magazine*.

12. I have used Pitcher's list of fiction in early American magazines as the basis for estimating that one in ten works published in American magazines before 1800 was an Oriental tale. I came to this estimate using the following figures. Pitcher lists approximately 2,880 tales, 215 of which he further classifies as "Oriental." Pitcher provides no general subject index of the stories, though he does provide an "Author, Signature, Special Subject" index of his catalog. The three "special subject" categories are "Indians," "Slavery," and "Oriental." Of these three subjects, "Oriental" contains 215 entries, compared with only 68 for "Slavery" and 56 for "Indians."

13. Pitcher cites the publication date of "The Meditation" as 1727. In the catalog entry that this chronological list cites, A1653, though, Pitcher lists the first publication date as 1746, the same date Mukhtar Ali Isani assigns the tale in "The Oriental Tale." Pitcher's note to catalog entry A1653, however, cites Bruce Granger as crediting Mather Byles with having first published this tale in the *New-England Weekly Journal* of September 1727. If one takes a broader definition of the Oriental tale than Pitcher does, though, some of Cotton Mather's discussions of Asia in his various writings might qualify as even earlier British American instances of the genre.

14. The chief rival to *The Turkish Spy* for first to attain popularity in America would seem to be Anton Galland's *The Arabian Nights*, first published in translation in London in 1704. We will examine the history of this text in the next chapter when we consider Poe's spoof of the collection of tales.

15. July 2, 1722 issue (No. 48) of the *New England Courant*, quoted in T. Wright 187.

16. Quoted in L. Wright 319.

17. *New York Magazine* 5 (September 1797): 533.

18. Ibid.

19. Kamrath 3 and 4.

20. Quoted in ibid., 7.

21. Bourdieu, *Distinction* 6.

22. Tchen 13.

23. Ballaster, "Narrative Transmigrations" 76.

24. Baepler discusses Franklin's letter, for instance, in the introduction to his collection of Barbary narratives, *White Slaves, African Masters* (8).

25. Histories of the various conflicts that took place between the United States and North Africa during this period abound. Allison provides the most thorough discussion of the relations between the Barbary states and the new United States. See also Baepler's introduction to *White Slaves, African Masters*, as well as Lambert and Leiner. Peskin explains how information about Barbary slavery, including narratives of captivity, circulated in the early United States, and he discusses the impact this information had on the formation of ideas about national identity in the new republic. For a very brief history of the early U.S.–Barbary relations set within the much larger context of a history of the Barbary Coast at large from 1500 to 1800, see Wolf 311–13. Hayes provides a very interesting discussion of the way Jefferson's reading of the *Koran* played a role in his negotiations to free Barbary captives in 1786. Hayes, "How Thomas Jefferson Read the *Qur'an*" 256.

26. *Papers of Benjamin Franklin*, vol. 31, 310. Subsequent passages from this story are

taken from the same page.

27. See Baepler's introduction to *White Slaves, African Masters* for a discussion of the fear expressed by colonial and early national Americans that they might convert to Islam. He extends this into later time periods in "The Barbary Captivity Narrative in American Culture." For a discussion of an earlier instance of the fear of "turning Turk," see Vitkus.

28. Stephen L. Carr calls it a "commonplace" that Blair "was the most widely published rhetorician of the eighteenth and nineteenth centuries" (75). Blair's *Lectures* were, Carr tells us, especially popular in America. They "far outpaced the circulation of any comparable rhetoric," he writes, "up through the 1820s" (83). See Tennenhouse for a discussion of the popularity of Blair's writings and their significance in understanding the history of American literature in the late eighteenth and early nineteenth centuries, esp. 35 and 137n31.

29. Blair 379–80.

30. All references to "An Arabian Tale" are from *Papers of Benjamin Franklin*, vol. 31, 309.

31. Lovejoy 201. Arthur Pitt points out this contradiction as well when he remarks, "The reasoning employed by Belubel amounts to a scientific demonstration of the goodness, greatness, and wisdom of God, and therefore allows one to cherish a happy faith in the ultimate goodness and rightness of things" (165).

32. Lovejoy makes a similar point when he discusses the evidence used by a wide variety of eighteenth-century writers in support of their belief in the Great Chain of Being: "[T]he notion of a Chain of Being, with the assumptions on which it rested, was obviously not a generalization derived from experience, nor was it, in truth, easy to reconcile with the known facts of nature" (183).

33. Douglas 122.

CHAPTER 4

1. Quoted in Lawson-Pebbles 221–22. For a thorough discussion of Poe's reaction to Transcendentalism in general, see Casale. For a discussion on the same topic that is more specifically directed at Poe's views on Emerson's writing, see Carlson.

2. Quoted in Lawson-Pebbles 218.

3. *Journals of Ralph Waldo Emerson, with Annotations*, ed. Edward Waldo Emerson and Waldo Emerson Forbes, vol. 4, 1836–38, 190.

4. Poe's use of the term "Arabesque" has received considerable attention from scholars. See, for instance, Cecil. For the most comprehensive discussion of Poe's use of the term, see Thompson, *Poe's Fiction*. See also Hoffman; Irwin 276–77; and Rippl 124–26. For a discussion of the terms "grotesque" and "arabesque" in literature in the eighteenth and nineteenth centuries, focusing on Europe, see Kayser. Naddaff offers a discussion that focuses on the significance of the "arabesque" in relation to the *1001 Nights*. Hansen and Pollin provide a brief but informative discussion of how Poe uses the term to fend off charges of "Germanism."

5. Emerson, vol. 9, 253–54; vol. 2, 31.

6. Emerson vol. 2, 31–32.

7. Cecil provides a thorough and convincing analysis of the considerable "impor-

tance" of the *Arabian Nights*' "literary influence" on Poe's writing. Indeed, Cecil goes so far as to say that Poe's late works show a "preoccupation with the Arabian tales" (61 and 62).

8. Mabbot makes the case that this reference to Montgomery constitutes one of the sources for Poe's "The Thousand-and-Second Story of Scheherazade" (1150).

9. Poe produces an almost identical entry in *Marginalia* 19.

10. Said discusses the way in which Pickerings's address suggests, in subtle ways, America's imperial ambitions in the East. See *Orientalism* 294.

11. Berman 3–4.

12. Pickering 5.

13. Scholars have recently examined nineteenth-century American literature in relation to Orientalist discourse. See, for instance, Lee; Obenzinger; and Obeidat. Scholars have also examined nineteenth-century American literature in relation to Asian religion. See, for instance, Dimock; Versluis.

Scholars have paid some attention to Poe's Orientalism in particular. In *Literary Culture and U.S. Imperialism*, for instance, Rowe argues that the "Orientalist fantasy" one finds underlying much of Edgar Allan Poe's work serves an explicitly "racist and imperialist" function. Erkkila explores in *Mixed Blood and Other Crosses* "the ways Orientalism intersects with Africanism and a whole series of social subordinations . . . in the formation of Poe's poetics of whiteness" (126). Schueller finds Poe "a particularly interesting" writer of the period to study in terms of his representation of the East, for in his work one finds, she argues, "a parodied Orientalist discourse, critical of imperial nationalism" that "intersects with raced discourses on Southern nationalism, resulting in epistemological crises of gendered and raced hierarchies of imperialism" (110). Trafton discusses Poe's work in relation to the mid-nineteenth-century Egyptology craze. Lyons analyzes the "American Pacific Orientalism" in *Pym*.

14. I do not offer a detailed reading of any of the translations of the *Nights*. Instead, I focus my analysis on Poe's use of the work in his story. For readings of the *Nights* in their eighteenth- and nineteenth-century English contexts, see Ballaster, esp. 101–13; Mahdi 127–63; and Sallis 108–42.

15. For a discussion of Galland's role in the emergence of what Said has famously called an "orientalist discourse," see Said 63–65. Mahdi provides a thorough examination of Galland's translation methods (11–50).

16. For a discussion of the controversy over the first publication of an English translation of the *Nights* in England, see MacDonald.

17. Caracciolo 6. Indeed, the nineteenth-century *Nights* differed from its eighteenth-century forebears in that, among other reasons, new translations appeared based on so-called more authentic material than Galland used in making his translations. The early nineteenth century saw several new translations, most notably one by Edward Lane that emphasized a more scholarly approach and considered the tales more as windows into life in the Arab world than as fantastic stories whose direct relationship to Arabian cultural practices was ambiguous at best. For a discussion of four different editions from the nineteenth century that claim to be translated from more "authentic" sources, see Mahdi 87–126. For a discussion of various English translations from the eighteenth and nineteenth centuries, see Sallis 43–64.

18. Sallis 44.

19. Quoted in Ali 42.

20. Ali 3.
21. Ibid., 69.
22. For a thorough discussion of the critical reaction to the *Nights* in nineteenth-century England, see Ali. For a brief discussion of the importance of these tales to English writers in the eighteenth and nineteenth centuries, see Caracciolo, "Introduction." See also the essays in *The Arabian Nights in English Literature*. Irwin examines the influence of the *Nights* on eighteenth- and nineteenth-century English and American literature; see especially 237–92.
23. Timothy Marr sees the American reaction to the *Nights* differently. He argues that the "negative tradition of islamicism had long been conditioned by the counterstrain of romantic exoticism, which arose from the imaginative opulence of the hugely popular *The One Thousand and One Nights* (known as *The Arabian Nights' Entertainments*)" (13).
24. For a discussion of the interest of nineteenth-century American readers in narratives relating to the Middle East as well as to the "East" more broadly conceived, see B. Harvey. For an analysis of nineteenth-century Americans' interest in materials dealing specifically with Islam, see Marr.
25. For a discussion of the influence of Melville's reading of *The Arabian Nights* on Melville's writings, see Finkelstein 26–41.
26. Ibid., 289.
27. *Literary World* (May 13, 1848): 284.
28. English commentators shared this view of the *Nights*. See Ali.
29. On the question of the way that the *Nights* taught Americans about Arabian culture and, in particular, about Islam, Marr calls the "book as important as the Qur'an for its influence on Western attitudes toward Islam" (13).
30. Nance argues, in fact, that Americans imagined themselves as Arabs with such frequency and in such a way before the 1930s that works such as *The Arabian Nights* can be said to have played a crucial role in Americans' self-understandings.
31. "The Thousand and One Nights," *American Review* 6 (December 1, 1847): 613.
32. Ibid., 614.
33. For a detailed discussion of the movement for literary nationalism in the United States, see McGill 187–216; Miller, *The Raven and the Whale;* Spencer; Widmer.
34. Hawthorne 3.
35. Simms 1.
36. Spencer 74.
37. Duyckinck believed the situation for American authors to be so dire that he spent three years working to convince a publisher to establish a series devoted solely to works by native authors; in 1845 he finally found a publisher willing to take the risk of issuing books that would be called the "Library of American Books," described by Ezra Greenspan as "the most important series of original works of American literature ever published to that date or since" (678).
38. Poe, *Selected Writings* 632.
39. Ibid.
40. Ibid.
41. Ibid. For a provocative, informative, and insightful reading of Poe's relation to the "Young America" movement that argued for a national literature, and with whom Poe was arguing in the passage I have cited, see McGill 187–217.

42. Denuccio argues that the story interrogates not the American literary scene in particular but the fate of the author in general. He equates, for instance, "[t]he fate of Scheherazade" with "the fate, in other words, of both author and story" (369). The story, in Denuccio's reading, has less to do with the particular historical moment at which Poe was writing, and more to do with the relation between author and reader in fiction in general.

43. Mabbott 1151. Further references to this text are parenthetical and are indicated by "M."

44. *Collected Writings of Edgar Allan Poe*, vol. 2, 8–9.

45. See "The Prose Writers of America," in Headley 284–98.

46. I have chosen not to discuss the personal animus that might also have driven Poe's rather odd reference to Griswold's work here. The relationship between Poe and Griswold has long been the subject of much analysis, especially given Griswold's behavior as Poe's literary executor. Their rivalry with and dislike for one another—and their attempts to undermine each other's work—are well documented. In this particular instance, I think it is important to note that Poe and Griswold were in the midst of a bitter exchange of letters about whether Poe would be included in an anthology of American prose writers then being compiled by Griswold.

47. Even so sensitive a critic as Denuccio can make a slip at precisely this issue. He claims, for instance, that Poe "summarizes the usual version of the *Arabian Nights* tales in which Scheherazade . . . stays the executioner's hand for one thousand and one nights, thereby inducing the king to repeal his vow to marry and have killed the next morning the most beautiful young women in his kingdom" (365–66). I have found no translation that Poe might have read that describes the king's vow as one in which he promises to execute "the most beautiful women in his kingdom."

48. Scott translation, 31.
49. Ibid.
50. Ibid.
51. Ibid.
52. Ibid.
53. Ibid.
54. Ibid., 34.
55. Ibid., 31.
56. Ibid.

57. Marr also reads the story of the more conventional translations in family terms. He writes, "After the despot witnesses the three sons whom Scheherazade had borne [*sic*] during the telling of the tales, he acknowledges her as a queen—an act that reconstitutes a stable family structure, redeeming both the brutal violence of the fraternal despots and the sensuality of their former wives" (45).

58. Poe, *Selected Writings* 680.

EPILOGUE

1. Scholars have begun to investigate the connections between sexuality and the East in relation to the Oriental tale in eighteenth-century American writing. See, for instance, Battistini; Kamrath, "An 'Inconceivable Pleasure' and the *Philadelphia Minerva*";

and Schueller, *U.S. Orientalisms*.

2. For work that begins to examine figures of the East in early American writing in relation to specifically American imperial and expansionist modes of thought, one might look at Schueller.

3. Marr's work, for instance, points in precisely this direction.

4. See C. Frank.

5. Transatlantic approaches to early American literature have come to dominate the field. Indeed, transatlantic approaches are so numerous that it would take far too much space to list them all here. For a list of instructive examples, see Slauter 180n2. Dimock's notion of "deep time" leads her to argue for a "planetary" approach. Burnham and Shapiro each argue for the applicability of Wallerstein's "world-system" theories to early American literature. For essays that focus specifically on hemispheric and various forms of global approaches to the study of early American literature, see "Special Issue: Projecting Early American Literary Studies," *ALH* 22. For studies that investigate the implications of hemispheric, global, and transnational approaches in American literary history more broadly, see *Hemispheric American Studies*. See also Arac; Boelhower; Doyle; and Giles. For a provocative discussion of the possibilities of global studies of early American history, see Coclanis.

WORKS CITED

Aldridge, Alfred Owen. *The Dragon and the Eagle: The Presence of China in the American Enlightenment.* Detroit, MI: Wayne State University Press, 1993.
Ali, Muhsin Jassim. *Scheherazade in England: A Study of Nineteenth-Century Criticism of the Arabian Nights.* Washington, DC: Three Continents Press, 1981.
Allison, Robert J. *The Crescent Obscured: The United States and the Muslim World, 1776–1815.* Chicago: University of Chicago Press, 2000. Originally published 1995.
Anderson, Benedict. *Imagined Communities.* Rev. ed. London: Verso, 1991.
Anonymous. "Domestick Occurrences in July." *Gentleman's Magazine* 2 (July 1732): 874.
Anonymous. "Benevolence: Or, the Good Samaritan." *Massachusetts Magazine: or, Monthly Museum of Rational Knowledge and Entertainment* 2 (February 1789): 76–77.
Anonymous. "The Thousand and One Nights." *American Review* 6 (December 1, 1847): 613.
Appleton, William W. *A Cycle of Cathay.* New York: Columbia University Press, 1951.
Arac, Jonathan. "Global and Babel: Language and Planet in American Literature." *Shades of the Planet: American Literature as World Literature.* Ed. Wai Chi Dimock and Lawrence Buell. Princeton, NJ: Princeton University Press, 2007. 19–38.
Aravamuden, Srinivas. "East and West Indies: Comparative Misapprehensions." *Anthropological Forum* 16 (2006): 291–309.
———. "In the Wake of the Novel: The Oriental Tale as National Allegory." *Novel: A Forum on Fiction* 33 (1999): 5–31.
———. *Tropicopolitans: Colonialism and Agency, 1688–1804.* Durham, NC: Duke University Press, 1999.
Armstrong, Nancy, and Leonard Tennenhouse. *The Imaginary Puritan: Literature, Intellectual Labor, and the Origins of Personal Life.* Berkeley: University of California Press, 1992.
Ashe, Thomas. *Carolina, or a Description of the Present State of that Country.* London, 1680.
Axelrod, Alan. "Benjamin Martyn (1699–1763)." *American Writers before 1800: A Biographical and Critical Dictionary.* Ed. James A. Levernier and Douglass R. Wilmes. Vol. 2. Westport, CT: Greenwood Press, 1983. 957–60.
Baepler, Paul Michel. "The Barbary Captivity Narrative in American Culture." *Early American Literature* 39.2 (2004): 217–46.
———. *White Slaves, African Masters: An Anthology of American Barbary Captivity Narratives.* Chicago: University of Chicago Press, 1999.
Baine, Rodney M. "James Oglethorpe and the Early Promotional Literature for Georgia."

The William and Mary Quarterly 45 (1988): 100–106.

Baine, Robert M., ed. *Creating Georgia: Minutes of the Bray Associates, 1730–1732 & Supplementary Documents*. Athens, GA, and London: University of Georgia Press, 1995.

Ballaster, Ros. *Fabulous Orients: Fictions of the East in England 1662–1785*. Oxford: Oxford University Press, 2005.

———. "Narrative Transmigrations: The Oriental Tale and the Novel in Eighteenth-Century Britain." *A Companion to the Eighteenth-Century English Novel and Culture*. Ed. Paula R. Backscheider and Catherine Ingrassia. Oxford: Blackwell Publishing, 2005. 75–96.

Barber, Edwin Atlee. *Pottery and Porcelain of the United States; an Historical Review of American Ceramic Art*. Watkins Glen, NY: Century House Americana, 1971.

Barbour, Richard. *Before Orientalism: London's Theatre of the East, 1576–1626*. Cambridge: Cambridge University Press, 2003.

Battistini, Robert. "Glimpses of the Other before Orientalism: The Muslim World in Early American Periodicals, 1785–1800." *Early American Studies* 2 (2010): 446–74.

Bauer, Ralph. *The Cultural Geography of Colonial American Literatures: Empire, Travel, Modernity*. Cambridge: Cambridge University Press, 2003.

Berg, Maxine. "Asian Luxuries and the Making of the European Consumer Revolution." *Luxury in the Eighteenth Century: Debates, Desires, and Delectable Goods*. Ed. Maxine Berg and Elizabeth Eger. London: Palgrave Macmillan, 2003. 228–44.

———. *Luxury and Pleasure in Eighteenth-Century Britain*. Oxford: Oxford University Press, 2003.

———, and Elizabeth Eger. "The Rise and Fall of the Luxury Debates." *Luxury in the Eighteenth Century: Debates, Desires, and Delectable Goods*. Ed. Maxine Berg and Elizabeth Eger. London: Palgrave Macmillan, 2003. 7–27.

Berman, Jacob Rama. "The Barbarous Voice of Democracy: American Captivity in Barbary and the Multicultural Specter." *American Literature* 79 (2007): 1–27.

Berry, Christopher J. *The Idea of Luxury: A Conceptual and Historical Investigation*. Cambridge: Cambridge University Press, 1994.

Bertelson, David. *The Lazy South*. New York: Oxford University Press, 1967.

Beurdeley, Michel. *Chinese Trade Porcelain*. Rutland, Vermont; and Tokyo, Japan: Charles E. Tuttle, 1962.

Blair, Hugh. *Lectures on Rhetoric and Belles Lettres*. New York: Garland Publishing, 1970.

Blair, Sara. "Cultural Geography and the Place of the Literary." *American Literary History* 10 (1998): 544–67.

Blaszczyk, Regina Lee. "Ceramics and the Sot-Weed Factor: The China Market in a Tobacco Economy." *Winterthur Portfolio* 19 (Spring 1984): 7–19.

Boelhower, William Q. "The Rise of the New Atlantic Studies Matrix." *American Literary History* 20 (2008): 83–101.

Boreman, Thomas. *A Compendious Account of the Whole Art of Breeding, Nursing, and Right Ordering of the Silk-Worm*. London, 1733.

Bosco, Ronald A. "Introduction." *The Poems of Michael Wigglesworth*. Ed. Ronald A. Bosco. Lanham, MD: University Press of America, 1989. ix–xliii.

———. "Michael Wigglesworth." *Dictionary of Literary Biography*. Vol. 24, *American Colonial Writers, 1606–1734*. Ed. Emory Elliott. Detroit, MI: Gale Research Co., 1984. 337–42.

———, ed. *The Poems of Michael Wigglesworth*. Lanham, MD: University Press of America, 1989.
Bourdieu, Pierre. *Distinction: A Social Critique of the Judgement of Taste*. Trans. Richard Nice. Cambridge, MA: Harvard University Press, 1984.
Bowen, H. V. *Elites, Enterprise, and the Making of the British Overseas Empire 1688–1775*. New York: St. Martin's Press, 1996.
Boys, Richard C. "General Oglethorpe and the Muses." *Georgia Historical Quarterly* 31 (1947): 19–30.
Bradstreet, Anne. *The Complete Works of Anne Bradstreet*. Ed. Joseph R. McElrath and Allan P. Robb. Boston: Twayne Publishers, 1981.
———. *Several Poems*. Boston. 1678.
———. *The Tenth Muse Lately Sprung Up in America*. London, 1650.
———. *The Works of Anne Bradstreet*. Ed. Jeannine Hensley. Cambridge, MA: Belknap Press of Harvard University Press, 1981.
Brockett, L. P. *The Silk Industry in America. A History: Prepared for the Centennial Exposition*. New York: George F. Nesbitt & Co., 1876.
Brotton, Jerry. *Trading Territories: Mapping the Early Modern World*. Ithaca, NY: Cornell University Press, 1997.
Brown, Laura. *Ends of Empire: Women and Ideology in Eighteenth-Century British Literature*. Ithaca, NY: Cornell University Press, 1993.
Brown, Roger H. "*American Magazine*, 1787–1788." *The Conservative Press in Eighteenth- and Nineteenth-Century America*. Ed. Ronald Lora and William Henry Longton. Westwood, CT, and London: Greenwood Press, 1999. 85–93.
Brown, Wallace Cable. "Prose Fiction and English Interest in the Near East, 1775–1825." *PMLA* 53 (1938): 827–36.
Brückner, Martin. *The Geographic Revolution in Early America: Maps, Literacy, and National Identity*. Chapel Hill: Published for the Omohundro Institute of Early American History and Culture by the University of North Carolina Press, 2006.
Brückner, Martin, and Hsuan L. Hsu, eds. *American Literary Geographies: Spatial Practice and Cultural Production, 1500–1900*. Newark: University of Delaware Press, 2007.
Buell, Lawrence. "American Literary Emergence as a Postcolonial Phenomenon." *American Literary History* 4 (1992): 411–42.
Burnham, Michelle. *Folded Selves: Colonial New England Writing in the World System*. Hanover, NH: Dartmouth College Press, 2007.
Bushman, Richard L. *The Refinement of America: Persons, Houses, Cities*. New York: Vintage Books, 1992.
Caldwell, Patricia. "Why Our First Poet Was a Woman: Bradstreet and the Birth of an American Poetic Voice." *Prospects* 13 (1988): 1–35.
Canup, John. "Cotton Mather and 'Criolian Degeneracy.'" *Early American Literature* 24 (1989): 20–34.
———. *Out of the Wilderness: The Emergence of American Identity in Colonial New England*. Middletown, CT: Wesleyan University Press, 1990.
Caracciolo, Peter L. *The Arabian Nights in English Literature: Studies in the Reception of The Thousand and One Nights into British Culture*. New York: St. Martin's Press, 1988.
Carlson, Eric W. "Poe's Ten-Year Frogpondian War." *Edgar Allan Poe Review* 3 (2002): 37–51.

Carpenter, Frederic Ives. *Emerson and Asia*. Cambridge, MA: Harvard University Press, 1930.

Carr, Stephen L. "The Circulation of Blair's Lectures." *Rhetoric Society Quarterly* 32.4 (2002): 75–104.

Casale, Ottavio M. "Edgar Allan Poe." *The Transcendentalists: A Review of Research and Criticism*. Ed. Joel Myerson. New York: Modern Language Association of America, 1984. 362–71.

Cavitch, Max. *American Elegy: The Poetry of Mourning from the Puritans to Whitman*. Minneapolis: University of Minnesota Press, 2007.

Cecil, L. Moffitt. "Poe's Arabesque." *Comparative Literature* 18 (1966): 55–70.

Certeau, Michel de. *The Practice of Everyday Life*. Trans. Steven Rendall. Berkeley: University of California Press, 1984.

———. *The Writing of History*. Trans. Tom Conley. New York: Columbia University Press, 1988.

Chaplin, Joyce. *An Anxious Pursuit: Agricultural Innovation and Modernity in the Lower South, 1730–1815*. Williamsburg, VA, and Chapel Hill: Published for the Institute of Early American History and Culture by the University of North Carolina Press 1993.

———. *The First Scientific American: Benjamin Franklin and the Pursuit of Genius*. New York: Basic Books, 2006.

———. *Subject Matter: Technology, the Body, and Science on the Anglo-American Frontier*. Cambridge, MA: Harvard University Press, 2001.

Chaudhuri, K. N. *The Trading World of Asia and the English East India Company, 1660–1760*. Cambridge: Cambridge University Press, 1978.

Chivers, T. H., and Richard Beale Davis. *Chivers' Life of Poe*. New York: Dutton, 1952.

Christy, Arthur E. *The Orient in American Transcendentalism: A Study of Emerson, Thoreau, and Alcott*. New York: Columbia University Press, 1932.

———. "The Sense of the Past." *The Asian Legacy and American Life: Essays Arranged and Edited by Arthur E. Christy*. Ed. Arthur E. Christy. New York: The John Day Company, 1945. 1–55.

Cigrand, Bernard John. *Story of the Great Seal of the United States: Or, History of American Emblems*. Chicago: Amberg & Co., 1903.

Clery, E. J. *The Feminization Debate in Eighteenth-Century England: Literature, Commerce, and Luxury*. Basingstoke, Hampshire: Palgrave Macmillan, 2004.

Cohen, Henig. "Two Colonial Poems on the Settling of Georgia." *Georgia Historical Quarterly* 37 (1953): 131–34.

Coclanis, Peter A. "Beyond Atlantic History." *Atlantic History: A Critical Appraisal*. Ed. Jack P. Greene and Philip D. Morgan. Oxford: Oxford University Press, 2009. 337–56.

Coleman, Kenneth. *Colonial Georgia: A History*. New York: Scribner's, 1976.

———, ed. *A History of Colonial Georgia*. Athens: University of Georgia Press, 1976.

Conant, Martha Pike. *The Oriental Tale in England in the Eighteenth Century*. New York: Columbia University Press, 1908.

Crane, Verner W. "The Promotion Literature of Georgia." *Biographical Essays: A Tribute to Wilberforce Eames*. Ed. George Parker Winship. Cambridge, MA: Harvard University Press, 1924. 281–98.

———. *The Southern Frontier, 1670–1732.* Durham, NC: Duke University Press, 1928.
Craven, Wesley Frank. *The Southern Colonies in the Seventeenth Century, 1607–1689.* Baton Rouge: Louisiana State University Press, 1949.
Davidson, Cathy. *Revolution and the Word: The Rise of the Novel in America.* New York: Oxford University Press, 1986.
Davis, Harold E. *The Fledgling Province: Social and Cultural Life in Colonial Georgia, 1733–1776.* Chapel Hill: Published for the Institute of Early American History and Culture, Williamsburg, VA, by the University of North Carolina Press, 1976.
Davis, Joseph Stancliffe. *Essays in the Earlier History of American Corporations.* Cambridge, MA: Harvard University Press, 1917.
Davis, Richard Beale. *Intellectual Life in the Colonial South, 1585–1763.* Vol. 1, *Promotion, Discovery, and History.* Knoxville: University of Tennessee Press, 1978.
Denker, Ellen Paul. *After the Chinese Taste: China's Influence in America, 1730–1930.* Salem, MA: Peabody Museum of Salem, 1985.
Denuccio, Jerome D. "Fact, Fiction, Fatality: Poe's 'The Thousand-and-Second Tale of Scheherazade.'" *Studies in Short Fiction* 27 (1990): 365–70.
de Prospo, R. C. "Marginalizing Early American Literature." *New Literary History* 23 (1992): 233–65.
———. *Theism in the Discourse of Jonathan Edwards.* Newark: University of Delaware Press, 1985.
Dimock, Wai Chee. "Hemispheric Islam: Continents and Centuries for American Literature." *ALH* (2008): 28–49.
———. "Planet and America: Set and Subset." *Shades of the Planet: American Literature as World Literature.* Ed. Wai Chee Dimock and Lawrence Buell. Princeton, NJ: Princeton University Press, 2007. 1–16.
———. *Through Other Continents: American Literature Across Deep Time.* Princeton, NJ: Princeton University Press, 2006.
Disraeli, Isaac, and Rufus W. Griswold. *Curiosities of Literature: And the Literary Character Illustrated.* New York: Appleton & Co, 1846.
Douglas, Mary. *Purity and Danger: An Analysis of the Concepts of Pollution and Taboo.* London: Routledge, 1966.
Doyle, Laura. "Toward a Philosophy of Transnationalism," *The Journal of Transnational American Studies* 1.1 (2009), http://escholarship.org/uc/item/9vr1k8hk (accessed July 15, 2010).
Dunn, Elizabeth E. "'A Wall Between Them Up to Heaven': Jonathan Edwards and Benjamin Franklin." *Benjamin Franklin, Jonathan Edwards, and the Representation of American Culture.* Ed. Barbara B. Obert and Harry S. Stout. New York and Oxford: Oxford University Press, 1993. 58–74.
Eberwein, Jane D. "Civil War and Bradstreet's 'Monarchies.'" *Early American Literature* 26 (1991): 119–44.
Eden, Trudy. "Food, Assimilation, and the Malleability of the Human Body in Early Virginia." *A Centre of Wonders: The Body in Early America.* Ed. Janet Moore Lindman and Michele Lise Tarter. Ithaca, NY: Cornell University Press, 2001. 29–42.
Egan, Jim. *Authorizing Experience: Refigurations of the Body Politic in Seventeenth-Century New England Writing.* Princeton, NJ: Princeton University Press, 1999.
———. "'The Long'd-for Aera' of an 'Other Race': Climate, Identity, and James Grainger's

The Sugar-Cane." *Early American Literature* 38 (2003): 189–212.
Ellis, John Harvard, ed. *The Works of Anne Bradstreet.* New York, 1867.
Emerson, Everett H. *Captain John Smith.* Boston: Twayne Publishers, 1971.
Emerson, Julie, Jennifer Chen, and Mimi Gardner Gates. *Porcelain Stories: From China to Europe.* Seattle and London: Seattle Art Museum in Association with the University of Washington Press, 2000.
Emerson, Ralph Waldo, Edward Waldo Emerson, and Waldo Emerson Forbes. *Journals of Ralph Waldo Emerson, with Annotations.* Boston: Houghton Mifflin, 1909. 10 volumes.
Emerson, Ralph Waldo, and William H. Gilman. *Journals and Miscellaneous Notebooks.* Cambridge, MA: Belknap Press of Harvard University Press, 1960.
Erkkila, Betsy. *Mixed Bloods and Other Crosses: Rethinking American Literature from the Revolution to the Culture Wars.* Philadelphia: University of Pennsylvania Press, 2005.
Falco, Raphael. *Conceived Presences: Literary Genealogy in Renaissance England.* Amherst: University of Massachusetts Press, 1994.
Feerick, Jean. *Strangers in Blood: Relocating Race in the Renaissance.* Toronto: University of Toronto Press, 2010.
Finch, Martha I. "'Civilized' Bodies and the 'Savage' Environment of Early New Plymouth." *A Centre of Wonders: The Body in Early America.* Ed. Janet Moore Lindman and Michele Lise Tarter. Ithaca, NY: Cornell University Press, 2001. 43–59.
Finkelstein, Dorothee Metlitsky. *Melville's Orienda.* Yale Publications in American Studies. New Haven, CT: Yale University Press, 1961.
Fletcher, Angus. *Allegory, the Theory of a Symbolic Mode.* Ithaca, NY: Cornell University Press, 1964.
Fliegelman, Jay. *Declaring Independence: Jefferson, Natural Language, and the Culture of Performance.* Palo Alto, CA: Stanford University Press, 1993.
Floyd-Wilson, Mary. *English Ethnicity and Race in Early Modern Drama.* Cambridge: Cambridge University Press, 2003.
Foerster, Norman, ed. *The Reinterpretation of American Literature.* New York: Harcourt, Brace and Co., 1928.
Foucault, Michel. *Discipline and Punish: The Birth of the Prison.* Trans. Alan Sheridan. New York: Vintage Books, 1979.
———. "Of Other Spaces." *Diacritics* 16 (1986): 22–27.
Frank, Andre Gunder. *Reorient: Global Economy in the Asian Age.* Berkeley: University of California Press, 1998.
Frank, Caroline. *Objectifying China, Imagining America: Chinese Commodities in Early America.* Chicago: University of Chicago Press, 2011.
Franklin, Benjamin. *Benjamin Franklin: Writings.* New York: The Library of America, 1987.
———. *The Papers of Benjamin Franklin.* Vol. 31, *November 1, 1779, through February 29, 1780.* Ed. Barbara B. Oberg. New Haven, CT: Yale University Press, 1995.
Franklin, Wayne. *Discoverers, Explorers, Settlers: The Diligent Writers of Early America.* Chicago: University of Chicago Press, 1979.
Frelinghuysen, Alice Cooney. *American Porcelain, 1770–1920.* New York: Metropolitan Museum of Art: Distributed by Harry N. Abrams, 1989.
Gee, Joshua. *The Trade and Navigation of Great-Britain Considered.* 3rd ed. London, 1731.

Giles, Paul. "Antipodean American Literature: Franklin, Twain, and the Sphere of Subalternity." *American Literary History* 20 (2008): 22–50.

———. "The Deterritorialization of American Literature." *Shades of the Planet: American Literature as World Literature*. Princeton, NJ: Princeton University Press, 2007. Ed. Wai Chee Dimock and Lawrence Buell. 39–61.

Gillespie, Katherine. "'This Briny Ocean Will O'erflow Your Shore': Anne Bradstreet's 'Second World' Atlanticism and National Narratives of Literary History." *Symbiosis* 3 (1999): 99–118.

Gillies, John. *Shakespeare and the Geography of Difference*. Cambridge: Cambridge University Press, 1994.

Glacken, Clarence J. *Traces on the Rhodian Shore: Nature and Culture in Western Thought from Ancient Times to the End of the Eighteenth Century*. Berkeley: University of California Press, 1967.

Goad, Caroline Mabel. "Horace in the English Literature of the Eighteenth Century." PhD diss., Yale University, 1916.

Goffman, Daniel. *The Ottoman Empire and Early Modern Europe*. Cambridge: Cambridge University Press, 2002.

Granger, Bruce. *American Essay Serials from Franklin to Irving*. Knoxville: University of Tennessee Press, 1978.

Gray, Lewis Cecil, and Esther Katherine Thompson. *History of Agriculture in the Southern United States to 1860*. Washington, DC: The Carnegie Institution of Washington, 1933. 2 volumes.

Green, James N., and Peter Stallybrass. *Benjamin Franklin: Writer and Printer*. New Castle, DE, and Philadelphia; London: Oak Knoll Press and the Library Company of Philadelphia: The British Library, 2006.

Greene, Jack. "Travails of an Infant Colony." *Forty Years of Diversity: Essays on Colonial Georgia*. Ed. Harvey H. Jackson and Phinizy Spalding. Athens: University of Georgia Press, 1984. 278–309.

———. "Travails of an Infant Colony." *Imperatives, Behaviors, and Identities: Essays in Early American Cultural History*. Charlottesville: University of Virginia Press, 1992. 113–42.

Greenspan, Ezra. "Evert Duyckinck and the History of Wiley and Putnam's Library of American Books, 1845–1847." *American Literature* 64 (1992): 676–93.

Griffith, Reginald Harvey. *Alexander Pope; a Bibliography*. Austin: University of Texas Press, 1922.

Griswold, Rufus. *The Prose Writers of America*. Philadelphia: A. Hart, 1852.

Gustafson, Sandra, and Gordon Hutner, eds. "Projecting Early American Literary Studies." Special issue, *American Literary History* 22 (2010): 245–500.

Hall, David D. "Learned Culture in the Eighteenth Century." *The History of the Book in America: The Colonial Book in the Atlantic World*. Ed. Hugh Amory and David D. Hall. Vol. 1. Cambridge: Cambridge University Press, 2000. 411–33.

———. *Worlds of Wonder, Days of Judgment: Popular Religious Belief in Early New England*. Cambridge, MA: Harvard University Press, 1990.

Hammond, Jeffrey. *The American Puritan Elegy: A Literary and Cultural Study*. New York: Cambridge University Press, 2000.

Hansen, Thomas S., and Burton Ralph Pollin. *The German Face of Edgar Allan Poe: A*

Study of Literary References in His Works. Columbia, SC: Camden House, 1995.

Hariot, Thomas. *A Briefe and True Report of the New Found Land of Virginia.* Francoforti ad Moenum: Typis Ioannis Wecheli, sumtibus vero Theodori de Bry, 1590.

Harvey, Bruce A. *American Geographics: U.S. National Narratives and the Representation of the Non-European World, 1830–1865.* Palo Alto, CA: Stanford University Press, 2001.

Harvey, Tamara. *Figuring Modesty in Feminist Discourse Across the Americas, 1633–1700.* Burlington, VT: Ashgate, 2008.

Hatch, Charles E. "Mulberry Trees and Silkworms: Sericulture in Early Virginia." *Virginia Magazine of History and Biography* 65 (1957): 3–61.

Hawthorne, Nathaniel, and William Charvat. *The Centenary Edition of the Works of Nathaniel Hawthorne.* 23 vols. Columbus: The Ohio State University Press, 1963.

Hayes, Kevin J. "How Thomas Jefferson Read the *Qur'an*." *Early American Literature* 39 (2004): 247–61.

Headley, Joel Tyler. *MISCELLANIES.* New York: Baker and Scribner, 1850.

Hegel, Georg Wilhelm Friedrich. *The Philosophy of History.* Trans. J. Sibree. New York: Dover Publications, Inc., 1956.

Heimert, Alan, and Andrew Delbanco, eds. *The Puritans in America: A Narrative Anthology.* Cambridge, MA: Harvard University Press, 1985.

Hensley, Jeannine. "Anne Bradstreet's Wreath of Thyme." *The Works of Anne Bradstreet.* Ed. Jeannine Hensley. Cambridge, MA: The Belknap Press of Harvard University Press, 1967. xxiii–xxxviii.

Hertz, Gerald B. "The English Silk Industry in the Eighteenth Century." *English Historical Review* 24.96 (1909): 710–27.

Hobson, John M. *The Eastern Origins of Western Civilization.* Cambridge: Cambridge University Press, 2004.

Hoffman, Daniel. *Poe Poe Poe Poe Poe Poe Poe.* Garden City, NJ: Doubleday, 1972.

Hubbell, Jay B. *The South in American Literature, 1607–1900.* Durham, NC: Duke University Press, 1954.

Hulme, Peter. *Colonial Encounters: Europe and the Native Caribbean, 1492–1797.* London: Methuen, 1986.

———. "Including America." *Ariel: A Review of International English Literature* 26 (1995): 117–23.

Inden, Ronald B. *Imagining India.* Bloomington: Indiana University Press. 2000.

Irwin, Robert. *The Arabian Nights: A Companion.* London: Allen Lane, 1994.

Isani, Mukhtar Ali. "Cotton Mather and the Orient." *New England Quarterly* 43 (1970): 46–58.

———. "Edward Taylor and the Turks." *Early American Literature* 7 (1972): 120–23.

———. "The Oriental Tale in America through 1865: A Study in American Fiction." PhD diss., Princeton University, 1962.

Ivic, Christopher. "'Our British Land': Anne Bradstreet's Atlantic Perspective." *Archipelagic Identities: Literature and Identity in the Atlantic Archipelago, 1550–1800.* Ed. Philip Schwyzer and Simon Mealor. Aldershot, UK; Burlington, VT: Ashgate, 2004. 195–204.

Jackson, Harvey H., and Phinizy Spalding, eds. *Forty Years of Diversity: Essays on Colonial Georgia.* Athens: University of Georgia Press, 1984.

Jacobson, Dawn. *Chinoiserie*. London: Phaidon, 1993.
Jordan, Winthrop D. *White Over Black: American Attitudes toward the Negro, 1550–1812*. Chapel Hill: University of North Carolina Press, 1968.
Kamrath, Mark. "An 'Inconceivable Pleasure' and the *Philadelphia Minerva:* Erotic Liberalism, Oriental Tales, and the Female Subject in Periodicals of the Early Republic." *American Periodicals* 14 (2004): 3–34.
Kamrath, Mark, and Sharon M. Harris. *Periodical Literature in Eighteenth-Century America*. Knoxville: University of Tennessee Press, 2005.
Kaplan, Amy. *The Anarchy of Empire in the Making of U.S. Culture*. Cambridge, MA: Harvard University Press, 2002.
———. "'Left Alone with America': The Absence of Empire in the Study of American Culture." *Cultures of United States Imperialism*. Ed. Amy Kaplan and Donald E. Pease. Durham, NC: Duke University Press, 1993. 3–21.
Kayser, Wolfgang Johannes. *The Grotesque in Art and Literature*. Gloucester, MA: P. Smith, 1968.
Kirkpatrick, James. "An Address to James Oglethorpe, Esq." *South Carolina Gazette* (10 February, 1732/33): 1.
———. *An Epistle to Alexander Pope, Esq.; from South Carolina*. London, 1737.
———. *The Sea-Piece: A Narrative, Philosophical, and Descriptive Poem. In Five Cantos*. London, 1750.
Kirsch, George B. "*Massachusetts Magazine,* 1789–1796." *The Conservative Press in Eighteenth- and Nineteenth-Century America*. Ed. Ronald Lora and William Henry Longton. Westwood, CT, and London: Westwood Press, 1999. 95–102.
Klamkin, Marian. *American Patriotic and Political China*. New York: Charles Scribner, 1973.
Kolodny, Annette. *The Land Before Her: Fantasy and Experience of the American Frontiers, 1630–1860*. Chapel Hill, NC, and London: University of North Carolina Press.
Kupperman, Karen Ordahl. "Fear of Hot Climates in the Anglo-American Colonial Experience." *William & Mary Quarterly* 41 (1984): 213–40.
———. "The Puzzle of the American Climate in the Early Colonial Period." *American Historical Review* 87 (1982): 1262–89.
Lambert, Frank. *The Barbary Wars: America's 1815 War Against the Pirates of North Africa*. New York: Hill and Wang, 2005.
Landa, Louis A. "Of Silkworms and Farthingales and the Will of God." *Studies in the Eighteenth Century*. Ed. R. F. Brissenden. Vol. 2. Toronto: University of Toronto Press, 1973. 259–78.
———. "Pope's Belinda, the General Emporie of the World, and the Wondrous Worm." *The South Atlantic Quarterly* 70 (1971): 215–35.
Larkin, Edward. *Thomas Paine and the Literature of Revolution*. Cambridge: Cambridge University Press, 2005.
Lawson-Pebbles, Robert. *American Literature before 1880*. Harlow, England: Pearson/Longman, 2003.
Leath, Robert A. "'After the Chinese Taste': Chinese Export Porcelain and Chinoiserie in Eighteenth-Century Charleston." *Historical Archaelogy* 33 (1999): 48–61.
Lee, Jee Yoon. "'The Rude Contact of Some Actual Circumstance': Hawthorne and Salem's East India Marine Museum." *ELH* 73 (2006): 949–73.

Lefebvre, Henri. *The Production of Space*. Trans. Donald Nicholson-Smith. Oxford: Blackwell, 1991.
Leiner, Frederick C. *The End of Barbary Terror: America's 1815 War Against the Pirates of North Africa*. New York: Oxford University Press, 2006.
Lemay, J. A. Leo. *A Calendar of American Poetry in the Colonial Newspapers and Magazines and in the Major English Magazines through 1765*. Worcester, MA: American Antiquarian Society, 1970.
———. *Men of Letters in Colonial Maryland*. Knoxville: University of Tennessee Press, 1972.
Levander, F. Caroline, and Robert S. Levine, eds. *Hemispheric American Studies*. New Brunswick, NJ: Rutgers University Press, 2008.
Lewis, Martin W., and Kären E. Wigen. *The Myth of Continents: A Critique of Metageography*. Berkeley: University of California Press, 1997.
Lewis, Richard. *Carmen Seculare, for the Year, M, DCC, XXXII to the Right Honourable Charles, Lord Baron of Baltimore*. Annapolis, MD, 1732.
Liu, Lydia He. *The Clash of Empires: The Invention of China in Modern World Making*. Cambridge, MA: Harvard University Press, 2004.
———. "Robinson Crusoe's Earthenware Pot." *Critical Inquiry* 25 (1999): 728–57.
Lovejoy, Arthur O. *The Great Chain of Being: A Study of the History of an Idea*. Cambridge, MA: Harvard University Press, 1942.
Luedtke, Luther S. *Nathaniel Hawthorne and the Romance of the Orient*. Bloomington: Indiana University Press, 1989.
Lyons, Paul. "Opening Accounts in the South Seas: Poe's Pym and American Pacific Orientalism." *ESQ* 42 (1996): 291–326.
Mabbott, Thomas Olive, ed. *Edgar Allan Poe: Tales & Sketches*. Vol. 2, *1843–1849*. Champaign: University of Illinois Press, 2000.
Macdonald, Duncan B. "A Bibliographical and Literary Study of the First Appearance of the *Arabian Nights* in Europe." *The Library Quarterly* 2 (1932): 387–420.
Mack, Maynard. *Alexander Pope: A Life*. New York and New Haven, CT: W. W. Norton Company in Association with Yale University Press, 1985.
Madsen, Deborah L. *Beyond the Borders: American Literature and Post-Colonial Theory*. London: Pluto Press, 2003.
Mahdi, Muhsin. *The Thousand and One Nights*. Leiden; New York; Koln: E. J. Brill, 1995.
Mapp, Paul W. "Atlantic History from Imperial, Continental, and Pacific Perspectives." *WMQ*, 3rd. series, 63 (2006): 713–25.
Maragou, Helena. "The Portrait of Alexander the Great in Anne Bradstreet's 'The Third Monarchy.'" *Early American Literature* 23 (1988): 70–81.
Marana, Giovanni. *Letters Writ by a Turkish Spy*. London, 1687.
Marr, Timothy. *The Cultural Roots of American Islamicism*. Cambridge: Cambridge University Press, 2006.
Martin, Wendy. *An American Triptych: Anne Bradstreet, Emily Dickinson, Adrienne Rich*. Chapel Hill: University of North Carolina Press, 1984.
Martyn, Benjamin. *Some Account of the Designs of the Trustees for Establishing the Colony of Georgia in America*. London, 1732.
———. *Reasons for Establishing the Colony of Georgia*. London 1732.
Mather, Cotton. "The Way to Prosperity." *The Wall and the Garden: Selected Massachusetts*

Election Sermons 1670–1775. Ed. A. W. Plumstead. Minneapolis: University of Minnesota Press, 1968. 115–39.
May, Henry F. *The Enlightenment in America*. Oxford: Oxford University Press, 1976.
McElrath, Joseph R., Jr., and Allan P. Robb, eds. *The Complete Works of Anne Bradstreet*. Boston: Twayne Publishers, 1981.
McGill, Meredith L. *American Literature and the Culture of Reprinting, 1834–1853*. Philadelphia: University of Pennsylvania Press, 2003.
McKinstry, Mary Thomas. "Silk Culture in the Colony of Georgia." *Georgia Historical Quarterly* 14 (1930): 225–29.
Meriton, George. *A Geographical Description of the World*. London, 1671.
Meroney, Geraldine. "The London Entrepot Merchants and the Georgia Colony." *The William and Mary Quarterly* 25 (April 1968): 230–44.
Miller, Perry. *Errand into the Wilderness*. Cambridge, MA: Harvard University Press, 1956.
———. *The Raven and the Whale: Poe, Melville, and the Literary Scene*. Baltimore and London: Johns Hopkins University Press, 1997. Originally published 1956.
Miller, Perry, ed. *The American Puritans: Their Prose and Poetry*. New York: Columbia University Press, 1982.
Mitchell, Jonathan. "A Modell For the Maintaining of Students & fellows. . . ." *Publications of the Colonial Society of Massachusetts* 31 (1935): 309–11.
Moss, Sidney P. *Poe's Literary Battles: The Critic in the Context of His Literary Milieu*. Durham, NC: Duke University Press, 1963.
Mott, Frank Luther. *A History of American Magazines 1741–1850*. Cambridge, MA: The Belknap Press of the Harvard University Press, 1966.
Mudge, Jean McClure. *Chinese Export Porcelain for American Trade, 1785–1835*. Newark: University of Delaware Press, 1981.
Mūsawī, Muḥsin Jāsim *Scheherazade in England: A Study of Nineteenth-Century English Criticism of the Arabian Nights*. 1st ed. Boulder, CO: L. Rienner, 1981.
Naddaff, Sandra. *Arabesque: Narrative Structure and the Aesthetics of Repetition in the 1001 Nights*. Evanston, IL: Northwestern University Press, 1991.
Nance, Susan. *How the Arabian Nights Inspired the American Dream, 1790–1935*. Chapel Hill: University of North Carolina Press, 2009.
Ng, Su Fang. "Global Renaissance: Alexander the Great and Early Modern Classicism from the British Isles to the Malay Archipelago." *Comparative Literature* 58 (2006): 293–312.
Nicholson, Colin. *Capital Satires of the Early Eighteenth Century*. Cambridge: Cambridge University Press, 1994.
Obeidat, Marwan M. *American Literature and Orientalism*. Berlin: K. Schwarz, 1998.
Obenzinger, Hilton. *American Palestine: Melville, Twain, and the Holy Land Mania*. Princeton, NJ: Princeton University Press, 1999.
Oglethorpe, James. *A New and Accurate Account of the Provinces of South Carolina and Georgia*. London, 1732.
Oldmixon, John. *The British Empire in America*. London, 1708.
Olson, Lester C. "Franklin on National Character and the Great Seal of the United States." *The Cambridge Companion to Benjamin Franklin*. Ed. Carla Mulford. Cambridge: Cambridge University Press, 2009. 117–31.
Orr, Bridget. *Empire on the British Stage, 1660–1714*. Cambridge: Cambridge University

Press, 2001.

Oser, Lee. "Almost a Golden World: Sidney, Spenser, and Puritan Conflict in Bradstreet's 'Contemplations.'" *Renascence* 52 (2000): 187–202.

Outram, Dorinda. *The Enlightenment.* Cambridge: Cambridge University Press, 1995.

Parks, A. Franklin. "James Kil(l)patrick (c. 1700–70). In *American Writers Before 1800: A Biographical and Critical Dictionary.* Ed. James A. Levernier and Douglass R. Wilmes. Westport, CT: Greenwood Press, 1983. 853–55.

Parrish, Susan Scott. *American Curiosity: Cultures of Natural History in the Colonial British Atlantic World.* Published for the Omohundro Institute of Early American History and Culture, Williamsburg, Virginia. Chapel Hill: University of North Carolina Press, 2006.

Peck, Linda Levy. *Consuming Splendor: Society and Culture in Seventeenth-Century England.* Cambridge; New York: Cambridge University Press, 2005.

Perceval, John, Earl. *Manuscripts of the Earl of Egmont. Diary of Viscount Percival afterwards First Earl of Egmont.* London: H. M. Stationery Off. 1920–23.

Peskin, Lawrence A. *Captives and Countrymen: Barbary Slavery and the American Public, 1785–1816.* Baltimore: Johns Hopkins University Press, 2009.

Pickering, John. "Address at the Annual First Meeting." *Journal of the American Oriental Society* 1 (1843): 1–78.

Pitcher, Edward W. R. *Fiction in American Magazines before 1800: An Annotated Catalogue.* Schenectady, NY: Union College Press, 1993.

Pitt, Arthur Stuart. "The Sources, Significance, and Date of Franklin's 'An Arabian Tale.'" *PMLA* 57 (1942): 155–68.

Poe, Edgar Allan. *The Selected Writings of Edgar Allan Poe.* Ed. G. R. Thompson. New York: W. W. Norton & Co., 2004.

———. *Collected Writings of Edgar Allan Poe.* Vol. 2, *The Brevities: Pinakidia, Marginalia, Fifty Suggestions, and Other Works.* Ed. and with an Introduction and Notes by Burton R. Pollin. New York: Gordian Press, 1985.

Polonsky, Rachel. "Poe's Aesthetic Theory." *The Cambridge Companion to Edgar Allan Poe.* Ed. Kevin J. Hayes. Cambridge: Cambridge University Press, 2002. 42–57.

Pomeranz, Kenneth. *The Great Divergence: China, Europe, and the Making of the Modern World Economy.* Princeton, NJ: Princeton University Press, 2000.

Pope, Alexander, Earl R. Wasserman, and Henry E. Huntington Library and Art Gallery. *Pope's Epistle to Bathurst: A Critical Reading with an Edition of the Manuscripts.* Baltimore, MD: Johns Hopkins University Press, 1960.

Porter, Carolyn. "What We Know We Don't Know: Remapping American Literary Studies." *American Literary History* 6 (1994): 467–526.

Porter, David. *Ideographia: The Chinese Cipher in Early Modern Europe.* Palo Alto, CA: Stanford University Press, 2001.

Preble, George Henry. *History of the Flag of the United States of America.* 4th ed. Boston: Houghton Mifflin, 1894.

Quilligan, Maureen. *The Language of Allegory: Defining the Genre.* Ithaca, NY: Cornell University Press, 1979.

Ralph, James. *Clarinda; or, The Fair Libertine.* London: 1729.

Raman, Shankar. *Framing "India": The Colonial Imaginary in Early Modern Culture.* Palo Alto, CA: Stanford University Press, 2002.

Ready, Milton L. "Philanthropy and the Origins of Georgia." In *Forty Years of Diversity: Essays on Colonial Georgia*. Ed. Harvey H. Jackson and Phinizy Spalding. Athens, GA: University of Georgia Press, 1984. 46–59.
Reese, Trevor Richard. *Colonial Georgia: A Study in British Imperial Policy in the Eighteenth Century*. Athens: University of Georgia Press, 1963.
———. "Benjamin Martyn, Secretary of the Trustees of Georgia." *Georgia Historical Quarterly* 38 (June 1954): 142–47.
Reps, John W. "C + L = S? Another Look at the Origins of Savannah's Town Plan." *Forty Years of Diversity: Essays on Colonial Georgia*. Ed. Harvey H. Jackson and Phinizy Spalding. Athens: University of Georgia Press, 1984. 101–51.
Reynolds, David S. *Faith in Fiction: The Emergence of Religious Literature in America*. Cambridge, MA: Harvard University Press, 1981.
Rippl, Gabriele. "Wild Semantics: Charlotte Perkins Gilman's Feminization of Edgar Allan Poe's Arabesque Aesthetics." *Soft Canons: American Women Writers and Masculine Tradition*. Ed. Karen L. Kilcup. Iowa City: University of Iowa Press, 1999.
Round, Phillip H. *By Nature and Custom Cursed: Transatlantic Civil Discourse and New England Cultural Production, 1620–1660*. Hanover, NH, and London: The University Press of New England, 1999.
Rowe, John Carlos. "Edward Said and American Studies." *American Quarterly* 56 (2004): 33–47.
———. *Literary Culture and U.S. Imperialism: From the Revolution to World War II*. Oxford; New York: Oxford University Press, 2000.
Rozbicki, Michal J. *The Complete Colonial Gentleman: Cultural Legitimacy in Plantation America*. Charlottesville: University Press of Virginia, 1998.
Said, Edward W. *Orientalism*. New York: Vintage Books, 1979.
Sallis, Eva. *Sheherazade through the Looking Glass: The Metamorphosis of* The Thousand and One Nights. Richmond, UK: Curzon, 1999.
Schmidt, Peter, and Amritjit Singh, eds. "Introduction." *Postcolonial Theory and the United States: Race, Ethnicity, and Literature*. Jackson: University Press of Mississippi, 2000. 3–69.
Schueller, Malini Johar. *U.S. Orientalisms: Race, Nation, and Gender in Literature, 1790–1890*. Ann Arbor: University of Michigan Press, 1998.
Schueller, Malini Johar, and Edward Watts. *Messy Beginnings: Postcoloniality and Early American Studies*. New Brunswick, NJ: Rutgers University Press, 2003.
Schumpeter, Elizabeth Boody. *English Overseas Trade Statistics 1697–1808*. Oxford: Clarendon Press, 1960.
Schweitzer, Ivy. "Anne Bradstreet Wrestles with the Renaissance." *Early American Literature* 23 (1988): 291–312.
———. *The Work of Self-Representation: Lyric Poetry in Colonial New England*. Chapel Hill: University of North Carolina Press, 1991.
Scott, Jonathan, trans. *The Arabian Nights Entertainments*. Philadelphia, 1830.
Sha'ban, Fuad. *Islam and Arabs in Early American Thought: Roots of Orientalism in America*. Durham, NC: Acorn Press, 1991.
Shapiro, Stephen. *The Culture and Commerce of the Early American Novel: Reading the Atlantic World System*. University Park: Pennsylvania State University Press, 2008.
Shields, David S. *Civil Tongues & Polite Letters in British America*. Chapel Hill: University

of North Carolina Press, 1997.

———. "Eighteenth-Century Literary Culture." In *The History of the Book in America. Volume One: The Colonial Book in the Atlantic World*. Ed. Hugh Armory and David D. Hall. American Antiquarian Society. Cambridge: Cambridge University Press, 2000. 434–76.

———. "Literature of the Colonial South." *Resources for American Literary Study* 19 (1993): 174–222.

———. "Dr. James Kirkpatrick: American Laureate." In *The Meaning of South Carolina History: Essays in Honor of George C. Rogers, Jr.* Columbia, SC: University of South Carolina Press, 1991. Ed. David R. Chesnutt and Clyde N. Wilson. 29–49.

———. *Oracles of Empire: Poetry, Politics, and Commerce in British America, 1690–1750.* Chicago: University of Chicago Press, 1990.

Shields, John C. *The American Aeneas: Classical Origins of the American Self.* Knoxville: University of Tennessee Press, 2001.

Silverman, Kenneth. *Edgar A. Poe: Mournful and Never-Ending Remembrance.* 1st ed. New York: HarperCollins Publishers, 1991.

Simms, William Gilmore. *The Wigwam and the Cabin: Selected Fiction of William Gilmore Simms.* Fayetteville: University of Arkansas Press, 2000.

Slauter, Eric. "History, Literature, and the Atlantic World." *Early American Literature* 43 (2008): 153–86.

Smith, John. *The Complete Works of Captain John Smith.* 3 vols. Ed. Philip Barbour. Chapel Hill: University of North Carolina Press, 1986.

Smith, W. Calvin. "Utopia's Last Chance? The Georgia Silk Boomlet of 1751." *Georgia Historical Quarterly* 69 (1975): 25–37.

Soja, Edward W. *Postmodern Geographies: The Reassertion of Space in Critical Social Theory.* London: Verso, 1989.

Solis-Cohen, Bertha. "Benjamin Franklin Defends Northwest Passage Navigation." *Princeton University Library Chronicle* 19 (1957): 15–33.

Spencer, Benjamin Townley. *The Quest for Nationality: An American Literary Campaign.* Syracuse, NY: Syracuse University Press, 1957.

Spengemann, William C. *A New World of Words: Redefining Early American Literature.* New Haven, CT, and London: Yale University Press, 1994.

———. *A Mirror for Americanists.* Hanover and London: University Press of New England, 1989.

Spiller, Robert E. et al., eds. *Literary History of the United States.* 3rd ed. Rev. ed. London: Macmillan Company, 1963.

Stanford, Ann. "Anne Bradstreet's Portrait of Sir Philip Sidney." *Critical Essays on Anne Bradstreet.* Ed. Pattie Cowell and Ann Stanford. Boston: G. K. Hall, 1983. 97–100.

———. *Anne Bradstreet: The Worldly Puritan.* New York: Burt Franklin & Company, 1974.

Stewart, Mart A. *"What Nature Suffers to Groe": Life, Labor, and Landscape on the Georgia Coast, 1680–1920.* Athens, GA; and London: University of Georgia Press, 2002.

Sweet, Julie Anne. *Negotiating for Georgia: British-Creek Relations in the Trustee Era, 1733–1752.* Athens: University of Georgia Press, 2005.

Sweet, Timothy. "Gender, Genre, and Subjectivity in Bradstreet's Early Elegies." *Early American Literature* 23 (1988): 152–74.

Szczesniak, Boleslaw. "The Seventeenth Century Maps of China: An Inquiry into the

Compliations of European Cartographers." *Imago Mundi* 13 (1956): 116–36.
Tailfer, Patrick, Hugh Anderson, Da. Douglass et al. *A True and Historical Narrative of the Colony of Georgia*. Charleston, SC, 1741.
Tarver, J. "Abridged Editions of Blair's Lectures on Rhetoric and Belles Lettres in America: What Nineteenth-Century College Students Really Learned about Blair on Rhetoric." *Biblotheck: A Scottish Journal of Bibliography and Allied Topics* 21 (1996): 55–68.
Taylor, Edward. *Edward Taylor's Gods Determinations and Preparatory Meditations*. Ed. Daniel Patterson. Kent, OH: Kent State University Press, 2003.
Tchen, John Kuo Wei. *New York before Chinatown: Orientalism and the Shaping of American Culture, 1776–1882*. Baltimore: Johns Hopkins University Press, 1999.
Tennenhouse, Leonard. *The Importance of Feeling English: American Literature and the British Diaspora, 1750–1850*. Princeton, NJ; Oxford: Princeton University Press, 2007.
Thompson, G. R. *Poe's Fiction: Romantic Irony in the Gothic Tales*. Madison: University of Wisconsin Press, 1973.
———, ed. *The Selected Writings of Edgar Allan Poe*. New York: W. W. Norton & Co., 2004.
Trafton, Scott. *Egypt Land: Race and Nineteenth-Century American Egyptomania*. New Americanists. Durham, NC: Duke University Press, 2004.
Treasure, Geoffrey. *The Making of Modern Europe 1648–1780*. London: Methuen, 1985.
Vainker, S. J. *Chinese Silk: A Cultural History*. New Brunswick, NJ: British Museum Press in Association with Rutgers University Press, 2004.
———. "Luxuries or Not? Consumption of Silk and Porcelain in Eighteenth-Century China." In *Luxury in the Eighteenth Century: Debates, Desires, and Delectable Goods*. Ed. Maxine Berg and Elizabeth Eger. London: Palgrave Macmillan, 2003. 207–18.
Versluis, Arthur. *American Transcendentalism and Asian Religions*. New York: Oxford University Press, 1993.
Vitkus, Daniel J. *Turning Turk: English Theater and the Multicultural Mediterranean, 1570–1630*. New York: Palgrave Macmillan, 2003.
W. De Gray Birch, L.L.D. *Catalogue of Seals in the Department of Manuscripts in the British Museum*. Vol. 6. London: Longmans and Co., 1900.
Waldstreicher, David. *Runaway America: Benjamin Franklin, Slavery, and the American Revolution*. New York: Hill & Wang, 2004.
Waring, Joseph Ioor, M.D. "James Killpatrick and Smallpox Incursion in Charlestown." *Annals of Medical History* 10 (1938): 301–8.
Warner, Michael. "What's Colonial about Colonial America?" *Possible Pasts: Becoming Colonial in Early America*. Ed. Robert Blair St. George. Ithaca, NY: Cornell University Press, 2000. 49–70.
Wasserman, Earl R. *Epistle to Bathurst: A Critical Reading with an Edition of the Manuscripts*. Baltimore: Johns Hopkins University Press, 1960.
Watts, Edward. *An American Colony: Regionalism and the Roots of Midwestern Culture*. Athens: Ohio University Press, 2002.
———. *Writing and Postcolonialism in the Early Republic*. Charlottesville: University Press of Virginia, 1998.
Watts, Emily Stripes. *The Poetry of American Women from 1632–1945*. Austin: University of Texas Press, 1977.

Wesley, Samuel. *Georgia, and Two Other Occasional Poems on the Founding of the Colony.* London, 1736.

Wheeler, Roxann. *The Complexion of Race: Categories of Difference in Eighteenth-Century British Culture.* 2000. Philadelphia: University of Pennsylvania Press.

White, Elizabeth Wade. *Anne Bradstreet: The Tenth Muse.* New York: Oxford University Press, 1971.

Widmer, Edward L. *Young America: The Flowering of Democracy in New York City.* Oxford: Oxford University Press, 2000.

Williams, Glyndwr. *Voyages of Delusion: The Northwest Passage in the Age of Reason.* London: HarperCollins, 2002.

Willis, John E., Jr. "European Consumption and Asian Production in the Seventeenth and Eighteenth Centuries." *Consumption and the World of Goods.* Ed. John Brewer and Roy Porter. London and New York: Routledge, 1993. 133–47.

Wolf, John B. *The Barbary Coast: Algiers Under the Turks, 1500–1830.* New York: W. W. Norton & Co., 1979.

Woodhead, Christine. "'The Present Terrour of the World?' Contemporary Views of the Ottoman Empire c. 1600." *History* 72 (1987): 20–37.

Wright, Louis B. *The First Gentlemen of Virginia: Intellectual Qualities of the Early Colonial Ruling Class.* San Marino, CA: The Huntington Library, 1940.

Wright, Nancy E. "Epitaphic Conventions and the Reception of Anne Bradstreet's Public Voice." *Early American Literature* 31 (1996): 243–63.

Wright, Thomas Goddard. *Literary Culture in Early New England, 1620–1730.* New Haven, CT: Yale University Press, 1920.

Yu, Beongcheon. *The Great Circle: American Writers and the Orient.* Detroit, MI: Wayne State University Press, 1983.

INDEX

Addison, Joseph, 81
"An Address to James Oglethorpe, Esq." (Kirkpatrick), 17, 45–46, 55–70, 72–74, 133n14, 133–34n15, 136n54; America as metonymy, 46, 70, 72–73; environmentalism, 62–63; importance of place, 73–74; India in poem, 59–61; publication history, 45, 55–57; race, 62–63; silk, 65–68; women, 65–69, 137n71
aesthetics, 53–55, 65–70, 97–98, 110–20
Aldridge, A. Owen, 8, 76
Alexander the Great: in Bradstreet's poetry, 19–20, 22–23, 26–33, 38–39; literary representation, 129n11; relation to the East, 21
Algiers, 84, 94
Ali, Muhsin Jassim, 99
allegory, 86–87, 90
American literary nationalism, 97, 102–3, 143n33
American literature: continuity, 11–12, 18; distinctive relation of American literature to figures of the East, 12–14, 16, 18, 124; East, Orient, and Orientalism before 1800, 8–10, 22, 127n27; global versus transatlantic and hemispheric approaches, 123–24; importance of geography, 7–8, 127n23; and postcolonial theory, 128n36
American Oriental Society, 96
American Review, 100

Anderson, Benedict, 11
Arabia, 42, 61, 87, 94, 96, 97, 109
"An Arabian Tale" (Franklin), 76, 86, 88–90
Arabic, 99
Arabian Nights Entertainments, 96–97, 98–101, 107, 108–9, 116, 118, 119, 142n17, 143n22
Aravamuden, Srinivas, 128n35
Ashe, Thomas, 47
Autobiography of Benjamin Franklin (Franklin), 78

Ballaster, Ros, 82
Barbary, 83
Barbary captivity narratives, 140n25, 141n27
Bauer, Ralph, 8
Berg, Elizabeth, 53, 135n31
Berkeley, Edmund, 79
Berman, Jacob Rama, 96, 126n16
Blair, Hugh, 87, 141n28
Boreman, Thomas, 50, 55
Bourdieu, Pierre, 81
Bradstreet, Anne, 1, 15, 16, 19–39, 96; Queen Elizabeth compared to Zenobia, 1; representation of Alexander, 19, 27–39, 130n20, 130n21; East, 20, 24–30, 38–39. *See also* "An Elegie . . ."; "The Four Monarchies"; *Several Poems*
Bradstreet, Simon, 36, 131n33
British Empire in America (Oldmixon), 79

Brotton, Jerry, 7
Brückner, Martin, 8
Buell, Lawrence, 13
Bushman, Richard, 125n9
Byrd, William, 78
Byron, Lord, 100

Caracciolo, Peter, 99
Carey, Matthew, 78
Carpenter, Frederic Ives, 8
Carr, Stephen L. 141n27
Cecil, L. Moffitt, 95
Chapin, Joyce, 125n8
China, 6, 42, 50–53, 55, 60, 76
chinoiserie, 52, 58, 132n9, 136n63
Christy, Arthur, 8
Clarinda (Ralph), 61
Coleridge, Samuel, 100
colonial seals, 47–48
Columbus, Christopher, 3
Conquest of Granada (Irving), 2
Crane, Verner, 51
"Curiosities of American Literature" (Griswold), 105
Curiosities of Literature (Disraeli), 105

Denuccio, James, 144n42
Dickens, Charles, 100
Disraeli, Isaac, 105
Douglas, Mary, 91
Dudley, Thomas, 36
Duyckinck, Evert, 103, 143n37, 144n47

East: changing boundaries, 4–7, 30; controversy over economic dominance, 126n17; cultural sophistication and civilizing figure, 4, 13–14, 25, 28, 72–74, 119–20; in seventeenth-century Anglo-America, 21–23; in eighteenth-century Anglo-America, 42; in nineteenth-century America, 96–97; marking literature as American, 13; object of desire, 3, 25; origins of modern notion, 7; products, 42–55; and race, 122; rhetorical style, 80; sexualized, 121; source of America's value, 3, 73–74; threat, 28–30, 38–39, 50, 77
East Indies, 3, 42, 43, 52, 60, 64, 65
Eastern imaginary, 96–97
Eberwein, Jane, 19
Egypt, 6, 42, 97
"An Elegie upon that Honourable and renowned Knight, Sir Philip Sidney" (Bradstreet), 16, 22, 30–39, 130n24, 131n32
Eliot, John, 38
Emerson, Ralph Waldo, 95
"Exordium to Critical Notices" (Poe), 103

Falco, Raphael, 32
Finkelstein, Dorothy Metlitsky, 8
Florida, 43, 45
Foerster, Norman, 127n22
"Four Monarchies" (Bradstreet), 16, 20–21, 22, 24–30, 128–29n2
Frank, Gunder, 126n17
Franklin, Benjamin, 2, 15, 17, 75–94; interest in China, 76; letter to his daughter, 75–76; Northwest Passage, 125n8; Oriental tales, 17, 139n7, 139n8; reason, 83–85, 87–94; reference to as China vase, 2, 138–39n6. *See also* "An Arabian Tale"; *Autobiography*; "A Turkish Apologue"; "Sidi Mehemet Ibrahim"

Galland, Antoine, 99
Gee, Joshua, 51
Gentleman's Magazine, 42, 57, 58, 64
A Geographical Description (Meriton), 126n12
Goldsmith, Oliver, 81
Georgia: eastern products, 40–42, 44, 47–55; seal, 40, 47–48
Georgia: A Poem (Wesley), 53–55, 65, 68–69
Godey's Magazine and Lady's Book, 99
Graham's Magazine, 103
"Grayling; Or, Murder Will Out" (Simms), 102
Greece, 5, 26, 126n12

Green, Samuel, 37
Greene, Jack, 66
Griswold, Rufus, 105, 144n46. *See also* "Curiosities of American Literature"
Grub Street, 99

Half-Way Covenant, 38
Hariot, Thomas, 47
Hawthorne, Nathaniel, 2, 102. See also *House of the Seven Gables* and *Scarlet Letter*
Headley, Joel T., 106
Hegel, Georg Wilhelm Friedrich, 6
Hensley, Jeannine, 129n3
Hertz, Gerald B., 50
Hobson, John M., 126 n17
Hoffman, Charles Fenno, 100
House of the Seven Gables (Hawthorne), 102
Hubbard, William, 37
Hunt, Leigh, 99

India, 4, 9, 42, 59–61, 64, 97, 126n11
Irving, Washington, 2. See also *Tales of the Alhambra* and *Conquest of Granada*
Isani, Mukhtar Ali, 79

Jackson, James, 83–84
Jerusalem, 6, 28
Johnson, Samuel, 81

Kamrath, Mark, 79
Kirkpatrick (Kilpatrick), James, 15, 16, 17, 45, 55–70, 72–74. *See also* "An Address to James Oglethorpe, Esq."
Knickerbocker, or New York Monthly magazine, 106

Landa, Louis, 50, 58–59
Lane, Edward William, 114
Lefebvre, Henri, 15
Letters Writ by a Turkish Spy (Marana), 78–79
Lewis, Martin, 6. See also *The Myth of Continents*

Lewis, Richard, 57, 136n60. *See also* "To Ld. Baltimore in Maryland"
Literary World, 100
Liu, Linda, 135n32
Lovejoy, David, 89

Mapp, Paul, 125
Maragou, Helen, 129n11, 130n16, 130n20
Marana, Giovanni, 78. See also *Letters Writ by a Turkish Spy*
Marr, Timothy, 9, 143n23, 143n29, 144n57
Martyn, Benjamin, 71–72. See also *Reasons for Establishing the Colony of Georgia*
Massachusetts Magazine, 87
Mather, Cotton, 37
Mather, Increase, 37. See also *A relation of the troubles which have hapned in New England*
Mathews, Cornelius, 103
McGill, Meredith, 143n41
Meriton, George, 126n12. See also *A Geographical Description*
metonomy, 46, 49, 70, 72–73
Mille et une nuit (Galland), 99
Miller, Perry, 10–11, 18, 37
Mitchell, Jonathan, 37
Montagu, Lady Mary Wortley, 81
Montesquieu, Baronde La Brède et de, 79
Mott, Frank, 78
The Myth of Continents (Lewis and Wigon), 6

A Narrative of the troubles with the Indians (Hubbard), 37
New York Magazine, 79
Nicholson, Colin, 138n78
North Africa, 6
North American Review, 100
Northwest Passage, 3

Obzinger, Hilton, 9
Oglethorpe, James, 43
Oldmixon, John, 47. See also *British*

166 • Index

Empire in America
"On the Use of Riches" (Pope), 71–72, 138n76
Oriental tale: definition, 79–80; generic conventions, 89; history in colonial America, 77–81, 140n12, 140n13; value, 81–82
Orientalism, 9, 22
Orientalism (Said), 8
Ottoman Empire, 21, 30, 129n12
Outram, Dorinda, 77

Peck, G. W., 100
Peck, Linda, 49
Persia, 6, 20, 26, 27, 29, 42, 51, 55, 101
"Philosophy of Composition" (Poe), 119
Pickering, John, 96, 97
Pinakidia (Poe), 96
Pitcher, Edward, 78, 140n12
Poe, Edgar Allan, 15, 17–18, 95–120; *Arabian Nights,* 95–96, 141n4; literary nationalism, 143n41; modern author, 117; references to Orient and Orientalism, 95, 142n13; romance aesthetic, 98, 119; women and aesthetics 112–13, 114–15, 118–19. *See also* "The Philosophy of Composition"; *Pinakidia;* "The Raven"; "The Thousand-and-Second Tale of Scheherazade"
Pomeranz, Kenneth, 126n17
Pope, Alexander, 71, 81. *See also* "On the Use of Riches"
Porter, David, 52
Pyrnne, Hester, 3

Ralph, James, 61. *See also Clarinda*
Raman, Shanker, 126n11, 126n18
"The Raven" (Poe), 119
Reasons for Establishing the Colony of Georgia (Martyn), 70–72, 137n74
A relation of the troubles which have hapned in New England (Increase Mather), 37
Reynolds, David, 8
romance, 102

Rosenmeier, Rosamond, 31
Rowlandson, Mary, 37. *See also The Sovereignty & Goodness of God*
Russia, 6

Said, Edward, 8. *See also Orientalism*
Scarlet Letter (Hawthorne), 2
Scheherazade, 101, 110–19
Schueller, Malini, 9
Scott, Jonathan, 114
Scott, Sir Walter, 100
Several Poems (Bradstreet), 22–23, 37–38, 42, 129–30n15
Sha'ban, Faud, 9
Shakespeare, William, 101
Shields, David, 45, 56, 135n53, 136–37n66 and 137n67
Shields, John, 130n19
"Sidi Mehemet Ibrahim" (Franklin), 76, 83–85
Sidney, Philip 32, 38
silk: eastern product, 42–43, 45–46, 51–53, 132n5; English importation, 49–51; object of display, 66–69; threat to English identity, 44; New World product, 46–48
Simms, William Gilmore, 102, 108
Sinbad, 101, 108–10, 113
Smith, John, 1, 47
Southern Literary Messenger, 107
South Carolina, 44, 45, 56
South Carolina Gazette, 45, 58
The Sovereignty & Goodness of God (Rowlandson), 37
Spain, 44
spatial theory, 15, 127n25
Spencer, Benjamin, 102
Spengemann, William, 20
symbolic spatial economy, 4–5, 8, 13, 77–78, 96, 124

Tales of the Alhambra (Irving), 2
Taylor, Edward, 1
Tchen, JohnWei, 81
Tennenhouse, Leonard, 13, 141n28
Tennyson, Lord, 100

"The Thousand-and-Second Tale of Scheherazade" (Poe), 17–18, 97, 102, 103–20; contrast with *Arabian Nights*, 116–17, 144n47; modern author, 117; women and aesthetics, 112–13, 114–15, 118–19
"To Ld. Baltimore in Maryland" (Lewis), 57
translatio imperii, 25
translatio studi, 25, 55
Turkey, 6, 30, 86, 87, 94
"Turkish Apologue" (Franklin), 76, 85–87, 90–93
Turner, Frederick Jackson, 8

turning Turk, 28, 29, 85–86

Vaughan, Benjamin, 76
Versluis, Arthur, 8
Vitkus, Daniel, 22

Warner, Michael, 9–10
Wesley, John, 53–55, 65, 68–69. See also *Georgia: A Poem*
White, Elizabeth, 36
Wigen, Kåren E., 6
Wigglesworth, Michael, 1
Williams, Glyndwr, 125n8
Winthrop, John, 36

TRANSOCEANIC STUDIES
Ileana Rodriguez, Series Editor

The Transoceanic Studies series rests on the assumption of a one-world system. This system—simultaneously modern and colonial and now postmodern and postcolonial (global)—profoundly restructured the world, displaced the Mediterranean *mare nostrum* as a center of power and knowledge, and constructed dis-centered, transoceanic, waterways that reached across the world. The vast imaginary undergirding this system was Eurocentric in nature and intent. Europe was viewed as the sole culture-producing center. But Eurocentrism, theorized as the "coloniality of power" and "of knowledge," was contested from its inception, generating a rich, enormous, alternate corpus. In disputing Eurocentrism, books in this series will acknowledge above all the contributions coming from other areas of the world, colonial and postcolonial, without which neither the aspirations to universalism put forth by the Enlightenment nor those of globalization promoted by postmodernism will be fulfilled.

Oriental Shadows: The Presence of the East in Early American Literature
    Jim Egan

www.ingramcontent.com/pod-product-compliance
Lightning Source LLC
Chambersburg PA
CBHW020949230426
43666CB00005B/234